CONTENTS

ABOUT THIS BOOK

The *Dorling Kindersley Eyewitness Travel Guide European Phrase Book* has been compiled by a team of language experts to provide all the key vocabulary you need to survive in the 14 main European countries. Each language section begins with a guide to pronunciation and special grammatical points, followed by general words and phrases (greetings, numbers, days of the week etc.), and features on communications, hotels, shopping, and eating out. Finally, a menu guide supplies core vocabulary for everyday foods and beverages, as well as regional specialities.

Typical replies to questions you may ask during your journey, and the signs or instructions you may see or hear, are shown in tinted boxes. In the main text, the pronunciation of words and phrases is imitated in English sound syllables – the unique, easy-to-use, "say it as you see it" system.

Other language and travel guide titles from Dorling Kindersley are shown at the back of this book.

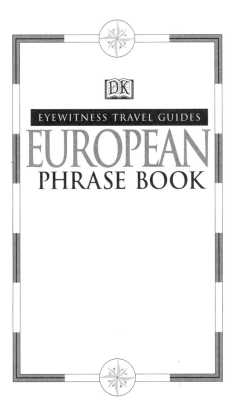

DK

EYEWITNESS TRAVEL GUIDES

EUROPEAN
PHRASE BOOK

A Dorling Kindersley Book

DK

LONDON, NEW YORK, MUNICH, MELBOURNE, AND DELHI

Produced for Dorling Kindersley by
g-and-w PUBLISHING 47A High St, Chinnor, OX9 4DJ

First published in Great Britain in 2001
by Dorling Kindersley Limited
80 Strand, London WC2R 0RL

Reprinted with corrections 2003

8 10 9 7

Dorling Kindersley books can be purchased in bulk quantities at
discounted prices for use in promotions or as premiums. We are
also able to offer special editions and personalized jackets, corporate
imprints, and excerpts from all of our books, tailored specifically to
meet your own needs. To find out more, please contact: Special Sales,
Dorling Kindersley Limited, 80 Strand, London WC2R 0RL;
Tel. 020 7010 3000.

A CIP catalogue record is available from the British Library.

ISBN-13: 978-0-7513-2144-9
ISBN-10: 0-7513-2144-3

Printed and bound in China by Leo Paper Products Limited

see our complete catalogue at
www.dk.com

Picture Credits

Jacket: JACKET PHOTOGRAPHY © Corbis/GEORGINA BOWATER (C)
All other images © Dorling Kindersley.
For further information see: www.dkimages.com

CZECH

CONTENTS

INTRODUCTION

PRONUNCIATION

When reading the imitated pronunciation stress the first syllable of each word. Pronounce each syllable as if it formed a part of an English word and you will be understood sufficiently well. Remember the points below, and your pronunciation will be even closer to the correct Czech.

a	as in the 'u' in 'up' except when it is followed by an *h* and is pronounced like the long 'a' in 'lather'
ay	as in 'pay'
e	as in 'bed' except when it is followed by *h* and the sound is longer
g	as in 'get'
h	as in the English 'h' in 'hand'
H	is similar to the 'ch' in the Scottish word 'loch'
i	as in 'bit'
I	as the 'i' sound in wine
o	as in 'hot' except when it is followed by an *h* and is pronounced *oh*
u	as in 'put'
y	always as in 'yes' apart from *ay* above
zh	like the 's' in 'leisure'

It is important to remember that when **e** comes at the end of a word, it must be pronounced as a separate syllable. For example, the word **moře** should be pronounced *morzheh*. The pronunciation guide in the phrase sections adds an *h* to a final *e* in cases where confusion could arise.

Summary of Special Characteristics in Czech

a	similar to the 'a' in 'ant' or the 'u' in 'up'
á	is a long 'a' as in 'lather'
c	as the 'ts' as in 'cats'
č	as the 'ch' in 'church'
d'	as the 'd' in 'duty'
é	is similar to the 'e' in 'bed' but longer
ě	as the 'ye' in 'yet'
h, ch	as the 'ch' in the Scottish word 'loch'
í	as the 'ee' in weed
j	as the 'y' in 'yes'
ň	as the first 'n' in 'companion'
ó	as the word 'awe'
ř	is similar to the Scots rolled 'r' run together with the 's' sound as in 'leisure'
š	as the 'sh' in 'ship'
t'	as the 't' in 'tune'
ú, ů	as the 'oo' in 'moon'
w	as the 'v' in 'van'
ý	as the 'ee' in 'weed'
ž	as the 's' in 'leisure'

The alternatives indicated by (*man*) and (*woman*) in the phrases show the forms to be used by a male or female speaker. Similarly, (*to a man*) and (*to a woman*) indicate the forms to be used when addressing a man or a woman.

USEFUL PHRASES

Yes/no
Ano/ne
ano/neh

Thank you
Děkuji
d-yeku-yi

No, thank you
Ne, děkuji
neh d-yeku-yi

Please
Prosím
prosseem

I don't understand
Nerozumím
nerozoomeem

Do you speak English/French/German?
Mluvíte anglicky/francouzsky/německy?
mlooveeteh anglitski/frantsohski/n-yemetski

I can't speak Czech
Nemluvím česky
nemluveem cheski

I don't know
Nevím
neveem

Please speak more slowly
Mluvte pomalu, prosím
mloovteh pomaloo prosseem

Please write it down for me
Napište mi to, prosím
napishteh mi to prosseem

My name is …
Jmenuji se …
y-menoo-yi seh

How do you do, pleased to meet you
Těší mě
t-yeshee m-yeh

Good morning
Dobré ráno
dobreh rahno

Good day *(common general greeting)*
Dobrý den
dobree den

Good evening
Dobrý večer
dobree vecher

Good night
Dobrou noc
dobroh nots

Goodbye
Nashledanou
nas-Hledanoh

How are you?
Jak se máte?
yak seh mahte

Excuse me, please
S dovolením
zdovoleneem

Sorry? *(pardon?)*
Prosím?
prosseem

Sorry! *(apology)*
Promiňte!
promin-yteh

I'm really sorry
Je mi to moc líto
yeh mi to mots leeto

Can you help me?
Můžete mi pomoci?
moozheteh mi pomotsi

Can you tell me …?
Můžete mi říci …?
moozheteh mi rzheetsi

Can I have …?
Mohu dostat …?
mo-hoo dostat

I would like …
Rád *(man)*/ráda *(woman)* bych …
raht/rahda biн

Is there … here?
Je tam … tady?
yeh tam … tadi

Where can I get …?
Kde mohu dostat …?
gdeh mo-hoo dostat

How much is it?
Kolik to stojí?
kolik to sto-yee

What time is it?
Kolik je hodin?
kolik yeh hodin

I must go now
Už musím jít
oozh moosseem yeet

I've lost my way
Zabloudil (*man*)/zabloudila (*woman*) jsem
zablohdil/zablohdila ysem

Cheers!
Na zdraví!
na zdravee

Do you take credit cards?
Berete karty?
bereteh karti

Where is the toilet?
Kde je záchod?
gdeh yeh zaнot

Go away!
Jděte pryč!
yd-yeteh prich

Excellent!
Výborně!
veeborn-yeh

I've lost my money/traveller's cheques/credit cards
Ztratil jsem peníze/cestovní šeky/kreditní karty
stradil ysem peneezeh/tsestovnee sheki/kreditnee karti

I've lost my passport
Ztratil jesm pas
stratil ysem pas

Where is the British/US embassy?
Kde je britská/americká ambasáda?
gdeh yeh britskah/ameritskah ambasahda

Is there wheelchair access?
Je tam bezbariérový přístup?
yeh tam besbari-yehrovee przheestup

Are guide dogs allowed?
Má sem přístup slepecký pes?
mah sem przheestup slepetskee pes

I'm deaf
Jsem hluchý (*man*)/hluchá (*woman*)
ysem hlutlee/hluttah

I'm blind
Jsem slepý (*man*)/slepá (*woman*)
ysem slepee/slepah

THINGS YOU'LL HEAR

Ahoj	Hello, Hi, Cheerio
Díky	Thanks
Dobrý den	Good day
Dobré ráno	Good morning
Jak máte?	How are you?
Nashledanou	Goodbye
Na zdraví!	Cheers!
Není zač	You're welcome; Not at all
Nerozumím	I don't understand
Nevím	I don't know
Omluvte mě	Excuse me
Pozor!	Look out!
Prosím vás	Excuse me
Správně	That's right
Vítáme vás	Welcome

DAYS, MONTHS, SEASONS

Sunday	neděle	*ned-yeleh*
Monday	pondělí	*pond-yelee*
Tuesday	úterý	*ooteree*
Wednesday	středa	*strzheda*
Thursday	čtvrtek	*chuhtvuhrtek*
Friday	pátek	*pahtek*
Saturday	sobota	*sobota*
January	leden	*leden*
February	únor	*oonor*
March	březen	*brzhezen*
April	duben	*dooben*
May	květen	*kv-yeten*
June	červen	*cherven*
July	červenec	*chervenets*
August	srpen	*suhrpen*
September	září	*zahrzhee*
October	říjen	*rzhee-yen*
November	listopad	*listopat*
December	prosinec	*prosinets*
Spring	jaro	*yaro*
Summer	léto	*lehto*
Autumn	podzim	*podzim*
Winter	zima	*zima*
Christmas	vánoce	*vahnotseh*
Christmas Eve	Štědrý večer	*sht-yedree vecher*
New Year	Nový rok	*novee rok*
New Year's Eve	Silvestr	*silvestuhr*

NUMBERS

0	nula *noola*	5	pět *p-yet*	
1	jedna *yedna*	6	šest *shest*	
2	dvě *dv-yeh*	7	sedm *sehduhm*	
3	tři *trzhi*	8	osm *ossuhm*	
4	čtyři *chuhtirzhi*	9	devět *dev-yet*	

10	deset *desset*	11	jedenáct *yedenahtst*
12	dvanáct *dvanahtst*	13	třináct *trzhinahtst*
14	čtrnáct *chuhtuhrnahtst*	15	patnáct *patnahtst*
16	šestnáct *shestnahtst*	17	sedmnáct *sehduhmnahtst*
18	osmnáct *ossuhmnahtst*	19	devatenáct *devatenahtst*

20	dvacet *dvatset*	
21	dvacet jedna *dvatset yedna*	
22	dvacet dva *dvatset dva*	
30	třicet *trzhitset*	
40	čtyřicet *chtirzhitset*	
50	padesát *padessaht*	
60	šedesát *shedessaht*	
70	sedmdesát *sehduhmdessaht*	
80	osmdesát *ossuhmdessaht*	
90	devadesát *devadessaht*	
100	sto *sto*	
110	sto deset *sto desset*	
200	dvě stě *dv-yeh st-yeh*	
300	tři sta *trzhi sta*	
400	čtyři sta *chtirzhi sta*	
500	pět set *p-yet set*	
600	šest set *shest set*	
700	sedm set *seduhm set*	
800	osm set *ossuhm set*	
900	devět set *dev-yet set*	
1,000	tisíc *tiseets*	
100,000	sto tisíc *sto tiseets*	
1,000,000	milion *mili-on*	

TIME

today	dnes	*dness*
yesterday	včera	*fchera*
tomorrow	zítra	*zeetra*
this week	tento týden	*tento teeden*
last week	minulý týden	*minulee teeden*
next week	příští týden	*przheeshtee teeden*
this morning		
(*early*)	dnes ráno	*dness rahno*
(*late*)	dnes dopoledne	*dness dopoledneh*
this afternoon	dnes odpoledne	*dness otpoledneh*
this evening	dnes večer	*dness vecher*
tonight (*early*)	dnes večer	*dness vecher*
(*late*)	dnes v noci	*dness vnotsi*
last night (*early*)	včera večer	*fchera vecher*
(*late*)	včera v noci	*fchera vnotsi*
in three days	za tři dny	*za trzhi dni*
three days ago	před třemi dny	*przhed trzhemi dni*
late	pozdě	*pozd-yeh*
early	časně	*chassn-yeh*
soon	brzy	*buhrzi*
later on	později	*pozd-yay-i*
at the moment	právě	*prahv-yeh*
second	sekunda	*sekunda*
minute	minuta	*minuta*
one minute	jedna minuta	*yedna minuta*
two minutes	dvě minuty	*dv-yeh minuti*
quarter of an hour	čtvrt hodiny	*chuhtvuhrt hodini*
half an hour	půl hodiny	*pool hodini*
three quarters	tři čtvrtě hodiny	*trzhi chuhtvuhrt-*
of an hour		*yeh hodini*
hour	hodina	*hodina*
that day	ten den	*ten den*
every day	každý den	*kazhdee den*
the next day	příští den	*przheeshtee den*

TELLING THE TIME

'It's one o'clock' is **je jedna hodina** (*yeh yedna hodina*); for 'it's two/three/four o'clock' use **jsou** (*yuhsoh*) followed by the number and **hodiny**; the remaining hours to twelve o'clock are simply **je** plus the appropriate number and **hodin**.

For time past the hour always refer to the next hour. For 'half past' use **půl** (*pool*) and specify the next hour. For example, 'half past one' is **půl druhé** (*pool drooheh*) literally 'half of the second'. Similarly for 'quarter past' use **čtvrt na** (*chuhtvuhrt na*) and specify the next hour. For example, 'quarter past one' is **čtvrt na dvě** (*chuhtvuhrt na dv-yeh*). For 'quarter to' use **tři čtvrtě na** (*trzhi chuhtvuhrt-yeh na*) and specify the next hour. For example, 'quarter to eight' is **tři čtvrtě na osm** (*trzhi chuhtvuhrt-yeh na ossuhm*).

Any of the expressions given above can be used with **v** meaning 'at', for example, 'at half past one' is **v půl druhé**.

am (*midnight to 5 am*)	v noci	*vnotsi*
am (*5 to 9 am*)	ráno	*rahno*
am (*9 to 12 am*)	dopoledne	*dopoledneh*
pm (*12 to 5 pm*)	odpoledne	*otpoledneh*
pm (*5 to 10 pm*)	večer	*vecher*
pm (*10 to 12 pm*)	v noci	*vnotsi*
one o'clock	jedna hodina	*yedna hodina*
ten past one	jedna hodina deset minut	*yedna hodina a desset minut*
quarter past one	čtvrt na dvě	*chuhtvuhrt na dv-yeh*
half past one	půl druhé	*pool drooheh*
twenty to two	za dvacet minut dvě	*za dvatset minoot dv-yeh*
quarter to two	tři čtvrtě na dvě	*trzhi chuhtvuhrt-yeh na dv-yeh*
two o'clock	dvě hodiny	*dv-yeh hodini*
midday	poledne	*poledneh*
midnight	půlnoc	*poolnots*

COMMUNICATIONS

Useful Words and Phrases

code	předčíslí	*przhetcheesslee*
dialling tone	volací tón	*volatsee tawn*
emergency	případ nouze	*przheepat nohzeh*
enquiries	informace	*informatseh*
extension	linka	*linka*
fax machine	fax	*fax*
internet	internet	*internet*
mobile phone	mobilní telefon	*mobilnee telefon*
number	číslo	*cheesslo*
operator (*exchange*)	ústředna	*oostrzhedna*
phonecard	telefonní karta	*telefonee karta*
receiver	sluchátko	*slooнahtko*
reverse charge call	hovor na účet volaného	*hovor na oochet volaneh-ho*
telephone	telefon	*telefon*
telephone box	telefonní budka	*telefonee bootka*
Web site	web site	*web site*
wrong number	špatné číslo	*shpatneh cheesslo*

Where is the nearest phone box?
Kde je nejbližší telefonní budka?
gdeh yeh nayblizhshee telefonee butka

I would like a number in …
Chtěl (*man*)/chtěla (*woman*) bych číslo v…
нt-yel/нt-yela biн cheesslo v

I would like to speak to …
Rád (*man*)/ráda (*woman*) bych mluvil/mluvila s …
raht/rahda biн mluvil/mluvila s

My number is …
Mé číslo je …
meh cheeslo yeh

Could you leave him a message?
Muzete mu nechat vzkaz?
moozheteh mu neнat fskas

Sorry, wrong number
Promite, mam spatně číslo
promin-yeteh mahm shpatneh cheesslo

What's your fax number/email address?
Jaké je tvé faxové číslo/e-mailová adresa?
yakeh yeh tveh faxoveh cheeslo/e-mailovah adresa

Can I send a fax/email from here?
Mohu odtud poslat fax/e-mail?
mo-hu odtud poslat fax/e-mail

THINGS YOU'LL HEAR

Koho voláte?
Who would you like to speak to?

Máte špatné číslo
You've got the wrong number

Kdo je u telefonu?
Who is speaking?

Mluví. Počkáte si?
The line is engaged. Will you wait?

Není tady
He's not in

Nezavěšujte!
Don't hang up!

Řeknu mu, že jste telefonoval
I'll tell him you called

Vrátí se v ... hodin
He'll be back at ...

THINGS YOU'LL SEE

fax	fax (machine)
informace	enquiries
kopírka	photocopier
meziměstský hovor	long-distance call
mezinárodní hovor	international call
místní hovor	local call
ohlašovna poruch	faults service
poplatky	charges
porucha	out of order
předvolba	code
přímá volba	direct dialling
případ nouze	emergency
telefon	telephone
telefonní budka	telephone box
telefonní kabina	telephone box (at post office)
telefonní seznam	telephone directory
ústředna	exchange (operator)
webová stránka	Web site
záloha	deposit

HOTELS

USEFUL WORDS AND PHRASES

balcony	balkón	*balkawn*
bathroom	koupelna	*kohpelna*
bed	postel	*postel*
bedroom	ložnice	*lozhnitseh*
bill	účet	*oochet*
breakfast	snídaně	*sneedan-yeh*
dining room	jídelna	*yeedelna*
dinner	večeře	*vechehr-zheh*
double room	pokoj s	*pokoy z*
	dvojlůžkem	*dvoyloozhkem*
foyer	předsálí	*przhetsahlee*
full board	plná penze	*puhlnah penzeh*
half board	polopenze	*polopenzeh*
hall of residence	studentská kolej	*stoodentskah kolay*
hotel	hotel	*hotel*
key	klíč	*kleech*
lift	výtah	*veetaн*
lounge	hala	*hala*
lunch	oběd	*ob-yet*
manager	ředitel	*rzheditel*
reception	recepce	*retseptseh*
receptionist	recepční	*retsepchnee*
restaurant	restaurace	*restowratseh*
room	pokoj	*pokoy*
room service	donáška do	*donahshka do*
	pokoje	*poko-yeh*
shower	sprcha	*spr-на*
single room	jednolůžkový	*yedno-loozhkovee*
	pokoj	*pokoy*
toilet	záchod	*zaнot*
twin room	dvoulůžkový	*dvohloozhkovee*
	pokoj	*pokoy*

Have you any vacancies?
Máte volné pokoje?
mahteh volneh poko-yeh

I have a reservation
Mám rezervovaný pokoj
mahm rezervovanee pokoy

I'd like a single/double room
Chtěl (*man*)/chtěla (*woman*) bych jednolůžkový pokoj/pokoj s
  dvoulůžkem
HT-yel/HT-yela biH yedno-loozhkovee pokoy/pokoy s dvoyloozhkem

I'd like a twin room
Chtěl (*man*)/chtěla (*woman*) bych s dvěma lůžky pokoj
HT-yel/HT-yela biH s dvyema loozhki pokoy

I'd like a room with a bathroom/with a balcony
Chtěl (*man*)/chtěla (*woman*) bych pokoj s koupelnou/s balkónem
HT-yel/HT-yela biH pokoy skohpelnoh/sbalkawnem

Is there satellite/cable TV in the rooms?
Je v pokojích satelit/kabelová televize?
yeh f-pokoyeeH satelit/kabelovah televize

I'd like a room for one night/for three nights
Chtěl (*man*)/chtěla (*woman*) bych pokoj na jednu noc/na tri noci
HT-yel/HT-yela biH pokoy na yednu nots/na trzhi notsi

I'm looking for private accommodation
Hledám ubytování v soukromí
hledahm ubitovahnee f-sohkromee

What is the charge per night?
Kolik stojí jedna noc?
kolik sto-yee yedna nots

I don't know yet how long I'll stay
Ještě nevím, jak dlouho tady zůstanu
yesht-yeh neveem yak dloh-ho tadi zoostanu

21

When is breakfast/dinner?
Kdy je snídaně/večeře?
gdi yeh sneedan-yeh/vecherzh-eh

Please call me at … o'clock
Prosím, zavolejte mi v … hodin
prosseem zavolayteh mi v … hodin

Can I have breakfast in my room?
Mohu snídat ve svém pokoji?
mo-hu sneedat veh svehm poko-yi

I'll be back at … o'clock
Vratím se v … hodin
vrateem seh v … hodin

My room number is …
Číslo mého pokoje je …
cheesslo meh-ho poko-yeh yeh

I'm leaving tomorrow
Odjíždim zítra
od-yeezhdeem zeetra

Can I have the bill, please?
Mohu dostat účet, prosím?
mo-hu dostat oochet prosseem

I'll pay by credit card
Budu platit úvěrovou kartou
budu platit oov-yerovoh kartoh

I'll pay cash
Budu platit v hotovosti
boodoo platit vhotovosti

Can you get me a taxi?
Můžete mi zavolat taxi?
moozheteh mi zavolat taksi

THINGS YOU'LL SEE

nouzový východ	emergency exit
obsazeno	no vacancies
poschodí	floor
pouze pro personál	staff only
recepce	reception
restaurace	restaurant
sem	pull
snídaně	breakfast
sprcha	shower
tam	push
tlačit	push
účet	bill
výtah	lift
zadáno	reservation

THINGS YOU'LL HEAR

Pokoje s dvoujlůžkem už nemáme
There are no double rooms left

Jednolůžkové pokoje už nemáme
There are no single rooms left

Jak budete platit?
How will you be paying?

Lituji, máme obsazeno
I'm sorry, we're full

Na kolik nocí?
For how many nights?

Platí se předem, prosím
Please pay in advance

SHOPPING

Where is the … department?
Kde je oddělení …?
gdeh yeh od-yelenee

Do you have …?
Máte …?
mahteh

How much is this?
Kolik to stojí?
kolik to sto-yee

Where do I pay?
Kde mohu zaplatit?
gdeh mo-hoo zaplatit

Have you anything cheaper?
Máte něco levnějšího?
mahteh n-yetso levn-yaysheeho

Could you wrap it for me?
Můžete mi to zabalit?
moozheteh mi to zabalit

Can I have a receipt?
Mohu dostat paragon?
mo-hu dostat paragon

Can I have a refund?
Mohu dostat zpátky peníze?
mo-hu dostat spahtki peneezeh

I'm just looking
Jenom se dívám
yenom seh deevahm

I'll come back later
Ještě se vrátím
yesht-yeh seh vrahteem

EATING OUT

Restaurants – **restaurace** (*restowratseh*) – are divided into four price categories. The first category – **cenová skupina** – and some of the second can be fairly expensive. A wide variety of both Czech and international food is available and Chinese and Indian restaurants are popular.

Food in cheaper restaurants varies depending on the season, region and initiative of the manager or owner. Small pubs in the mountain region of Bohemia often serve interesting local dishes. Roast pork with dumplings and sauerkraut (**vepřová pečeně s knedlíky a se zelím**, *veprzhovah pechen-yeh sknedleeki a se zeleem*) is a popular dish. In big hotels and more upmarket restaurants, game is available in season, and haunch of venison in cream sauce (**srnčí kýta na smetane**, *sruhnchee keeta na smetan-yeh*) is recommended. Those who like fresh-water fish, should try trout in herb butter (**pstruh na másle**, *puhstrooн na mahsleh*). While meat still plays an important role in Czech food culture, some vegetarian dishes are available.

Popular snacks in lower-priced restaurants include tripe soup (**dršťková polévka**, *druhzht-yehkovah polehfka*), goulash soup (**gulášová polévka**, *goolashovah polehfka*) and stewed pork with paprika and rice (**vepřové na paprice rýží**, *veprzhoveh na papritseh s reezhee*). Goulash with dumplings, or just with a roll as a snack, should be of reasonable quality anywhere.

Beer is at its best in Bohemia, but there is some good beer in Brno and a few locally brewed beers in Northern Moravia and Slovakia are worth trying. A visit to one of the wine cellars in Southern Moravia is recommended. The best wines come from South Moravia. The white wines **Rulandské bílé** (*roolantskeh beeleh*), **Müller Thurgau** and the red **Kláštorné červené** (*klashtorneh cherveneh*) are among the most popular. **Mattoniho kyselka** (*matoniho kiselka*) is the best type of mineral water.

A service charge may be shown on the bill, but a tip of about 10% is customary.

USEFUL WORDS AND PHRASES

beer	pivo	*pivo*
bill	účet	*oochet*
bottle	láhev	*lah-hef*
bowl	miska	*miska*
cake	zákusek	*zahkoossek*
chef	kuchař	*kooнarzh*
coffee	káva	*kahva*
cup	šálek	*shahlek*
fork	vidlička	*vidlichka*
glass	sklenice	*sklenitseh*
hors d'oeuvre	předkrm	*przhetkuhruhm*
knife	nůž	*noozh*
menu	jídelní lístek	*yeedelnee leestek*
milk	mléko	*mlehko*
plate	talíř	*taleerzh*
receipt	stvrzenka	*stuhruhrzenka*
sandwich	obložený chléb	*oblozhenee нlehp*
serviette	ubrousek	*oobrohsek*
snack	rychlé	*riнleh*
	občerstvení	*opcherstuhvenee*
soup	polévka	*polehfka*
spoon	lžíce	*lzheetseh*
sugar	cukr	*tsookuhr*
table	stůl	*stool*
tea	čaj	*chɪ*
teaspoon	čajová	*chɪ-ovah*
	lžička	*luzhzhichka*
tip	spropitné	*spropitneh*
waiter	číšník	*cheeshneek*
waitress	číšnice	*cheeshnitseh*
water	voda	*voda*
wine	víno	*veeno*
wine list	nápojový	*nahpo-yovee*
	lístek	*leestek*

A table for one, please
Stůl pro jednoho, prosím
stool pro yednoho prosseem

A table for two, please
Stůl pro dva, prosím
stool pro dva prosseem

Is there a highchair?
Mají tam dětskou židličku?
mayee tam dyetskoh zhidlichku

Can I see the menu?
Mohu dostat jídelní lístek?
mo-hoo dostat yeedelnee leestek

Do you have a vegetarian menu?
Máte vegetariánskou nabídku jídel?
mah-te vegetari-yahnskoh nabeedku yee-del

Call the manager, please!
Zavolejte vedoucího, prosím!
zavolayteh vedohtseeho prosseem

Can I see the wine list?
Mohu dostat nápojovy lístek?
mo-hoo dostat nahpo-yovee leestek

Do you do children's portions?
Děláte dětské porce?
d-yelahte d-yetskeh portse

Can you warm this bottle/baby food for me?
Můžete ohřát tuto láhev/kojeneckou výživu?
moozheteh o-hrzhaht tuto lah-hef/ko-yenetskoh veezhivu

What would you recommend?
Co byste mi doporučil (*to a man*)/doporučila (*to a woman*)?
tso bisteh mi doporuchil/doporuchila

Is this suitable for vegetarians?
Je to vhodné pro vegetariány?
yeh to vhodneh pro vegetari-yahni

I'm allergic to nuts/shellfish
Jsem alergický (man)/alergická (woman) na ořechy/korýše
ysem alergitskee/alergitskah na orzhetti/koreeshe

I'd like …
Rád (man)/ráda (woman) bych …
raht/rahda biн

Just a cup of coffee, please
Jenom šálek kávy, prosím
yenom shahlek kahvi prosseem

Waiter/waitress!
Pane/paní vrchní!
paneh/panee vuhruнnee

A beer/two beers, please
Pivo/dvě piva, prosim
pivo/dv-yeh piva prosseem

Can we have the bill, please?
Můžeme dostat účet, prosím?
moozhemeh dostat oochet prosseem

I only want a snack
Chci jenom něco malého k jídlu
нtsi yenom n-yetso maleh-ho k-yeedloo

I didn't order this
Toto jsem si neobjednal (man)/neobjednala (woman)
toto yuhsem si ne-ob-yednal/ne-ob-yednala

The meal was very good, thank you
Jídlo bylo velmi dobré, děkuji
yeedlo bilo velmi dobreh d-yekoo-yi

MENU GUIDE

aperitiv aperitif
banán banana
bažant pheasant
bez ledu without ice
biftek s vejcem steak with an egg
bílé víno white wine
bramborák potato pancake
bramborová kaše mashed potatoes
bramborová polévka potato soup
bramborové hranolky chips
bramborové knedlíky potato dumplings
bramborové placky potato pancake
bramborový guláš potato goulash
brambory potatoes
broskev peach
brynza sheep's cheese
burské oříšky peanuts
celer celery
celerový salát celeriac salad
chlupaté knedlíky se zelím Bohemian potato dumplings with cabbage (dumplings made from a mixture of raw grated potatoes, flour and egg)
chřest asparagus
cibule onions
cibulová omáčka onion sauce
citrón lemon
cukr sugar
cukroví biscuits
čaj tea
čaj s mlékem tea with milk
černá káva black coffee
čerstvý fresh
červené víno red wine
červená řepa beetroot
česnek garlic
čočka lentils
čočková polévka lentil soup

daněk venison
datle dates
divoký kanec wild boar
divoký králík wild rabbit
do krvava rare
domácí home-made
dort cream cake
dršťková polévka tripe soup
drůbež poultry
dušená kapusta stewed curly kale
dušené hovězí maso beef stew
dušené telecí maso veal stew
dušené vepřové maso pork stew
dušený stewed
džem jam
džus juice
fazole beans
fazole na kyselo sour beans (beans boiled in water, thickened with flour and seasoned with vinegar)
fíky figs
guláš goulash
guláš z dančího masa venison goulash
guláš z husích žaludků goulash made with goose's stomach
gulášová polévka goulash soup (made with meat and spices)
hašé minced beef, hash
hlávkové zelí cabbage
hlávkový salát lettuce
hodně vypečený well done
holub pigeon
horké kakao hot chocolate
horký hot
hořčice mustard
houbová omáčka mushroom sauce
houby mushrooms
houskové knedlíky bread dumplings

hovězí (maso) beef
hovězí játra na slanině calf's liver stewed with onions and bacon
hovězí maso s houbovou omáčkou boiled beef in mushroom sauce
hovězí maso s koprovou omáčkou boiled beef in dill sauce
hovězí maso s rajskou omáčkou boiled beef with tomato sauce
hovězí pečeně stewed beef
hovězí polévka se žemlovým svítkem meat broth with bread omelette
hovězí polévka beef broth
hovězí polévka s knedlíčky beef broth with dumplings
hovězí polévka s masovými knedlíčky meat broth with meatballs
hovězí polévka s noky beef broth with gnocchi (flour and potato dumplings)
hovězí polévka s rýží beef broth with rice
hovězí tokáň beef stewed in wine
hrách peas
hráškový krém cream of pea soup
hroznové víno grapes
hruška pear
humr lobster
husa goose
husí játra goose liver
chléb bread
chuťovky savouries
játra liver
játrová omáčka liver sauce
jablko apple
jablkový závin apple strudel
jahody strawberries
jednotlivá jídla à la carte
jehněčí maso lamb
jelení maso venison
kachna duck
kachna pečená roast duck

kakao hot chocolate or cocoa
kančí (maso) wild boar
kapr carp
kapr pečený baked carp
kapr na rožni carp on a skewer
kapr smažený fried carp
kapusta curly kale
karotka carrots
kaše buckwheat cereal
káva coffee
kaviár caviar
kedlubny kohlrabi
klobása smoked sausage
klopsy na smetaně stewed meatballs
knedlíky dumplings
koblihy doughnuts
koláč pie
koláčky small sweet pies or tartlets
koprová omáčka dill sauce
krém cream or custard
krocan turkey
krupicová kaše semolina purée
krupicové noky semolina dumplings
krupicový nákyp semolina pudding
křehký koláč s jablky apple pie
křenová šlehačka horse-radish sauce
kuře chicken
kuře na rožni chicken on a skewer
květák cauliflower
kynuté knedlíky dumplings made from yeast dough filled with jam
kyselé zelí sauerkraut
lískové ořechy hazelnuts
livance pancakes with jam
losos salmon
majonéza mayonnaise
maliny raspberries
máslo butter
maso meat
masová směs na roštu mixed grill
menu table d'hôte, set menu

meruňky apricots
minerálka/minerální voda mineral water
mléko milk
mořské ryby salt-water fish
moučník dessert
mouka flour
na jehle on a skewer
na roštu grilled
nanukový dort ice-cream gâteau
ne moc vypečený medium-rare
nealkoholické nápoje soft drinks
nešumivá minerálka still mineral water
noky gnocchi (potato dumplings)
nudle noodles
nudlový nákyp s tvarohem noodle
    pudding baked with cottage cheese
oběd lunch
obložený chlebíček open sandwich
ocet vinegar
okurky cucumbers
omáčka sauce
omeleta omelette
opékané brambory fried potatoes
ovoce fruit
párek sausage, frankfurter
párek s hořčicí sausage with mustard
párek v rohlíku hot dog
paprika pepper (green or red)
pařížský krém whipped cream and
    chocolate cream
paštika pâté
pečená husa roast goose
pečené hovězí maso roast beef
pečený roast, baked or grilled
pepř pepper
pivo beer
plněné rajče zapečené stuffed tomato
plněné žampióny stuffed mushrooms
plněný telecí řízek stuffed veal steak
polévka soup
pórek leek

pomeranč orange
pomerančová šťáva orange juice
přesnídávka mid-morning snack
přesnídávková polévka thick soup
přílohy side dishes
pstruh trout
pšeničný chléb white bread
ragú ragoût
rajčatový salát tomato salad
rajská tomatoes
rohlík roll
rybí polévka z kapra carp soup
rybíz currants
ryby fish
rýže rice
rýže dušená stewed rice
řízek fillet
s ledem with ice
s octem in vinegar
salát salad
sekaná pečeně meat loaf
sekané maso minced meat
sekaný chopped
skopová kýta leg of mutton
skopové (maso) mutton
skopové ragú mutton ragoût
sladkovodní ryby freshwater fish
sladký sweet
slanina bacon
sled' herring
slepice chicken
sluka snipe
smažené bramborové hranolky chips
smažené bramborové lupínky crisps
smažené kuře fried chicken
smažené telecí maso fried veal
smažené vepřové maso fried pork
smažený fried, fried in breadcrumbs
smažený karbanátek fried meatballs
smetana cream, full-cream milk
snídaně breakfast

srnčí (maso) venison
studené předkrmy hors d'oeuvres
studený cold
sůl salt
šumivá minerálka fizzy mineral water
sýr cheese
šampaňské champagne
šlehačka whipped cream
špenát spinach
šunka ham
švestkové knedlíky plum dumplings
švestky plums
telecí (maso) veal
telecí na paprice veal in paprika sauce
telecí řízek přírodní veal steak
teplá šunka boiled ham (served hot)
teplé předkrmy entrées
teplý hot or warm
těstoviny noodles
treska cod
třešně cherries
tvaroh cottage cheese
uzené maso vařené boiled smoked meat
uzené vepřové maso smoked pork
uzeniny smoked meats
uzený úhoř smoked eel
vaječná jídla egg dishes
vařené boiled
večeře supper
vejce egg
veka white French-style bread
vepřové dušené v kedlubnách pork
  stewed with kohlrabi
vepřová kýta na paprice stewed leg of
  pork with paprika
vepřová pečeně roast pork
vepřová žebírko přírodní stewed rib of
  pork
vepřové na kmíně pork stew with
  caraway seeds
vepřové (maso) pork

vepřové maso uzené smoked pork
vepřové ražniči pork on skewer with
  bacon and onions
vepřový bůček nadívaný stuffed side
  of pork
vepřový guláš pork goulash
vídeňský telecí řízek fried veal fillet in
  breadcrumbs
víno wine
višně morello cherries
voda water
voda s ledem water with ice
zadělávané in white sauce
zadělávané dršťky tripe in white sauce
zajíc hare
zajíc na černo stewed hare in thick,
  dark, sweet and sour sauce
zajíc na smetaně, přírodní hare in
  cream sauce
zapečená šunka s vejci ham and eggs
zapékané brambory se sýrem potatoes
  baked with cheese
zastřené vejce poached egg
zavařenina preserves, jam
zelenina vegetables
zeleninová polévka vegetable soup
zeleninové rizoto rice with vegetables
zeleninový řízek fried vegetable rissole
zelený hrášek green peas
zelná polévka cabbage soup
zelná polévka s klobásou cabbage soup
  with smoked sausage
zmrzlina ice cream
zmrzlinový pohár sundae
znojemská roštěná Znojmo-style sirloin
  (fried, then stewed with onions)
zvěřina game
žampióny mushrooms
žemlovka pudding made from bread,
  apples, cinnamon, eggs and milk
žitný chléb rye bread

DANISH

CONTENTS

INTRODUCTION

Pronunciation

When reading the imitated pronunciation, stress the part which is underlined. Pronounce each syllable as if it formed part of an English word, and you will be understood sufficiently well. Remember the points below, and your pronunciation will be even closer to the correct Danish.

ai	as in 'fair' or 'stair'
ī	the 'i' sound in 'wine'
ew	like the sound in 'dew' (or the French 'u')
g	always hard as in 'get'
s	as in 'hiss', never as in 'his'
th	as in 'smooth', never as in 'smith'

Danish Alphabetical Order

In the lists of Things You'll See and in the Menu Guide we have followed Danish alphabetical order. The following letters are listed after **z**: **æ, ø, å**.

'You'

The informal word **du** *[doo]* has recently become very common and you may even find yourself addressed with this form by total strangers. All the same, many Danes would still use the more formal **De** *[dee]* to address people they don't know – and this is the form generally given in this book. The verb stays the same whether you use **du** or **De**.

The Definite/Indefinite Articles

The definite article ('the') in Danish is a suffix: ie **en** or **et** (or **ne** for plural) added to the end of a word. When you see translations given in the form **hus(et)** or **bil(en)**, the form **huset** will mean 'the house' and **bilen** 'the car'. The indefinite article ('a', 'an') is again **en** or **et**, but placed as a separate word *before* the noun, as in English: **et hus** ('a house'), **en bil** ('a car'). If the noun is used with an adjective then the definite article changes to the word **den** or **det** and comes before the noun: eg **den tyske bil** ('the German car'), **det smukke hus** ('the beautiful house').

USEFUL PHRASES

Yes/no
Ja/nej
ya/nī

Thank you/no, thank you
Tak/nej tak
tak/nī tak

Please *(offering)*
Værsgo
vairsgoh

Please *(accepting something)*
Ja tak
ya tak

I don't understand (you/it)
Jeg forstår (Dem/det) ikke
yī forstor (dem/day) igger

Do you speak English/French/German?
Taler De engelsk/fransk/tysk?
tahlor dee engelsk/fransk/tewsk

I can't speak Danish
Jeg kan ikke tale dansk
yī ka igger tahler dansk

I don't know
Det ved jeg ikke
day vayth yī igger

Please speak more slowly
Vær venlig at tale langsommere
vair venlee or tahler langsommorer

Please write it down for me
Vær venlig at skrive det ned for mig
vair venlee or skreever day nayth for mī

My name is …
Mit navn er …
mit nown air

How do you do, pleased to meet you
Goddag, det glæder mig at træffe Dem
gohdah, day glaythor mī or treffer dem

Good morning/good afternoon/good evening
Godmorgen/goddag/godaften
gohmorn/gohdah/goh-aften

Good night
Godnat
gohnat

Goodbye
Farvel
farvel

How are you?
Hvordan går det?
vordan gor day

Excuse me, please *(introducing a question)*
Undskyld
awnskewl

Excuse me *(trying to move forward)*
Tillader De?
tillahthor dee

Sorry!
Undskyld
awnskewl

I'm really sorry
Det må De meget undskylde
day maw dee mi-et awnskewler

Can you help me?
Kan De hjælpe mig?
ka dee yelber mi

Can you tell me …?
Kan De sige mig …?
ka dee see mi

Can I have …?
Må jeg bede om …?
maw yi bay om

I would like …
Jeg vil gerne have …
yi vil gairner ha

Would you like …?
Ønsker De …?
urnskor dee

Is there … here?
Er der … her?
air dair … hair

Where can I get …?
Hvor kan jeg få …?
vor ka yi faw

How much is it?
Hvad koster det?
va k_ostor day

What time is it?
Hvad er klokken?
va air kl_oggen

Is there wheelchair access?
Er der adgang for korestole?
air dair _athg_ang for k_urrer-st_ohler

Are there facilites for the disabled?
Er der handicap faciliteter?
air dair 'handicap' faseeleet_ehteh

Where is the British embassy?
Hvor er den britiske ambassade?
vor air den br_itiske ambas_ather

I must go now
Jeg må afsted nu
yī maw ast_eth noo

I've lost my way
Jeg er faret vild
yī air f_ahret veel

Cheers!
Skål!
skawl

Do you take credit cards?
Tager De credit-card?
tar dee 'credit-card'

Where is the toilet?
Hvor er toilettet?
vor air toh-ahle̱ddet

Excellent!
Fint!
feent

THINGS YOU'LL HEAR

dav	hello
det forstår jeg ikke	I don't understand
det går godt	very well, thank you
– og De?	– and you?
det ved jeg ikke	I don't know
farvel	goodbye
goddag, det glæder mig	how do you do,
at træffe Dem	nice to meet you
hvadbehager?	pardon?
hvordan går det?	how are you?
højre	right
ja (det er rigtigt)	yes, that's right
kvinder	women
lige et øjeblik	just a moment
mænd	men
nej	no
pas på!	look out!
selv tak	you're welcome
tak	thanks
tillader De?	excuse me
undskyld	excuse me
venstre	left
vi ses	see you later
virkelig?	is that so?
værsgo	here you are

DAYS, MONTHS, SEASONS

Sunday	søndag	*surnda*
Monday	mandag	*manda*
Tuesday	tirsdag	*teersda*
Wednesday	onsdag	*awnsda*
Thursday	torsdag	*torsda*
Friday	fredag	*frayda*
Saturday	lørdag	*lurda*
January	januar	*yanoo-ar*
February	februar	*fibbroo-ar*
March	marts	*marts*
April	april	*apreel*
May	maj	*mi*
June	juni	*yoonee*
July	juli	*yoolee*
August	august	*owgawst*
September	september	*septembor*
October	oktober	*awktohber*
November	november	*nohvembor*
December	december	*dissembor*
Spring	forår	*for-or*
Summer	sommer	*sommor*
Autumn	efterår	*efter-or*
Winter	vinter	*vindor*
Christmas	jul	*yool*
Christmas Eve	juleaften	*yooler-aften*
New Year	nytår	*newdor*
New Year's Eve	nytårsaften	*newdorsaften*
Easter	påske	*pawsker*
Whitsun	pinse	*pinser*

NUMBERS

0	nul	*nawl*	5	fem *fem*
1	et	*it*	6	seks *sex*
2	to	*toh*	7	syv *seeoo*
3	tre	*tray*	8	otte *awder*
4	fire	*feerer*	9	ni *nee*

10 ti *tee*
11 elleve *elver*
12 tolv *tull*
13 tretten *tredden*
14 fjorten *fyorden*
15 femten *femden*
16 seksten *sisten*
17 sytten *surden*
18 atten *adden*
19 nitten *nedden*
20 tyve *tewver*
21 enogtyve *aynor-tewver*
22 toogtyve *toh-or-tewver*
30 tredive *trethver*
31 enogtredive *aynor-trethver*
32 toogtredive *toh-or-trethver*
40 fyrre *fur-rer*
50 halvtreds *hahl-tres*
60 tres *tres*
70 halvfjerds *hahl-fyairs*
80 firs *feers*
90 halvfems *hahl-fems*
100 hundrede *hoonrerther*
110 hundredeogti *hoonrerther-ortee*
200 to hundrede *toh hoonrerther*
300 tre hundrede *tray hoonrerther*
1,000 tusind *toosen*
1,000,000 en million *ayn milliohn*

TIME

today	idag	_ee<u>dah</u>_
yesterday	igår	_ee<u>gor</u>_
tomorrow	imorgen	_eem<u>or</u>n_
the day before yesterday	i forgårs	_ee for<u>gor</u>s_
the day after tomorrow	i overmorgen	_ee <u>aw</u>-wor-m<u>or</u>n_
this week	i denne uge	_ee d<u>e</u>nner <u>oo</u>er_
last week	sidste uge	_s<u>ee</u>ster <u>oo</u>er_
next week	næste uge	_n<u>e</u>ster <u>oo</u>er_
this morning (_said later in the day_)	her til morgen i morges	_hair til m<u>or</u>n_ _ee mors_
this afternoon	i eftermiddag	_ee efdormidd<u>ah</u>_
this evening	i aften	_ee <u>a</u>ften_
tonight	i aften	_ee <u>a</u>ften_
yesterday afternoon	igår eftermiddag	_eegor efdormidd<u>ah</u>_
last night	i aftes	_ee <u>a</u>ftes_
tomorrow morning	imorgen tidlig	_eem<u>or</u>n t<u>ee</u>thlee_
in three days	om tre dage	_om tray dah_
three days ago	for tre dage siden	_for tray dah s<u>ee</u>then_
late	sent	_saynt_
early	tidligt	_t<u>ee</u>thleet_
soon	snart	_snart_
later on	senere	_s<u>ay</u>nerer_
at the moment	i øjeblikket	_ee <u>oy</u>erbligget_
second	et sekund	_sikk<u>aw</u>nt_
minute	et minut	_it minn<u>oo</u>t_
one minute	et minut	_it minn<u>oo</u>t_
two minutes	to minutter	_toh minn<u>oo</u>ddor_
quarter of an hour	et kvarter	_it kvart<u>ai</u>r_
half an hour	en halv time	_in hahl t<u>ee</u>mer_
three quarters of an hour	tre kvarter	_tray kvart<u>ai</u>r_
hour	time	_t<u>ee</u>mer_

day	en dag	*dah*
fortnight	fjorten dage	*fyorden dah*
month	en måned	*mawneth*
year	et år	*or*

TELLING THE TIME

In everyday speech the 12-hour clock is quite common, but the 24-hour clock is preferred for timetables, radio and television programmes and theatre performances etc. Using the 12-hour system, the minutes, followed by **i** (to) or **over** (past), come before the hour, eg **fem minutter i/over seks** (*fem minnoodor ee/aw-wor sex*) is 'five to/past six' (with the word **minutter** following the minute number). Using the 24-hour clock, the minute numbers (without **minutter**) follow the hour, eg '17.55' is **sytten femoghalvtreds** (*surden femmor-hahl-tres*); '18.05' is **atten nul fem** (*adden nawl fem*). To express the half hour Danish refers ahead to the next full hour, eg 'half past six' is **halv syv** (*hahl seeoo*) – literally 'half seven'.

am (*until 10*)	morgen	*morn*
(*after 10*)	formiddag	*formiddah*
pm (*afternoon*)	eftermiddag	*efdormiddah*
(*evening*)	aften	*aften*
one o'clock	klokken et	*kloggen it*
quarter past one	et kvarter over et	*it kvartair aw-wor it*
half past one	halv to	*hahl toh*
twenty to two	tyve minutter i to	*tewver minnoodor ee toh*
quarter to two	et kvarter i to	*it kvartair ee toh*
two o'clock	klokken to	*kloggen toh*
13.00	klokken tretten	*kloggen tredden*
16.30	klokken seksten tredive	*kloggen sisten trethver*
at half past five	klokken halv seks	*kloggen hahl sex*
at seven o'clock	klokken syv	*kloggen seeoo*
noon	middag	*midda*
midnight	midnat	*meethnat*

COMMUNICATIONS

Useful Words and Phrases

code	kaldenummer(et)	_kahler-nawmor_
dialling tone	klartone(n)	_klar-tohner_
email address	email adresse(n)	_'email' adrasser_
emergency	en nødsituation	_nurth-sittoo-ashohn_
enquiries	oplysningen	_oplewsningen_
extension	et lokalnummer	_lohkahl-nawmor_
mobile phone	mobiltelefon(en)	_mobeeltillerfohn_
number	nummer(et)	_nawmor_
operator (faults)	fejlkontor(et)	_fil-kontor_
(overseas)	udenrigstelefon(en)	_oothenrees-tillerfohn_
reverse charge call	en opringning hvor modtageren betaler	_oprengning vor mohth-tjoren betahlor_
telephone	en telefon	_tillerfohn_
telephone box	en telefonboks	_tillerfohn-boks_
wrong number	forkert nummer	_forkairt nawmor_

Where is the nearest phone box?
Hvor er den nærmeste telefonboks?
vor air den nairmerster tillerfohn-boks

How much is a call to …?
Hvad koster en opringning til …?
va kostor in oprengning til

I would like to reverse the charges
En samtale, hvor modtageren betaler, tak
in samtahler vor mohth-tjoren betahlor tak

I'd like to send a fax
Jeg vil gerne sende en fax
yi vil gairner senner in fax

I would like a number in …
Må jeg bede om et nummer i …
maw yī bay om it n<u>aw</u>mor ee

Hello, this is … speaking
Hallo, det er …
hahl<u>oh</u>, day air

Speaking
Det er (+ name)
day air

I would like to speak to …
Jeg vil gerne tale med …
yī vil <u>ga</u>irner t<u>a</u>hler meth

My number is …
Mit nummer er …
mit n<u>aw</u>mor air

Could you leave him a message?
Kunne De give ham en besked?
koo dee gee ham in besk<u>ay</u>th

I'll ring back later
Jeg ringer igen senere
yī r<u>e</u>ng-er igg<u>e</u>n s<u>ay</u>norer

What's your fax number/email address?
Hvad er dit faxnummer/din email adresse?
va air dit faxn<u>aw</u>mor/deen email ad<u>ra</u>sser

Can I send an email/fax from here?
Kan jeg sende en email/fax herfra?
ka ya s<u>e</u>nner in email/fax hairfrah

THINGS YOU'LL HEAR

Hvem ønsker De at tale med?
Who would you like to speak to?

Hvem taler jeg med?
Who's speaking?

Hvad er Deres nummer?
What is your number?

Han er her desværre ikke
Sorry, he's not in

Han kommer igen klokken …
He'll be back at … o'clock

Vær så venlig at ringe igen i morgen
Please call again tomorrow

Jeg skal sige, De ringede
I'll tell him you called

THINGS YOU'LL SEE

drej	dial
fejlkontoret	faults service
HJÆLP	emergency (dial 112)
læg røret	replace the receiver
mønt(er)	coin(s)
opkald	call
optaget	engaged
tag røret	lift the receiver
ude af drift	out of order
udenbys-	long-distance call
udenrigs-	international call
udenrigstelefonen	international calls service

HOTELS

Useful Words and Phrases

balcony	en balkon	*balkong*
bathroom	et badeværelse	*bahther-vairelser*
bed	en seng	*seng*
bedroom	et værelse	*vairelser*
bill	en regning	*rining*
breakfast	morgenmad(en)	*mornmath*
dining room	en restaurant	*restohrang*
dinner	en middag	*midda*
double room	et dobbeltværelse	*dobbelt-vairelser*
farmhouse	en bondegård	*bawner-gor*
foyer	en foyer	*foh-ah-yay*
full board	helpension	*haylpang-shohn*
half board	halvpension	*hahlpang-shohn*
hotel	et hotel	*hohtel*
key	en nøgle	*noyler*
lift	en elevator	*ellervahtor*
lounge	opholdsstue(n)	*opholsstooer*
lunch	frokost(en)	*frawkost*
manager	direktør(en)	*direktur*
reception	reception(en)	*ressepshohn*
receptionist *(male)*	portier(en)	*porchay*
(female)	receptionist(en)	*ressepshohnist*
restaurant	en restaurant	*restohrang*
room	et værelse	*vairelser*
room service	servering på værelset	*sairvairing paw vairelset*
shower	et brusebad	*brooser-bath*
single room	et enkeltværelse	*enggelt-vairelser*
toilet	et toilet	*toh-ahlet*
twin room	et to-sengs værelse	*toh-sengs-vairelser*

Do you have any vacancies?
Har De et ledigt værelse?
har dee it laythit vairelser

I have a reservation
Jeg har bestilt et værelse
yī har bestilt it vairelser

I'd like a single/double room
Jeg vil gerne have et enkelt/dobbelt værelse
yī vil gairner ha it enggelt/dobbelt vairelser

I'd like a twin room
Jeg vil gerne have et to-sengs værelse
yī vil gairner ha it toh-sengs vairelser

I'd like a room with a bathroom/balcony
Jeg vil gerne have et værelse med bad/balkon
yī vil gairner ha it vairelser meth bath/balkong

I'd like a room for one night/three nights
Jeg vil gerne have et værelse for en nat/tre nætter
yī vil gairner ha it vairelser for ayn nat/tray neddor

What is the charge per night?
Hvad koster det pr. nat?
va kostor day pair nat

Is there satellite/cable TV in the rooms?
Er der satellit/kabel TV på værelserne?
air dair saddeleet/kahbel tay vay paw vairelsorne

I don't know yet how long I'll stay
Jeg ved endnu ikke, hvor længe jeg bliver
yī vayth ennoo igger vor leng-er yī bleer

When is breakfast/dinner?
Hvornår serveres der morgenmad/middag?
vornor sairvaires dair mornmath/midda

Please call me at ... o'clock
Vær venlig at vække mig klokken ...
vair venlee or vegger mī kloggen

Can I have breakfast in my room?
Kan jeg få morgenmad på værelset?
ka yī faw mornmath paw vairelset

I'll be back at ... o'clock
Jeg vil være tilbage klokken ...
yī vil vairer tilbah-yer kloggen

My room number is ...
Mit værelsesnummer er ...
mit vairelses-nawmor air

I'm leaving tomorrow
Jeg rejser i morgen
yī risor ee morn

Can I have the bill, please?
Må jeg bede om regningen?
maw yī bay om riningen

I'll pay cash/by credit card
Jeg betaler kontant/med credit-card
yī betahlor kontant/meth 'credit card'

Can you get me a taxi?
Kan De skaffe mig en taxa?
ka dee skaffer mī in taxa

Things You'll See

bad	bath(room)
betjening	service
brandtrappe	fire escape
bruser/brusebad	shower
dobbeltværelse	double room
enkeltværelse	single room
fuldt optaget	no vacancies
ingen adgang	no admittance
kro	country inn
nødudgang	emergency exit
opholdsstue	lounge
oplysning	information
tryk/træk	push/pull
udgang	exit

Things You'll Hear

Vi beklager, alt er optaget
I'm sorry, we're full

Vi har ikke flere enkeltværelser
There are no single rooms left

For hvor mange nætter?
For how many nights?

Hvad er Deres navn?
What is your name?

Hvordan vil De betale?
How will you be paying?

Betal venligst forud
Please pay in advance

SHOPPING

Where is the … department?
Hvor er … afdelingen?
vor ai … <u>ow</u>dayling-en

Do you have …?
Har De …?
har dee

How much is this?
Hvad koster det?
va <u>k</u>ostor day

Do you have any more of these?
Har De flere af disse her?
har dee <u>fla</u>irer ah <u>di</u>sser hair

Where do I pay?
Hvor er kassen?
vor air <u>k</u>assen

Have you anything cheaper?
Har De noget, der er billigere?
har dee nawth dair air <u>bee</u>leeyorrer

Could you wrap it for me?
Vil De godt pakke det ind?
vil dee got <u>pa</u>gger day in

Can I have a receipt?
Kan jeg få en kvittering?
ka yi faw in kvitt<u>ai</u>ring

Can I have a refund?
Kan jeg få det refunderet?
ka yi faw day reffoond<u>ai</u>ret

I'm just looking
Jeg kigger bare
yi <u>kee</u>ggor bar

EATING OUT

Denmark has several kinds of eating establishments. There is the **restaurant** (*restohrang*), which serves a wide variety of dishes including the famous **koldt bord** (*kult bor*), or cold buffet, and **smørrebrød** (*smurrerbrurth*) or garnished open sandwiches. If you feel like **smørrebrød** ask the waiter for the **smørrebrødsseddel** (*smurrerbrurths-sethel*) – the sandwich list.

A **bodega** (*bohdayga*) is less formal and has a less ambitious menu. The **cafeteria** (*kaffertair-ya*) is similar to its British equivalent but with a larger choice of cold food and a very reasonably priced **dagens ret** (*dahns ret*), or dish of the day. Cafeterias are often found in department stores and large supermarkets.

A country restaurant or inn is called a **kro** (*kroh*) and, as mentioned in the Hotels section, these are much frequented by Sunday visitors wanting afternoon coffee (which can be quite an elaborate affair). Many **kroer** also have a local reputation for their **kroplatte** (*kroh-pladder*), which is an assortment of marinated herring, beautifully garnished cold meats, a small hot dish and cheese.

Danish cafés serve snacks such as quiches, patés and sandwiches. If you have a sweet tooth, go to a **konditori** (*kondiddoree*) where you can enjoy delicious cakes, sumptuous gateaux and mouth-watering pastries with your tea, coffee or hot chocolate (with whipped cream, of course). Service is always included in your bill.

The most common drink by far is beer or **øl** (*url*). In Denmark this normally means **pilsner** lager (*peelsnor*]. A bottle of Carlsberg (*karlsbair*) and a bottle of Ceres (*saires*) are known as **en hof** (*in hof*) and **en top** (*in top*) respectively. Draught lager is called **fadøl** (*fath-url*).

Beer (or cold soft drinks), never wine, accompanies a **koldt bord**, and it is normal to enjoy one or two ice-cold **snaps** at the beginning with **sild** (*seel*), or marinated herring, and often at the end with the **ost** (*awst*), or cheese. **Snaps**, sometimes called **akvavit** (*agvaveet*) – the water of life – is a spirit made from potatoes and often flavoured with caraway. There are various kinds, including the popular dark and bitter **Gammel Dansk** (*gahmel dansk*), or 'Old Danish', but if you want to try the classic **snaps**, ask for **Rød Ålborg** (*rurth olbor*), or 'Red Ålborg'. The Danish word for 'cheers' is **skål** (*skawl*). This literally means 'bowl' and was what the Vikings would shout to each other whenever the need for mead came over them.

USEFUL WORDS AND PHRASES

beer	øl(let)	*url*
bill	regning(en)	*rining*
bottle	en flaske	*flasker*
bowl	en skål	*skawl*
cake	en kage	*kah-yer*
chef	kok(ken)	*kok*
coffee	kaffe(n)	*kaffer*
cup	en kop	*kop*
fork	en gaffel	*gaffel*
glass	et glas	*glas*
knife	en kniv	*kneeoo*
menu	menu(en)	*menew*
milk	mælk(en)	*melk*
plate	en tallerken	*tahlairken*
receipt	en kvittering	*kvittairing*
sandwich	et stykke smørrebrød	*sturger smurrerbrurth*
serviette	en serviet	*sairveeyet*
snack	en snack	*snak*
soup	suppe(n)	*sawbber*
spoon	en ske	*skay*
sugar	sukker(et)	*sawgor*
table	et bord	*bor*
tea	te(en)	*tay*
teaspoon	en teske	*tayskay*
tip	drikkepenge(ne)	*dregger-peng-er*
waiter	en tjener	*chaynor*

waitress	en servitrice	*sairveetreeser*
water	vand(et)	*van*
wine	vin(en)	*veen*
wine list	vinkort(et)	*veenkort*

A table for one/two, please
Et bord til en person/to, tak
it bor til ayn pairsohn/toh tak

Can I see the menu/wine list?
Må jeg se menuen/vinkortet?
maw yi say menewen/veenkordet

Is there a highchair/baby changing room?
Er der en høj stol/et puslerum?
air dair in hoy stohl/it puwsler-rum

What would you recommend?
Hvad kan De anbefale?
va ka dee anbefahler

Do you do children's portions?
Har I børneportioner?
har ee burnerpawshohnor

Do you have a vegetarian menu?
Har I en vegetarisk menu?
har ee in veggetarisk menew

I'd like …
Må jeg bede om …
may yi bay om

Just a cup of coffee, please
Kun en kop kaffe, tak
kawn in kop kaffer tak

Waiter/waitress!
Tjener/frøken!
chaynor/frurggen

Can we have the bill, please?
Må vi bede om regningen, tak?
maw vee bay om rī ningen-eng tak

I only want a snack
Jeg skal bare have en snack
yī ska bar ha in snak

Is there a set menu?
Er der en fast menu?
air dair in fast menew

I didn't order this
Jeg bad ikke om dette
yī bath igger om dedder

May we have some more …?
Må vi bede om lidt mere …?
maw vee bay om lit mair

The meal was very good, thank you
Måltidet var udmærket, tak
molteethet var oothmair-get tak

YOU MAY HEAR

Velbekomme!
Enjoy your meal

MENU GUIDE

agerhøne partridge
agurk cucumber
akvavit aquavit, a potato-based liquor
and duck
ansjos anchovy
appelsin- orange…
appelsinfromage orange mousse
artiskokker artichokes
asier pickled cucumber chunks
asparges asparagus
bagt(e) baked
bajerske pølser frankfurters
benløse fugle beef (or veal) olives
bladselleri celery
blodpølse black pudding
blomkål cauliflower
blomme- plum…
blåmuslinger mussels
boller meat and flour dumplings; buns
bouillon broth
brasede kartofler sauté potatoes
brisler sweetbread
brombær- blackberry…
brændende kærlighed mashed
  potatoes with bacon and onions
brød bread
butterdej puff pastry
bækforel trout
bøf beef
bønner beans
bønnespirer bean sprouts
børnemenu children's menu
champignons mushrooms
chokoladeis chocolate ice cream
citron lemon
citronfromage lemon mousse
citronvand lemonade
crepinetter pork rissoles

dagens ret dish of the day
dampet, dampkogt steamed
dansk bøf minced beef steak
dansk vand mineral water
dild dill
dildsild dill herring
dildsmør dill butter
drueagurk gherkin
druer grapes
engelsk bøf steak and onions
farseret stuffed
fasan pheasant
fedt dripping
fersken, ferskner peach(es)
ferskrøget laks smoked salmon
figner figs
fisk fish
fiskeboller fish ball or dumpling
fiskefrikadeller fish rissoles
fjerkræ poultry
flæsk belly of pork
flæskekarbonade minced pork steak
fløde cream
flødeost cream cheese
fløderand vanilla mousse
flødeskum whipped cream
flødestuvet creamed
forel trout
forloren hare meat loaf
forretter starters
fransk bøf steak with parsley butter
franskbrød white bread
franske kartofler crisps
frikadeller pork rissoles
frisk(e) fresh(ly)
friteret, friturestegt deep-fried
frokostretter lunch dishes
frugt(er) fruit

57

frugttærte fruit tart of flan
fyldt(e) filled, stuffed
gaffelbidder bite-sized pieces of
  marinated herring fillet
gammeldags, gammaldaws traditional
gammelost very mature cheese
gemyse vegetables
gravad laks marinated salmon
grillstegt grilled
grovbrød whole-kernel ryebread
gryderet casserole
græskar pickled pumpkin or marrow
grøn salat green salad, tossed salad
grøn(t)sager vegetables
grønkål curly kale
grønlandske rejer Greenland prawns
grønne bønner green beans
grønærter green peas; creamed peas
gule ærter med flæsk yellow split-pea
  soup with belly of pork
gulerødder carrots
gås goose
gåsesteg roast goose
hachis minced beef in gravy
hakket, hakkede chopped
hamburgerryg smoked pork loin
haresteg roast hare
hasselnødder hazelnuts
havregrød porridge
hellefisk flounder
helleflynder halibut
hindbær- raspberry...
hjemmebag(t) home-baked (pastries)
hjemmelavet home-made
hjerter heart
hornfisk garfish
hovedretter main courses
hummer- lobster...
hummerhaler lobster tails
husets of the house
hvide bønner broad beans

hvide kartofler boiled potatoes
hvidkål white cabbage
hvidkålsrulle stuffed cabbage
hvidkålssuppe cabbage soup
hvidløg garlic
højreb saddle of beef
høns chicken
hønsefrikassé creamy chicken stew
håndmadder plain open sandwiches
hårdkogt æg hard-boiled egg
is ice cream
jomfruhummer Norwegian crayfish
jordbær- strawberry...
jordbæris strawberry ice cream
jordbærsyltetøj strawberry jam
julienne with thin vegetable strips
kaffe coffee
kage(r) cake(s)
kalkun turkey
kalv(ekød) veal
kalvelever veal liver
kalvesteg roast veal
kande pot
kanel cinnamon
kanin rabbit
karamelrand caramel custard
karbonade minced pork steak
karse cress
kartoffel, kartofler potato(es)
kartoffelmos mashed potatoes
kartoffelsalat potato salad
kastanie- chestnut...
kiks crackers, biscuits
kirsebær- cherry...
klipfisk salt cod
knækbrød crispbread
kogt(e) boiled
kold(t) cold
kompot stewed fruit
kotelet chop
kransekage marzipan cake

krydder- savoury, spicy
kryddersild spicy red marinated herring
krydderurter herbs
krydret spiced
kylling chicken
kyllingelever chicken liver
kyllingelår chicken leg
kærnemælk buttermilk
kød meat
kødboller meatballs, meat dumplings
kødgratin meat soufflé
kødpølse sliced pork sausage
kødretter meat dishes
kål cabbage
labskovs meat and potato stew
lage marinade
lagkage gâteau
laks salmon
lam lamb
lammekoteletter lamb chops
lammekølle leg of lamb
lammeryg saddle of lamb
lammesteg roast lamb
lever liver
leverpostej pâté
løg onions
løgsovs onion sauce
løse ris boiled rice
majs corn, maize
makrel mackerel
marineret, marinerede marinated
medisterpølse fried pork sausage
melboller flour dumplings (in broth)
millionbøf minced beef in gravy
mineralvand fizzy mineral water
morgencomplet, morgenmad breakfast
muslinger mussels
mørbrad fillet
nudler noodles
nyrer kidneys
nødder nuts

oksefilet fillet of beef
oksehalesuppe oxtail soup
oksehøjreb saddle of beef
oksemørbrad roast sirloin
oksesteg roast beef
oksetyksteg roast beef
olie oil
ost cheese
osteanretning cheese board
pandekager pancakes
paneret coated with breadcrumbs
peber pepper
peberbøf peppered steak
peberrod horseradish
pighvar turbot
pikant savoury, spicy, herb-flavoured
platte cold buffet served at table
pocheret, pocherede poached
porrer leeks
portvin port
purløg chives
pære- pear...
pølse(r) sausage(s)
radiser radishes
ragout stew
rasp breadcrumbs
rejer prawns, shrimps
ret(ter) dish(es), course(s)
revelsben spare ribs
reven(t), revne grated
ribbensteg roast spare ribs
ribsgelé redcurrant jelly
ris rice
ristet franskbrød toast
ristet, ristede fried, toasted
rogn fish roe
rosenkål Brussels sprouts
rosiner raisins
roulade sponge roll; rolled-up stuffed
    slice of meat; rolled-up joint of meat
rugbrød ryebread

rullepølse sliced streaky pork sausage
rødbeder beetroot
rødspætte plaice
røget smoked
røget makrel smoked mackerel
røget sild smoked herring
røræg scrambled egg
rå raw
råcreme cold vanilla cream sauce
saft juice
salathoved lettuce
selleri celery
sennep mustard
sild herring
sildesalat marinated herring salad
skaldyr shellfish
skinke ham
skipperlabskovs meat and potato stew
smør butter
smørrebrød open sandwiches
småkager cookies, biscuits
solbær- blackcurrant...
sovs sauce, gravy
spegepølse salami
spegesild marinated herring
spejlæg fried egg
spinat- spinach...
spisekort menu
sprængt boiled
steg roast (joint)
stegt(e) fried, roast(ed)
stikkelsbær- gooseberry...
sukker sugar
suppe(r) soup(s)
surkål sauerkraut
surt pickles
svampe mushrooms
sveske- prune...
svine- pork...
svinekam roast pork
svinekød pork

svær pork crackling
sylte brawn
syltet, syltede preserved, pickled
syltetøj jam
sød(t), søde sweet
sød-og-sur sweet-and-sour
sødlig medium-sweet
søtunge sole
te, the tea
torsk cod
trøfler truffles
tunge tongue, sole
tyttebær- cranberry...
tærte(s) tart(s)
urter herbs
vaffel, vafler waffle(s)
vagtel quail
valnødde- walnut
vand still water
vanillecreme custard
vegetarretter vegetarian dishes
vildt game
vildtsovs redcurrant sauce
vin(e) wine(s)
vinbjergsnegle snails
vindruer grapes
wienerbrød flaky Danish pastry
wienerschnitzel pork or veal escalope
ymer milk curd, junket
æble- apple...
æblemost apple juice
æbleskiver warm doughnuts
æg egg(s)
æggekage omelette (with bacon)
ærter peas
øl beer
øllebrød beer-and-bread soup
ørred trout
østers oysters
ål eel
ål i gelé jellied eel

DUTCH

CONTENTS

INTRODUCTION

Pronunciation

When reading the imitated pronunciation, stress the part that is underlined. Pronounce each syllable as if it formed part of an English word, and you will be understood sufficiently well. Remember the points below, and your pronunciation will be even closer to the correct Dutch.

CH	represents the guttural sound of 'ch' as in Scottish 'loch' (*don't* pronounce this as 'lock')
ey	should be as in 'day'
oo	as in 'book'
OO	is like the French sound 'du', or similar to the 'eau' in 'beauty'
ow	as in 'cow', *not* as in 'low'

In vocabulary lists, where a Dutch word is pronounced the same as in English, then the English word is given, in quotation marks, for the pronounciation guide.

USEFUL PHRASES

Yes/No
Ja/Nee
ya/ney

Thank you
Dank u wel
dank oo vel

No thank you
Nee, dank u
ney, dank oo

Please
Alstublieft
alstoobleeft

I don't understand
Ik begrijp het niet
ick beCHreyp et neet

Do you speak English/French/German?
Spreekt u Engels/Frans/Duits?
spreykt oo engels/frans/dowts

I can't speak Dutch
Ik spreek geen Nederlands
ick spreyk CHeyn nederlands

Please speak more slowly
Wilt u alstublieft wat langzamer spreken
vilt oo alstoobleeft vatt langzahmer spreykeh

Please write it down for me
Wilt u het alstublieft voor mij opschrijven
vilt oo et alstoobleeft foor mey opscHreyfeh

Good morning/good afternoon/good night
Goedemorgen/goedemiddag/goedenavond
cHoodemorcHen/cHoodemiddacH/cHoodenahfont

Goodbye
Tot ziens
tot zeens

How are you?
Hoe gaat het met u?
hoo cHaht et met oo

Excuse me, please
Neem me niet kwalijk, alstublieft
neym mey neet kvalek alstoobleeft

Sorry!
Sorry!
sorry

I'm really sorry
Het spijt me echt
et speyt mey ecHt

Can you help me?
Kunt u mij helpen?
kuhnt oo mey helpeh

I've lost my passport/money/room key/traveller's cheques
Ik heb mÿn paspoort/geld/kamer sleutel/reischeques verloren
Ick hep meyn paspohrtcHeld/kahmeh slurrtel/reys sjecks verlohreh

Can you tell me …?
Kunt u mij vertellen …?
kuhnt OO mey fertelleh

Can I have …?
Mag ik … hebben?
mahCH ick … hebbeh

I would like …
Ik zou graag …
ick zow CHrahCH

Is there a … here?
Is er hier een …?
iss er here en

Where can I get …?
Waar kan ik … krijgen?
vahr kan ick … kreyCHeh

Where is the British embassy?
Waar is de Britse ambassade?
vahr iss de Britseh ambassahde

How much is it?
Hoeveel is het?
hooveyl iss et

Do you take credit cards?
Accepteert u credit cards?
acksepteert OO 'credit cards'

Can I pay by cheque?
Kan ik met een cheque betalen?
kan ick met en sheck betahleh

Where are the toilets?
Waar zijn de toiletten?
vahr zeyn de tvaletteh

What time is it?
Hoe laat is het?
hoo laht iss et

I must go now
Ik moet nu gaan
ick moot noo CHahn

Go away!
Ga weg!
CHa veCH

Cheers!
Proost!
prohst

Is there wheelchair access?
Waar is de ingang voor rolstoelen?
vahr iss de inchang voor rolstoohleh

Are there facilities for the disabled?
Zÿn er gehandicapte faciliteiten?
zeyn er CHehandikapt fahciliteyteh

Are guide dogs allowed?
Mogen blindengeleide honden naar binnen?
mooCHeh blihndehCHeleydeh hondeh nahr binnen?

THINGS YOU'LL SEE OR HEAR

aan de voorkant	at the front
aanbellen	ring
aankomst	arrival
achter	at the back
attentie	attention
a.u.b.	please
beneden	at the bottom, downstairs
betalen	pay
bezet	engaged
binnengaan	enter
boven	at the top, above, upstairs
controle	check, inspection
dames	women
defect	out of order
dicht	shut
douane	customs
duwen	push
geen, geen een	none, not any
geopend	open
gereserveerd	reserved/booked
gesloten	closed
gevaar	danger
gratis	free
heren	men
ingang	way in, entry
kapot	out of order
kassa	till, cash desk
kinderen	children
kloppen	knock
langzaam	slow
let op de opstap/ afstap	mind the step (literally step up or down)
links	left
niet roken a.u.b.	no smoking

→

niet ...	do not ...
omkeren	to turn
onder	under
open	open
openingstijden	opening hours
paspoort	passport
prijs	price
rechts	right
snel	fast
stad	town, city
stop	stop
straat	street
strafbaar	punishable
tarief	charges, price list
tijd	time
toegang	access
tot	until
trekken	pull
uitgang	way out/exit
vanuit, van	from, of
verboden	prohibited
verhuren	to rent
verkopen	to sell
vertrek	departure
voetgangers	pedestrians
volwassenen	adults
voorzichtig	take care

DAYS, MONTHS, SEASONS

Sunday	zondag	*z*o*ndaCH*
Monday	maandag	*mahndaCH*
Tuesday	dinsdag	*dinsdaCH*
Wednesday	woensdag	*voonsdaCH*
Thursday	donderdag	*donderdaCH*
Friday	vrijdag	*freydaCH*
Saturday	zaterdag	*zahterdaCH*
January	januari	*yanooary*
February	februari	*febrooary*
March	maart	*mahrt*
April	april	*ahpril*
May	mei	*mey*
June	juni	*yooni*
July	juli	*yooli*
August	augustus	*owchustus*
September	september	*september*
October	oktober	*oktober*
November	november	*november*
December	december	*deysember*
Spring	lente	*lenteh*
Summer	zomer	*zohmer*
Autumn	herfst	*herfst*
Winter	winter	*vinter*
Christmas	Kerstmis	*kerstmiss*
Christmas Eve	Kerstnacht	*kerstnaCHt*
Good Friday	Goede Vrijdag	*CHoodeh freydaCH*
Easter	Pasen	*pahseh*
New Year	Nieuwjaar	*neewyahr*
New Year's Eve	Oudejaarsavond	*owdehyahrsahfont*

NUMBERS

0 nul *nool*
1 een *eyn*
2 twee *tvey*
3 drie *dree*
4 vier *feer*

5 vijf *feyf*
6 zes *zess*
7 zeven *zeyveh*
8 acht *aCHt*
9 negen *neyCHeh*

10 tien *teen*
11 elf *elf*
12 twaalf *tvahlf*
13 dertien *derteen*
14 veertien *feyrteen*
15 vijftien *feyfteen*
16 zestien *zessteen*
17 zeventien *zeyvehteen*
18 achttien *aCHteen*
19 negentien *neyCHenteen*
20 twintig *tvintiCH*
21 eenentwintig *eynentvintiCH*
22 tweeëntwintig *tveyentvintiCH*
30 dertig *dertiCH*
40 veertig *feyrtiCH*
50 vijftig *feyftiCH*
60 zestig *zesstiCH*
70 zeventig *zeyventiCH*
80 tachtig *taCHtiCH*
90 negentig *neyCHentiCH*
100 honderd *hondert*
110 honderd tien *hondert-teen*
200 tweehonderd *tvey hondert*
1000 duizend *dowzend*
1,000,000 een miljoen *eyn milyoon*

TIME

today	vandaag	*fandahCH*
yesterday	gisteren	*CHistereh*
tomorrow	morgen	*morCHeh*
this week	deze week	*deyzeh veyk*
last week	vorige week	*foriCHeh veyk*
next week	volgende week	*folCHende veyk*
this morning	vanmorgen	*fanmorCHeh*
this afternoon	vanmiddag	*fanmiddaCH*
this evening	vanavond	*fanahfont*
tonight	vanavond, vannacht	*fanahfont, fannaCHt*
last night	gisteravond	*CHisterafont*
tomorrow morning	morgenochtend	*morCHeh-oCHtent*
tomorrow night	morgenavond	*morCHeh-ahfont*
in three days	over drie dagen	*ofer dree dahCHeh*
three days ago	drie dagen geleden	*dree daCHeh CHeleydeh*
late	laat	*laht*
early	vroeg	*frooCH*
soon	gauw	*CHow*
later on	later	*lahter*
at the moment	op het moment	*op et moment*
second	een seconde	*sekondeh*
minute	een minuut	*minoot*
ten minutes	tien minuten	*teen minooteh*
quarter of an hour	een kwartier	*kvarteer*
half an hour	een half uur	*hulf oor*
three quarters of an hour	drie kwartier	*dree kvarteer*
hour	een uur	*oor*
day	een dag	*daCH*
week	een week	*veyk*
month	een maand	*mahnt*
year	een jaar	*yahr*

TELLING THE TIME

Telling the time has similarities with English. Minutes past the hour being **over** and minutes before being **voor**. Thus 6.10 is **tien over zes**, literally 'ten beyond six' and 5.50 is **tien voor zes**, 'ten before six'. The half hour is different; it is always related to the following hour rather than the previous one, so 5.30 is **half zes**, literally 'half (before) six'.

You will also hear people refer to the time in relation to the half hour. 5.20 can be either **twintig over vijf** 'twenty past five' or **tien voor half zes** 'ten to half past five'. Similarly, 5.40 can be either **twintig voor zes** 'twenty to six' or **tien over half zes** 'ten past half past five'. The quarter hour is always **kwart voor** 'quarter to' or **kwart over** 'quarter past'. The twenty-four hour clock is used in all public transport timetables.

one o'clock	een uur	*eyn OOr*
ten past one	tien over een	*teen ofer eyn*
quarter past one	kwart over een	*kvahrt ofer eyn*
twenty past one	twintig over een	*tvintiCH ofer eyn*
half past one	half twee	*hulf tvey*
twenty to two	twintig voor twee	*tvintiCH foor tvey*
quarter to two	kwart voor twee	*kvahrt foor tvey*
ten to two	tien voor twee	*teen foor tvey*
two o'clock	twee uur	*tvey OOr*
13.00 (1 pm)	dertien uur	*derteen OOr*
16.30 (4.30 pm)	zestien uur dertig	*zessteen OOr dertiCH*
20.10 (8.10 pm)	twintig uur tien	*tvintiCH OOr teen*
at half past five	om half zes	*om half zess*
at seven o'clock	om zeven uur	*om zeyveh OOr*
noon	twaalf uur's middags	*tvahlf OOr smiddaCHs*
midnight	middernacht	*middernaCHt*

COMMUNICATIONS

Useful Words and Phrases

code	het netnummer	_netnummer_
dialling tone	de kiestoon	_keestone_
email address	het email adres	_email ahdres_
emergency	spoedgeval	_spootchefal_
enquiries	inlichtingen	_inlichtingeh_
extension	het toestel	_toostell_
fax machine	de fax machine	_fax mahsjeneh_
mobile phone	de mobiele telefoon	_mobeyleh telephone_
number	het nummer	_noomer_
operator	de telefoniste	_telefone-ist_
payphone	de telefooncel	_telephonecell_
reverse charge call	het collect call gesprek	_'collect call' chespreyk_
telephone	de telefoon	_telephone_
Web site	de Web site	_'web site'_
wrong number	verkeerd nummer	_ferkeyrt noomer_

Where is the nearest phone box?
Waar is de dichtstbijzijnde telefooncel?
vahr iss dey dichtsbeyzeyndeh telephonecell

I would like a number in …
Ik wil graag een nummer hebben van …
ick vill chrahch en noomeh hebbeh fan

I would like to speak to …
Kan ik … spreken?
kan ick … spreykeh

My number is …
Mijn nummer is …
meyn noomeh iss

Could you leave him a message?
Kunt u een boodschap voor hem achterlaten?
kuhnt oo en bohdscHap foor hem acHterlahteh

I'll ring back later
Ik bel straks wel terug
ick bell straks vell terrucH

What's your fax number/email address?
Wat is uw fax nummer/email adres?
vhat iss oo fax nummer/email ahdres

Can I send an email/fax from here?
Kan ik hiervandaan een fax/email sturen?
kan ich heervandahn en fax/email stooren

THINGS YOU'LL HEAR

Daar spreekt u mee
Speaking

Het spijt me, hij is er niet
Sorry, he's not in

Met wie spreek ik?
Who's calling?

Kan hij u terugbellen?
Can he call you back?

Met wie wilt u spreken?
Who do you want to speak to?

U bent verkeerd verbonden
You've got the wrong number

Hij is om … terug
He'll be back at …

THINGS YOU'LL SEE

antwoord apparaat	answering machine
brand	fire
brandweer	fire brigade
defect	out of order
email adres	email address
fotokopieer apparaat	photocopier
gesprek	call, conversation
gouden gids	yellow pages
haak	hook
in het buitenland	abroad
inwerpen	insert
interlokaal gesprek	long-distance call
kiesschijf	the dial (on the telephone)
lokaal gesprek	local call
lokaal	local
maak het kort!	be brief!
munt, geldstuk	coin(s)
mobiele telefoon	mobile telephone
opnemen	lift (the receiver)
storingsdienst	faults service
tarief	charges
telefoniste	operator
telefoon	telephone
telefoonboek	telephone directory
telefooncel	telephone box
telefoon kaart	phonecard
telefoonnummer	number
tik	unit
wachten	wait

HOTELS

Useful Words and Phrases

balcony	het balkon	*balkon*
bathroom	de badkamer	*batkahmeh*
bed	het bed	*bet*
bedroom	de slaapkamer	*slahpkahmeh*
bill	de rekening	*reykening*
breakfast	het ontbijt	*ontbeyt*
dining room	de eetkamer	*eytkahmeh*
double room	de tweepersoonskamer	*tveypersohnskahmeh*
foyer	de foyer	*foyeh*
full board	volpension	*follpenshon*
half board	halfpension	*halfpenshon*
hotel	het hotel	*hotel*
key	de sleutel	*slurrtel*
lift	de lift	*lift*
lounge	de conversatiezaal	*konversasiesahl*
lunch	de lunch	*'lunch'*
manager	de manager, de chef	*manager, shef*
reception	de receptie	*resepsie*
receptionist		
(female)	de receptioniste	*resepshonisteh*
(male)	de receptionist	*resepshonist*
restaurant	het restaurant	*restorant*
room	de kamer	*kahmeh*
room service	de roomservice	*roomservis*
shower	de douche	*doosh*
single room	de eenpersoonskamer	*eynpersohnskahmeh*
toilet	het toilet	*tvalet*
twin room	een kamer met twee eenpersoonsbedden	*kahmeh met tvey eynpersohnsbeddeh*

Have you any vacancies?
Hebt u een kamer vrij?
hept OO en k_ahmeh frey

I have a reservation
Ik heb een kamer besproken
ick hep en k_ahmeh besprohkeh

I'd like a single room
Ik wil graag een eenpersoonskamer
ick vill CHRACH en eynpersohnsk_ahmeh

We'd like a double room
Wij willen graag een tweepersoonskamer
vey villeh CHRACH en tveypersohnsk_ahmeh

I'd like a room with a bathroom/balcony
Ik wil graag een kamer met bad/balkon
ick vill CHRACH en k_ahmeh met bat/balk_on

Is there satellite/cable TV in the rooms?
Hebben de kamers satelliet/kabel TV?
heppeh de kahmehs saht_eleet/k_ahbel tch veh

I'd like a room for one night/three nights
Ik wil graag een kamer voor een nacht/drie nachten
ick vill CHRACH en k_ahmeh foor eyn naCHt/dree n_aCHteh

What is the charge per night?
Hoeveel is het per nacht?
hoov_eyl iss et per naCHt

I don't know yet how long I'll stay
Ik weet nog niet hoelang ik blijf
ick vate noCH neet hool_ang ick bleyf

When is breakfast/dinner?
Hoe laat is het ontbijt/diner?
hoo laht iss et ontbeyt/deeney

Would you have my luggage brought up?
Wilt u mijn bagage naar boven laten brengen?
vilt oo meyn bacHage nahr bohfeh lahteh brengeh

Please call me at … o'clock
Roep me alstublieft om … uur
roop mey alstoobleeft om … oor

Can I have breakfast in my room?
Kan ik in mijn kamer ontbijten?
kan ick in meyn kahmeh ontbeyteh

I'll be back at … o'clock
Ik ben om … uur terug
ick ben om … oor terrucH

My room number is …
Mijn kamernummer is …
meyn kahmehnoomer iss

I'm leaving tomorrow
Ik vertrek morgen
ick fer-treck morcHeh

May I have my bill, please?
Kan ik afrekenen, alstublieft?
kan ick afreykeneh, alstoobleeft

Can you get me a taxi?
Kunt u voor mij een taxi bestellen?
kuhnt oo foor mey en taxi bestelleh

THINGS YOU'LL SEE

bad	bath
bagage	luggage
begane grond	ground floor
diner	dinner
douche	shower
duwen	push
kamer	room
kamers vrij	vacancies
kinderen	children
logies met ontbijt	bed and breakfast
nacht	night
nooduitgang	emergency exit
overnachting	overnight stay
reservering	reservation
toeslag	supplement
trekken	pull
verdieping	storey, floor
vol, volgeboekt	no vacancies

THINGS YOU'LL HEAR

Alle tweepersoonskamers zijn bezet
We have no double rooms left

Het spijt me, we zitten vol
I'm sorry, we're full

Verlaat uw kamer alstublieft om …
Please vacate the room by …

Wilt u alstublieft vooruit betalen
Please pay in advance

SHOPPING

Where is the ...-department?
Waar is de ...-afdeling?
vahr iss deh ...-afdeyling

Do you have ...?
Hebt u ...?
hept OO

How much is this?
Hoeveel kost dit?
hooveyl kost dit

Do you have any more of these?
Hebt u er hier nog meer van?
hept OO er here noCH meyr fan

Where do I pay?
Waar moet ik afrekenen?
vahr moot ick afreykeneh

Have you anything cheaper?
Hebt u iets goedkopers?
hept OO eets CHoodkopers

Can I have a receipt?
Hebt u een kassabon voor me?
hept OO en kassabon foor meh

Can I have a refund?
Kan ik mijn geld terugkrijgen?
kan ick meyn CHeld terruCH-kreyCHeh

I'm just looking
Ik kijk alleen wat rond
ick keyk alleyn vatt rond

EATING OUT

There is a wide selection of good-quality restaurants in Holland, to suit all tastes and price brackets. The most common types are traditional Dutch, French, Italian, Chinese and Indonesian.

You can also eat in a cafeteria (but don't confuse this with the English variety!); it is a combined bar, café and restaurant with service provided at the counter or – for a little extra – at the table. There is usually a good variety of set menus at reasonable prices.

Another establishment whose name could be confusing to those used to the English interpretation is the café-bar or **eet-café**. Like the cafeteria, it sells all kinds of food and drink, and is well worth trying if all you want is a quick snack. Full meals are often available.

USEFUL WORDS AND PHRASES

beer	het bier	'*beer*'
bill	de rekening	*reykening*
bottle	de fles	*fless*
bowl	de schaal	*sCHahl*
cake	het gebak	*CHebak*
chef	de chef-kok	*sheff-kok*
coffee	de koffie	*koffee*
cup	het kopje	*kop-ye*
fork	de vork	'*fork*'
glass	het glas	*CHlass*
knife	het mes	*mess*
menu	het menu	*menoo*
milk	de melk	*melk*
plate	het bord	*bort*
recipe	het recept	*resept*
receipt	het bonnetje	*bonneht-ye*
sandwich	de boterham	*bohterham*
serviette	het servet	*serfett*

snack	het hapje	*hap-ye*
soup	de soep	*'soup'*
spoon	de lepel	*leypel*
sugar	de suiker	*sowker*
table	de tafel	*tahfell*
tea	de thee	*tey*
teaspoon	de theelepel	*teyleypel*
tip	de fooi	*fohy*
waiter	de kelner/ober	*kelner*
waitress	de serveerster	*serveyrsteh*
water	het water	*vahter*
wine	de wijn	*veyn*

A table for one/two, please
Een tafel voor een persoon voor/twee personen, alstublieft
en tahfell foor eyn persohn/tvey persohneh, alstoobleeft

Can we see the menu/wine list?
kunnen we de kaart/de wijnkaart krijgen?
kuhneh vey deh kahrt/deh veynkahrt kreyCHeh

Do you do children's portions?
Heeft u een kindermenu?
heyft oo en kindermenoo

What would you recommend?
Wat beveelt u aan?
vaht behfehlt oo ahn

I'd like …
Ik wil graag …
ick vill CHrahCH

Just a cup of coffee, please
Alleen een kopje koffie, alstublieft
alleyn en kop-ye koffee, alstoobleeft

Waiter!
Ober!
ober

Can we have the bill, please?
Kunnen we afrekenen, alstublieft?
kuhnen vey afreykeneh, alstoobleeft

I only want a snack
Ik wil alleen maar een hapje eten
ick vill alleyn mahr en hap-ye eyteh

Is there a set menu?
Hebt u een menu van de dag?
hept oo en menoo fan deh dacн

Do you have a vegetarian menu?
Heeft u een vegetarisch menu?
heyft oo en vecнetaris menoo

I'm allergic to nuts/shellfish
Ik ben allergisch voor noten/schaaldieren
ick ben allecнees foor nohten s-chahldeereh

I didn't order this
Ik heb dit niet besteld
ick hep dit neet bestelt

May we have some more …?
Kunnen we nog wat … krijgen?
kuhneh vey nocн vatt … kreycheh

The meal was very good, thank you
De maaltijd was erg lekker, dank u
deh mahlteyt vass ercн lekker, dank oo

MENU GUIDE

aardappelen potatoes
aardappelpuree mashed potatoes
aardbeien strawberries
abrikozenjam apricot jam
abrikozenvlaai apricot flan
amandelen almonds
ananas pineapple
andijvie endive
ansjovissen anchovies
appelcompote stewed apples
appelflap apple turnover
appelmoes apple sauce
appelsap apple juice
appeltaart applecake
artisjok artichoke
asperges asparagus
aubergine aubergine
augurken gherkins
azijn vinegar
baars bass
bak-en braadvet cooking fat
balkenbrij white pudding
banaan banana
banketletter roll of puff pastry with
    almond paste filling
basilicum basil
bearnaise saus sauce hollandaise
bediening service
belegen kaas mature cheese
beschuit type of rusk
bessenjenever blackcurrant liqueur
biefstuk beef steak
biefstuk van de haas fillet steak
bier van het vat draught beer
bieslook chives
bieten beetroot
bijgerecht side dish
bitterballen deep fried meatballs

blauw rare
bloedworst black pudding
bloemkool cauliflower
boerenjongens brandy with raisins
boerenkaas farmhouse cheese
boerenkool Scotch kale
boerenmeisjes apricots in brandy
boerenmetworst coarse sausage
boerenomelet omelette with ham and
    potatoes
bokking (gerookte) red herring (smoked)
bokking (verse) bloater
bonensla bean salad
bosbessen bilberries
boterham met …… sandwich
boterham met kaas cheese sandwich
boterhamworst sliced sausage
boterletter roll of puff pastry with
    almond paste filling
bouillon consommé
braadschotel casserole
brandewijn brandy
brood bread
broodje roll
broodje kaas cheese roll
bruine bonen dried brown beans
bruine bonensoep brown bean soup
bruine suiker brown sugar
casselerrib pickled smoked rib of pork
cassis blackcurrant cordial
champignon mushroom
champignonsoep mushroom soup
Chinese kool Chinese cabbage
chips crisps
chocoladepasta chocolate spread
chocoladevla chocolate custard
chocomel tinned or bottled chocolate
    drink

citroen lemon
citroenthee lemon tea
compote stewed fruit
croquetje, kroket croquette
dame blanche ice cream with chocolate
   sauce
doorbakken, doorbraden well done
doperwten garden peas
droog dry
druiven (blauwe) grapes (black)
druiven (witte) grapes (white)
Duitse biefstuk minced beef and onion
   steaks served
   on onion rings
Edammer Edam cheese
eieren eggs
eierkoeken flat round sponge cakes
erwtensoep (met spek/worst) pea soup
   (with bacon/sausage)
fazant pheasant
fijngehakt finely minced
forel trout
frambozen raspberries
frikandel rissole
garnalencocktail prawn cocktail
gebakje small cake
gebakken fried
gebakken kip fried chicken
gebakken mosselen fried mussels
gebakken paling fried eel
gebakken spierling fried smelt
gebonden thickened
gebonden soep thickened soup
gebraden roast
gebraden eend roast duck
gebraden fazant roast pheasant
gebraden gehakt roast meatloaf
gebraden konijn roast rabbit
gedistilleerde dranken spirits
gehakt mince
gehaktbal minced beef and pork rissole

gekookt boiled
gekookte kip boiled chicken
gekookte mosselen boiled mussels
gekruid seasoned with herbs or spices
gemarineerd marinated
gemarineerd rundvlees marinated beef
gember (poeder) ginger (ground)
gemberkoek gingerbread
gepocheerde eieren poached eggs
gerecht dish, course
gerookt smoked
gerookte paling smoked eel
gerookte zalm smoked salmon
geroosterd grilled
geroosterd brood toast
gestoofd stewed
gestoofd konijn stewed rabbit
gestoofde paling stewed eel
gevulde koek pastry with almond filling
Goudse kaas Gouda cheese
groene haring lightly salted herring,
   first of the season
groene/rode paprika green/red pepper
groenten vegetables
groentesoep vegetable soup
gulasch, goulash goulash
haas hare
hachée finely chopped meat
halfvolle melk skimmed milk
halvarine half butter and half margarine
ham ham (smoked or salted)
hamlappen belly of pork
haring herring
heilbot halibut
hertevlees venison
hete bliksem potatoes and apples
   mashed together
hollandse biefstuk thick slice of frying
   steak
hom soft roe
honing honey

honingkoek type of gingerbread
hutspot (met klapstuk) mashed
  potatoes with carrots, onions and
  breast or rib of beef
huzarensalade potato salad with
  beetroot, gherkin, salmon,
  sardines etc
ijs ice cream
jachtschotel shepherd's pie
janhagel kind of biscuit
jenever Dutch gin
jeneverbessen juniper berries
jonge kaas new cheese
jonge klare young Dutch gin
kaas cheese
kaassoesjes cheese puff
kabeljauw cod
kadetje soft roll
kalfslever calf's liver
kalfsniertjes calf's kidneys
kalfsoester escalope of veal
kalfsschnitzel veal schnitzel
kalfstong calf's tongue
kalfsvlees veal
kalkoen turkey
karbonade chop
karnemelk buttermilk
karper carp
kasserole casserole
kastanjes chestnuts
kerriesoep curry soup
kersen cherries
kersenvlaai cherry flan
kervilsoep chervil soup
kikkerbilletjes frogs' legs
kippesoep chicken soup
knåckebrod crispbread
knakworst frankfurter
knoflook garlic
koekjes biscuits
koffie coffee

koffietafel cold buffet lunch (usually
  bread, cold meats and cheese)
kogelbiefstuk thick end of rump
komijnekaas cheese with cumin seeds
komkommer cucumber
koninginnesoep cream of chicken soup
kool cabbage
koolraap swede
korst crust
kotelet cutlet
kreeft lobster
kreeftesoep lobster soup
krenten currants
krentenbrood currant loaf
kroepoek prawn crackers
kropsla cabbage lettuce
kruiden herbs
kruidenboter herb butter
kruisbessen gooseberries
kuit hard roe
kwark soft white cheese
kwarktaart cheesecake
kwast lemon squash
lamskotelet lamb cutlet, lamb chop
lamsragout lamb stew
landwijn simple wine, vin ordinaire
laurierblad bayleaf
lekkerbekjes deep-fried whiting fillets
leverworst liver sausage
Limburgse vlaai open fruit flan
limonade lemonade
linzen lentils
loempia spring roll (Indonesian)
magere kaas skimmed-milk cheese
magere melk skimmed milk
makreel mackerel
marsepein marzipan
melk milk
mierik horseradish
moesappelen cooking apples
mosselen mussels

mosselensoep mussel soup
mosterd mustard
munt mint
nagerecht dessert
nasi goreng Indonesian fried rice dish
  with meats and vegetables
nieren kidneys
nieuwe haring salted herring
nootmuskaat nutmeg
oesters oysters
oliebol doughnut
olijfolie olive oil
olijven olives
omelet omelette
ontbijtkoek type of gingerbread
ontbijtspek (lean, smoked) bacon
ossestaart oxtail
ossestaartsoep oxtail soup
oude kaas mature cheese
paling eel
palingworst type of sausage
paneermeel breadcrumbs
pannekoek pancake
patates frites chips
patrijs partridge
peper pepper
perenmoes puréed pears
perziken peaches
peterselie parsley
piccalilly pickles
pikant piquant
pils type of lager
pindakaas peanut butter
pocheren to poach
pommes frites French fries
pompelmoes grapefruit
pompelmoessap grapefruit juice
pompoen pumpkin
prei leek
preisoep leek soup
pruimedant type of prune

pruimen plums
pruimenjam plum jam
rabarber rhubarb
radijs radish
ree/reebok roe/roebuck
reebout leg of venison
regenboogforel rainbow trout
rijst rice
rijstebrij rice pudding
rijstevlaai rice tart
rivierkreeft crayfish
riviervis fresh water fish
rode kool red cabbage
rode wijn red wine
roerei scrambled eggs
roggebrood ryebread
rookworst smoked sausage
room cream
roomboter dairy butter
roomijs ice cream
rosbief roast beef
rozijnen currants
rundervlees beef
Russisch ei egg salad
sardientjes sardines
saucijzenbroodje sausage roll
saus sauce
savooiekool savoy cabbage
schartong lemon sole
schelvis haddock
schnitzel veal cutlet
schol plaice
schuimpje meringue
selderij celery
sinaasappel orange
sinaasappelsap orange juice
slaatje salad
slagroom whipped cream
slakken snails
slaolie salad oil
slasaus salad cream

slavinken minced pork rolled in bacon
smeerkaas cheese spread
snijbonen string beans
snoekbaars perch
soep van de dag soup of the day
spa water mineral water
specerijen spices
speculaas spiced biscuit
spek bacon, usually rather fatty
sperziebonen French beans
spiegelei fried egg
spiering smelt
spijskaart menu
spinazie spinach
spirituosa spirits
spruiten, spruitjes Brussels sprouts
stokbrood French loaf
stokvis stockfish
stoofperen stewing pears
stroopwafel waffle with syrup filling
taart cake
tarwebrood wheaten bread
tomatensoep tomato soup
tong sole
tongrolletjes rolled fillets of sole
tonijn tuna
tosti/toastie toasted sandwich
tuinbonen broad beans
uien onions
uiensoep onion soup
uitgebreide koffietafel buffet lunch
  with soup and dessert
vanillevla custard saucea
varkensbiefstuk pork fillet
varkenshaas pork fillet
varkensoester pork escalope
varkenspoot leg of pork
varkensrib pickled smoked rib of pork
varkensrollade rib, tailend (rolled)
varkensvlees pork
venkel fennel

vermout vermouth
verse haring fresh herring
verse oesters fresh oysters
verse worst sausage
vet fat
vis fish
vissoep fish soup
vleet skate
vlierbessen elderberries
volkorenbrood wholemeal bread
voorgerecht starter
voorn roach
vruchten fruit
vruchtensap fruit juice
vruchtensla fruit salad
wafel waffle, wafer
walnoot walnut
waterkers watercress
wijn wine
wijting whiting
witte bonen dried white beans
wittebrood white bread
wittekool white cabbage
witte wijn white wine
wortel carrot
zalm salmon
zeepaling sea-eel
zeetong Dover sole
zilveruitjes pickled silverskin onions
zoet sweet
zoetwatervis fresh-water fish
zoet-zuur sweet-sour
zout salt
zoute haring salted herring
zoutjes salty/savoury meatballs
zult brawn
zure haring pickled herring
zwarte bessen blackcurrants
zwarte bessenjam blackcurrant jam
zwarte kersenjam black cherry jam
zwezerik sweetbread

FINNISH

CONTENTS

INTRODUCTION

Pronunciation

When reading the imitated pronunciation, the first syllable of each word is underlined and should be stressed. Try and pronounce each syllable clearly. The intonation is flat without extremes. The following sounds need special attention:

Letter	Approximate Pron.	Symbol	Example
Consonants			
h	as in hot whatever its position in the word	h	lahti <u>lah</u>hti
j	like y as in you	y	ja yah
r	always rolled	r	raha <u>rah</u>hah
s	s as in set	s	sillä <u>sil</u>la
ng	pronounced as in singer	ng	sangen <u>sah</u>ngayn
Vowels			
a/aa	like a as in car	ah	matala <u>mah</u>tahlah
e	like ay as in lay	ay	kolme <u>koal</u>may
i	like i as in pin	i	takki <u>tah</u>kki
ii	ee as in see	ee	siitä <u>see</u>ta
o/oo	a sound between aw in law and oa in coat	oa	olla <u>oal</u>lah
u/uu	like oo as in pool	oo	hupsu <u>hoop</u>soo
y/yy	like u in French sur or ü in German über	ew	yksi <u>ewk</u>si
ä/ää	like a as in hat;	a	äkkiä <u>ak</u>kia
ö/öö	like ur as in fur, but without any r sound	ur	tyttö <u>tewt</u>tur

When a double consonant appears in the original Finnish word, try to make sure that the letter is clearly pronounced twice.

Finnish Alphabetical Order

In the lists of Things You'll See and in the Menu Guide we have followed Finnish alphabetical order. The following letters are listed after z: å, ä, ö.

USEFUL PHRASES

Yes, No, OK, etc.

Yes/No
Kyllä/Ei
_kew_lla/ay

OK
Selvä
_say_lva

That's fine
Hyvä on
_hew_va on

That's right
Aivan niin
_ah_vahn neen

Greetings, Introductions

How do you do, pleased to meet you
Päivää, hauska tutustua
_pah_vah _haoo_skah _too_toostooah

Good morning
Huomenta
_hooa_mentah

Good evening/Good night
Iltaa/Hyvää yötä
_el_taah/_hewaah_ _ewur_tah

Goodbye
Näkemiin
_na_kaymeen

How are you?
Mitä kuuluu?
_mi_tta _koo_loo

My name is
Nimeni on
nimmayni on

What's your name?
Mikä teidän nimenne on?
mikka taydan nimmaynnay on

(familiar form)
Mikä sinun nimesi on?
mikka sennoon nimmaysi on

This is …
Tämä on …
tamma on

Hello/Hi!
Terve/ Hei!
tayrvay/hey

PLEASE, THANK YOU, APOLOGIES

Thank you/No, thank you
Kiitos/Ei kiitos
keetoss/ay keetoss

Please
Olkaa/Ole hyvä
oalkaa/oalay hewvah

Excuse me!/Sorry!
Anteeksi!
ahntayksi

WHERE, HOW, ASKING

Excuse me, please
Anteeksi
ahntayksi

Can you tell me …?
Voitteko sanoa minulle …?
voatteaykoa sahnoah minnoollay

Can I have …?
Voinko saada …?
_voan_koa _saa_dah

Would you like a …?
Haluaisitteko …?
_hahloo_ahsittekoa

Would you like to …?
Haluaisitteko …?
_hahloo_ahsittekoa

What's that?
Mitä se on?
_mit_ta say on

How much is it?
Paljonko se on?
_pahl_yoankoa say on

Where is the …?
Missä on …?
_mis_sa on

Is there wheelchair access?
Voiko sinne mennä rullatuolissa oleva henkilö?
_voa_koa _sin_nay _maynnah _roolla_toooa_lissah _oala_yvah _hayn_kiloe

Are guide dogs allowed?
Onko opaskoirilla pääsy sinne?
_oan_koa _oapahskoa_rillah _paa_sew _sin_nay

ABOUT ONESELF

I'm from …
Olen … sta/lta
_oa_layn … stah/ltah

I'm … years old
Olen … vuotta vanha
_oa_layn … _vooa_ttah _vaon_hah

FINNISH • USEFUL PHRASES

I'm a …
Olen …
oalayn

I'm married/single/divorced
Olen naimisissa/naimaton/eronnut
oalayn naoimisissah/naoimahtoan/ayroannoot

I have … sisters/brothers/children
Minulla on … sisaria/veljiä/lapsia
minnoollah on … sissahrriah/vayllyeea/lapseea

HELP, PROBLEMS

Can you help me?
Voitteko auttaa minua?
voattaykoa ahoottaa minnooah

I don't understand
En ymmärrä
ayn ewmmarrah

Does anyone here speak English?
Puhuuko joku täällä englantia?
poohookoa yokoo taalla aynglahntiah

I can't speak Finnish
En puhu suomea
ayn poohoo sooamayah

I don't know
En tiedä
ayn tiayda

Please speak more slowly
Puhukaa hitaammin olkaa hyvä?
poohookaa hihtaammin oalkaa hewva

Please write it down for me
Voisitteko kirjoittaa sen minulle?
voasittaykoa keeryoattaa sayn minnoollay

I've lost my way
Olen eksynyt
oalayn eksewnewt

Go away!
Menkää pois!
maynkaa poais

LIKES, DISLIKES, SOCIALIZING

I like/love …
Pidän/Rakastan …
pidan/rahkahstahn

I don't like …
En pidä …
ayn pida

I hate…
Vihaan …
veehaan

Do you like …?
Pidätkö …?
peedatkur

It's delicious/awful!
Se on herkullista/kauheaa!
say on hayrkoollistah/kaoohayah

I don't drink/smoke
En juo/polta
ayn yooah/poaltah

Do you mind if I smoke?
Pahastutteko jos poltan?
paohaostoottaykoa yoas poaltahn

What would you like to drink?
Mitä haluaisitte juoda?
mitta haolooasittay yooahdah

I would like a …
Haluaisin …
hahlooahsin

Nothing for me, thanks
Kiitos, ei mitään minulle
keetoss, ay mittaan minnoollay

Cheers! (toast)
Kippis/Skål!
kippiss/skoal

THINGS YOU'LL HEAR

anteeksi	excuse me
anteeksi	sorry!/pardon?
ei kestä	don't mention it
hei/terve	hello
henkilöllisyystodistus, olkaa hyvä	identification papers, please
hyvä	fine
hyvää matkaa!	have a good trip!
hyvästi	goodbye
mitä sanoitte?	what did you say?
näkemiin	see you later
niinkö?	is that right?
olkaa hyvä	here you are
ottakaa itse	help yourself
selvä	right! OK!
tulkaa sisään	come in
varo!	look out!

DAYS, MONTHS, SEASONS

Sunday	sunnuntai	*soonnoontah*
Monday	maanantai	*maanahntah*
Tuesday	tiistai	*teestah*
Wednesday	keskiviikko	*kayskiveekkoa*
Thursday	torstai	*toarstah*
Friday	perjantai	*payryahntah*
Saturday	lauantai	*lahoontah*

January	tammikuu	*tahmmikkoo*
February	helmikuu	*haylmikoo*
March	maaliskuu	*maalisskoo*
April	huhtikuu	*hoohtikkoo*
May	toukokuu	*toaookoakoo*
June	kesäkuu	*kayssakoo*
July	heinäkuu	*haynakoo*
August	elokuu	*ayloakoo*
September	syyskuu	*sewskoo*
October	lokakuu	*loakahkoo*
November	marraskuu	*mahrrahskoo*
December	joulukuu	*yoaoolookoo*

Spring	kevät	*kayvat*
Summer	kesä	*kayssa*
Autumn	syksy	*sewksew*
Winter	talvi	*tahlvi*

Christmas	joulu	*yoaooloo*
Christmas Eve	jouluaatto	*yoaooloo-aahttoa*
Good Friday	pitkäperjantai	*pitkapayryahntah*
Easter	pääsiäinen	*paassiaynen*
New Year	uusi vuosi	*ooossi vooassi*
New Year's Eve	uuden vuoden aatto	*ooodayn vooaden aahttoa*
Pentecost	helluntai	*haylloontah*

NUMBERS

0	nolla _noallah_	6	kuusi _koo_ssi
1	yksi _ewk_si	7	seitsemän _sayt_sayman
2	kaksi _kahk_si	8	kahdeksan _kah_dayksahn
3	kolme _koal_may	9	yhdeksän _ewh_dayksan
4	neljä _nayl_ya	10	kymmenen _kewm_maynayn
5	viisi _vee_ssi		

11 yksitoista _ewk_si_toas_tah
12 kaksitoista _kahk_si_toas_tah
13 kolmetoista _koal_may_toas_tah
14 neljätoista _nayl_ya_toas_tah
15 viisitoista _vee_ssi_toas_tah
16 kuusitoista _koo_ssi_toas_tah
17 seitsemäntoista _sayt_sayman_toas_tah
18 kahdeksantoista _kah_dayksahn_toas_tah
19 yhdeksäntoista _ewh_dayksan_toas_tah

20 kaksikymmentä _kahk_si_kewm_maynta
21 kaksikymmentäyksi _kahk_si_kewm_maynta_ewk_si
22 kaksikymmentäkaksi _kahk_si_kewm_maynta_kahk_si
30 kolmekymmentä _koal_may_kewm_maynta
40 neljäkymmentä _nayl_ya_kewm_maynta
50 viisikymmentä _vee_ssi_kewm_maynta
60 kuusikymmentä _koo_ssi_kewm_maynta
70 seitsemänkymmentä _sayt_sayman_kewm_maynta
80 kahdeksankymmentä _kah_dayksahn_kewm_maynta
90 yhdeksänkymmentä _ewh_dayksan_kewm_maynta
100 sata _sah_tah
110 satakymmenen _sah_tah_kewm_maynayn
200 kaksisataa _kahk_si_sah_taah
1,000 tuhat _too_haht
10,000 kymmenentuhatta _kewm_maynayn_too_hattah
20,000 kaksikymmentätuhatta _kahk_si_kewm_maynta_too_hattah
100,000 satatuhatta _sah_tah_too_hattah
1,000,000 miljoona _mil_yoanah

TIME

today	tänään	*tanan*
yesterday	eilen	*aylayn*
tomorrow	huomenna	*hooaomaynnah*
this week	tällä viikolla	*talla veekoallah*
last week	viime viikolla	*veemay veekoallah*
next week	ensi viikolla	*aynsi veekoallah*
this morning	tänä aamuna	*tanna aahmoonnah*
this afternoon	tänä iltapäivänä	*tanna iltahpayvana*
this evening/ tonight	tänä iltana/ yönä	*tanna iltahnnah/ ewurna*
in three days	kolmen päivän kuluttua	*koalmayn payvan kooloottooah*
three days ago	kolme päivää sitten	*koalmay payvaa sittayn*
late	myöhään	*mewrhaan*
early	aikaisin	*ahikahisin*
soon	pian	*peeahn*
later on	myöhemmin	*myerhammin*
at the moment	tällä hetkellä	*talla haytkaylla*
second	sekunti	*saykoontti*
minute	minuutti	*minnootti*
ten minutes	kymmenen minuuttia	*kewmmaynayn minnoottiah*
quarter of an hour	neljännes tuntia	*nayljannays toontiah*
half an hour	puoli tuntia	*pooahli toontiah*
hour	tunti	*toonti*
day	päivä	*paiva*
everyday	joka päivä	*yoakah paiva*
all day	koko päivän	*koakoa paivan*
week	viikko	*veekkoa*
fortnight	kaksi viikkoa	*kahksi veekkoah*
month	kuukausi	*kookahoosi*
year	vuosi	*vooahsi*

TELLING THE TIME

The 24-hour clock is always used in the written form in
timetables and for appointments, and also verbally in enquiry
offices and if talking about the times of television and radio
programmes. However, in most other situations, people will
use the 12-hour clock.

'What time is it?' is **Mitä kello on**?. 'O'clock' is translated as
kello. '(It's) one (o'clock)' is (**Kello on**) **yksi**; '(It's) four
(o'clock)' is (**Kello on**) **neljä** and so on. Note that the half
hour (**puoli**) refers forward to the next hour, so 'half past five'
is **puoli kuusi**, literally 'half (to) six'.

To express minutes after the hour, state the number of
minutes followed by **yli** (past) and the hour. For example, 'ten
past five' is **kymmentä yli viisi**. For minutes to the hour use
vaille, which means 'towards'. For example, 'twenty to eleven'
is **kaksikymmentä vaille yksitoista**.

'Quarter' is **neljännes**, so 'quarter past three' is **neljännestä
yli kolme**, and 'quarter to eight' is **neljännestä vaille
kahdeksan**.

one o'clock	kello yksi	_kaylloa ewksi_
ten past one	kymmentä yli yksi	_kewmmaynta ewli ewksi_
quarter past one	neljännestä yli yksi	_naylyannaysta ewli ewksi_
twenty past two	kaksikymmentä yli kaksi	_kahksikewmmaynta ewli kahksi_
1.30	yksi kolmekymmentä	_ewksi koalmaykewmmaynta_
twenty to two	kaksikymmentä vaille kaksi	_kahksikewmmaynta vahillay kahksi_
quarter to two	neljännestä vaille kaksi	_naylyannaysta vahillay kahksi_
two o'clock	kello kaksi	_kaylloa kahksi_
midday	keskipäivä	_kayskipaiva_
midnight	keskiyö	_kayskiewur_

COMMUNICATIONS

Useful Words and Phrases

code	koodi	_koaoad_i
dialling tone	soittoääni	_soattoaah_ni
email address	sähköpostiosoite	_sahkoepoastiossoatay_
emergency	hätätilanne	_hatatillahnnay_
enquiries	tiedusteluja	_tiaydoostaylooyah_
extension	posti, alanumero	_poasti, ahlahnoomayroa_
fax machine	faksi	_fahks_i
internet	internet	_internet_
mobile phone	kännykkä	_kannewkka_
number	numero	_noommayroa_
operator	operaattori	_oapayraattoar_i
phonecard	puhelinkortti	_poohaylinkoart_ti
reverse charge call	vastapuhelu	_vahstahpoohayloo_
telephone	puhelin	_poohaylin_
telephone box	puhelinkioski	_poohaylinkioa_ski
Web site	web-sivusto	_web-sivoostoa_
wrong number	väärä numero	_vaara noommayroa_

Where is the nearest phone box?
Missä on lähin puhelinkioski?
missa on lahin poohaylinkioaski

I would like a number in …
Haluaisin numeron … ssa/lla
hahlooahsin noommayroan … ssah/llah

I would like to speak to …
Haluaisin puhua … kanssa
hahlooahsin puuhooah … kahnssah

My number is …
Numeroni on …
noommayroani on

Could you leave him/her a message?
Voisitteko jättää hänelle sanoman?
voysittaykoa jatta hanayllay sahnoamahn

I'll ring back later
Soitan myöhemmin uudestaan
soatahn mewurhaymmin oodaystaan

What's your fax number/email address?
Mikä on teidän faksinumero/sähköpostiosoite?
mikka on taydan fahksinoommayroh/sahkoepoastioasoytay

Can I send an email/fax from here?
Voinko lähettää täältä sähköpostia?
voynkoa lahayttaa taalta sahkoepoastiah

THINGS YOU'LL HEAR

Kenen kanssa haluaisitte puhua?
Who would you like to speak to?

Teillä on väärä numero
You've got the wrong number

Anteeksi, kuka kysyy?
May I ask who's calling?

Puhelimessa
Speaking

Hetkinen olkaa hyvä
Hold the line

Voitteko soittaa uudestaan myöhemmin?
Could you call back later?

Valitettavasti hän ei ole paikalla
Sorry, he/she is not in

EMERGENCIES

accident	onnettomuus	_oannayttoamoos_
ambulance	ambulanssi	_ahmboolahnssi_
breakdown	epäkunto	_aypakkoontoah_
burglary	murtovarkaus	_moortoavahrkahoos_
crash	yhteenajo	_ewhtaynahyoa_
emergency	hätätilanne	_hatatillahnnay_
fire	tulipalo	_toollipahloa_
fire brigade	palokunta	_pahloakkoontah_
police	poliisi	_poaleessi_
police station	poliisiasema	_pohleessiahsaymah_

Help!
Apua!
ahpooah

Stop!
Pysähdy!/Pysähdyttäkää!
pewrsahdew/pewrsahdewttakaa

Get an ambulance!
Kutsukaa ambulanssi!
kootsookaa ahmboolahnssi

Hurry up!
Kiirehtikää!
keerayhtikaa

My address is …
Osoitteeni on …
oasoattayni on

My passport/car has been stolen
Passini/ autoni on varastettu
pahssihni/aootoani on vahrahstayttoo

HOTELS

Useful Words and Phrases

balcony	parveke	_pahr_vaykay
bathroom	kylpyhuone	_kewlpewhooa_nay
bed	vuode	_vooa_day
bed & breakfast	huone aamiaisella	_hooa_nay _aami_ahssayllah
bill	lasku	lahskoo
breakfast	aamiainen	_aami_ahinayn
car park	parkkipaikka	_pahrkkipahikkah_
dining room	ruokasali	_rooa_kah_sahli_
dinner	päivällinen	_pai_vallinnayn
double room	kahden hengen huone	_kahdayn_ _hayngayn_ _hooa_nay
full board	täysihoito	_tawursihoahtoa_
guesthouse	täysihoitola	_tawursihoahtoalah_
half board	puolihoito	_pooa_lihoatoa
hotel	hotelli	_hoat_aylli
key	avain	_ah_vahin
lift	hissi	_his_si
lunch	lounas	_loaoo_nahss
maid	siivooja	_see_voahyah
manager	johtaja	_yohht_ahyah
receipt	kuitti	_koo_itti
reception	vastaanotto	_vah_staan_ott_oa
receptionist	vastaanottoapulainen	_vah_staamn_ott_oa-poollahinayn
room	huone	_hooa_nay
room service	huonepalvelu	_hooa_nay_pahl_vayloo
shower	suihku	_sooi_hkoo
single room	yhden hengen huone	_ewh_dayn _hayn_gayn _hooa_nay
toilet	toiletti	_toal_aytti
twin room	kaksi eri vuodetta	_kahk_si _ay_ri _vooa_dayttah

Do you have any vacancies?
Onko teillä vapaita huoneita?
_oan_koa _tay_lla _vah_paotah _hooa_naytah

I have a reservation
Minulla on varaus
_min_noollah on _vah_rahoos

I'd like a single room
Haluaisin yhden hengen huoneen
_hah_looahsin _ewh_dayn _hayn_gayn _hooa_nayn

I'd like a room with a bathroom/balcony
Haluaisin huoneen jossa on kylpyhuone/parveke
_hah_looahsin _hooa_nayn _yoas_sah on _kewl_pew_hooa_nay/_pahr_vaykay

Is there satellite/cable TV in the rooms?
Onko huoneissa satelliitti/kaapeli-teeveetä?
_oan_koa _hooa_nayssah _sah_taylleetti/_kaah_paylli-_tay_vayta

I'd like a room for one night/three nights
Haluaisin huoneen yhdeksi/kolmeksi yöksi
_hah_looahsin _hooa_nayn _ewh_dayksi/_koal_maykksi _ewurk_si

What is the charge per night?
Mitä maksaa yksi yö?
_mit_ta _mahk_saah _ewk_si ewur

When is breakfast/dinner?
Koska on aamiainen/päivällinen?
_koas_kah on _aa_miahnayn/ _pai_vallinnayn

Please wake/call me at one o'clock
Herättäkää minut kello yksi
_hay_rattakaa _min_noot _kayl_loa _ewk_si

Can I have breakfast in my room?
Voinko saada aamiaisen huoneeseeni?
_voan_koa _saa_dah _aa_miahssayn _hooa_naysayni

My room number is …
Huoneeni numero on …
hooanayni noommayroa on

There is no toilet paper in the bathroom
Kylpyhuoneessa ei ole toilettipaperia
kewlpewhooanayssah ay oalay toalayttipahpayriah

The window won't open
Ikkuna ei avaudu
ikkoonah ay ahvaoodoo

There isn't any hot water
Ei ole kuumaa vettä
ay oalay koomaa vaytta

I'm leaving tomorrow
Lähden huomenna
lahhdayn hooamaynnah

When do I have to vacate the room?
Koska minun on luovutettava huone?
koaskah minnoon on looavootayttahvah hooanay

Can I have the bill, please?
Saisinko laskuni?
saosinkoa lahskooni

I'll pay by credit card
maksan luottokortilla
mahksahn looattoakoartillah

I'll pay cash
Maksan käteisellä
mahksahn kataysaylla

Can you get me a taxi?
Voitteko hankkia minulle taksin?
voattaykoa hahnkkiah minnoollay tahksin

Things You'll See

aamiainen	breakfast
hissi	lift
hätäuloskäytävä	emergency exit
kylpyhuone	bathroom
lasku	bill
lounas	lunch
portaat	stairs
pääsy kielletty	no admission
sisäänkäynti	entrance
suihku	shower
työnnä	push
täynnä	no vacancies
vedä	pull

Things You'll Hear

Valitan, mutta hotelli täynnä
I'm sorry, we're full

Ei ole enää kahden/yhden hengen huoneita jäljellä
There are no double/single rooms left

Kuinka moneksi yöksi?
For how many nights?

Kuinka maksatte?
How will you be paying?

Voitteko maksaa etukäteen
Please pay in advance

Huone on luovutettava puoleen päivään mennessä
You must vacate the room by noon

SHOPPING

Excuse me, where is/are …?
Anteeksi, missä on …?
ahntayhksi, missa on

Do you have …?
Onko teillä…?
oankoa taylla …

How much is this?
Paljonko tämä maksaa?
pahlyoankoa tama mahksaa

Where do I pay?
Missä voin maksaa?
missa voan mahksaa

Do you take credit cards?
Hyväksyttekö luottokortteja?
hewvaksewttaykur looattoakoarttayjah

Can I have a receipt?
Voinko saada kuitin?
voankoa saadah kooitin

Have you anything cheaper?
Onko teillä mitään halvempaa?
oankoa taylla mittan hahlvaympaa

Can I have a refund?
Voinko saada hyvityksen?
voankoa saadah hewvitewksayn

That's fine. I'll take it
Se on hyvä. Otan sen
say on hewva. oatahn sayn

It isn't what I wanted
Se ei ole mitä haluan
say ay oalay mitta hahlooahn

EATING OUT

It is not difficult to eat well and fairly inexpensively in Finland. Menus are often displayed on the window or door of an eating establishment, so you can readily fit your choice of restaurant to your budget. It is not customary to leave a tip for the waiter or waitress, but if you are especially pleased with the service, you may leave some small change or something more substantial. Note that the same tipping guidelines apply to taxi drivers, barbers and hairdressers.

Every town has a number of cafés, often called **kahvila** or **baari**, where, at lunchtime, you can order an open sandwich, consisting of white or rye bread with a cheese, ham or egg topping, plus a salad garnish, various pasties filled with minced meat, chopped salmon, rice and eggs, etc. Do not forget to taste the delicious pastries, such as the Finnish equivalent of Danish pastries, which are called **viineri** ('Viennese').

There is a variety of small restaurants with a selection of traditional dishes or snacks. Meatballs are a typical dish, and also a variety of frankfurter sausages, sold in street kiosks at night. Other popular dishes are pea soup and cabbage rolls. As well as salmon from the northern rivers – often served as **raavi lohi** or **gravad lax**, a Scandinavian speciality – freshwater fish such as **kuha** and **siika** (resembling hake or haddock in flavour) are plentiful. Smoked or grilled Baltic herring can also be recommended, not forgetting salted herring, which is an unmissable classic. If your visit falls in August, you can join in crayfish parties downing a few chilled vodkas to accompany it!

Beer, lager and vodka are popular, but a wide selection of wines is also available. Finns, like other Scandinavians, are great coffee drinkers and coffee is often served very strong with a dash of cream, which the more health-conscious Finns now sometimes leave out.

Traditional sweets consist mostly of berries, either the wild varieties or cultivated ones. Finnish ice cream and chocolates are highly recommended.

Useful Words and Phrases

beer	olut	_oa_loot
bill	lasku	_lahs_koo
bread	leipä/ä	_layp_a/a
butter	voi/ta	_voa_/tah
cake	leivos	_lay_voas
child's portion	lasten annos	_lahs_tayn _ahn_noss
coffee	kahvi/a	_kahh_vi/ah
cup	kuppi	_koop_pi
dessert	jälkiruoka	_jalk_ki_rooak_kah
fork	haarukka	_haah_rookkah
glass	lasi	_lah_si
knife	veitsi	_vayt_si
main course	pääruoka	_pah_rooakah
menu	menu/ruokalista	_may_noo/_rooak_ah_lis_tah
milk	maito/a	_mah_to/ah
napkin	servietti	_sayr_viaytti
pepper	pippuri/a	_pip_poori/ah
plate	lautanen	_laoo_tahnayn
receipt	kuitti	_kooit_ti
salt	suola/a	_sooa_lah/ah
sandwich	voileipä	_voa_laypa
snack	välipala	_val_ip_pah_lah
soup	keitto/a	_kayt_to/ah
spoon	lusikka	_loo_sikkah
starter	alkuruoka	_ahl_koo_rooa_kah
sugar	sokeri/a	_soa_kayri/ah
table	pöytä	_purew_ta
tea	tee/tä	_tayh_/ta
teaspoon	teelusikka	_tayh_loosikkah
tip	juomaraha	_yooa_mah_rahh_hah
waiter	tarjoilija	_tahr_yoaliyah
waitress	tarjoilijatar	_tahr_yoaliyahtahr
water	vesi/vettä	_vay_si/_vayt_ta
wine	viini/ä	_vee_ni/a
wine list	viinilista	_vee_ni_lis_tah

A table for one, please
Pöytä yhdelle, kiitos
_purew_ta _ewh_dayllay _kee_toss

A table for two/three, please
Pöytä kahdelle/kolmelle, kiitos
_purew_ta _kah_dayllay/_koal_mayllay, _kee_toss

Is there a highchair?
Onko teillä lastentuolia?
_oan_koa _tayl_la _lah_stayn _too_aliah

Can we see the menu/wine list?
Saammeko nähdä ruoka/viinilistan
_saam_maykoa _nah_da _rooa_kah/_veeni_listahn

What would you recommend?
Mitä suosittelisitte?
_mit_ta _sooa_sittaylissittay

I'd like …
Saisinko …
_sah_sinkoah

Just a cup of coffee/tea, please
Vain kuppi kahvia, kiitos
_vahin _koop_pi _kahh_viah, _kee_toss

I only want a snack
Haluaisin vain välipalan
_hah_looahsin vahin _valli_pahlahn

Is there a set menu?
Onko teillä päivänannos?
_oan_koa _tayl_la _pa_van _ahn_noss

A carafe of house red, please
Pullo talon viiniä, kiitos
_pool_loa _tah_loan _vee_nia _kee_toss

Do you have any vegetarian dishes?
Onko teillä kasvisruokia?
oankoa taylla kahsvisrooakiah

Could we have some water?
Voisimmeko saada vettä?
voasimmekoa saadah vaytta

Can you warm this bottle/baby food for me?
Voisitteko lämmittää tämän pullon/vauvanruoan minulle?
voasittekoa lammittaa taman poolloan/vahoovahnroohan minnoollay

Waiter/waitress!
Tarjoija/Neiti!
tahryoaliyah/nayhti

We didn't order this
Tämä ei ole sitä mitä tilasimme
tama ay oalay sitta mitta tillahsimmay

May we have some more …?
Saammeko hieman lisää …?
saammekoa hayamahn lissaa

Can I have another knife/fork?
Voinko saada toisen veitsen/haarukan?
voankoa saadah toahsayn vaytsayn/haahrookkahn

Can we have the bill, please?
Saammeko laskun, kiitos?
saammaykoa lahskoon keetoss

Could I have a receipt, please?
Voisinko saada kuitin?
voasinkoa saadah kooitin

The meal was very good, thank you
Ateria oli oikein hyvä, kiitos
ahtayriah oali oakayn hewva keetoss

MENU GUIDE

aamiainen breakfast
alkuruoka starter
ananas pineapple
anjovis anchovies
ankka duck
ankkapasteijaa duck pâté
apprikoosi apricot
artisokka artichoke
avokaado avocado
baari café
banaani banana
beef stroganoff beef casserole
blinis buckwheat pancakes served with
   burbot roe
bortsch beetroot soup served with sour
   cream
crêpes Suzette pancakes flambéed with
   orange sauce
etanoita snail
fasaania pheasant
gratinoitu baked in a milk, cream and
   cheese sauce
gravad lax semi-raw salmon
grillattu grilled
haarukka fork
hanhi goose
hapoton kivennäisvesi still mineral
   water
haudukas braised
hedelmäsalaatti fruit salad
herneitä peas
hillo jam
hirvenlihaa venison
hummeri lobster
hummerikeitto lobster soup
huoneen lämpötilassa room
   temperature
hyvin kuiva/brut very dry

häränkieltä ox tongue
iso katkarapu prawn
jauhelihaa minced beef
jukurttia yoghurt
juomaraha tip
juussi juice
juustoa cheese
juustotarjotin cheese board
jälkiruoka dessert
jälkiruoka-astia dessert dish
jäätelöä ice cream
kaakao hot chocolate
kaali cabbage
kahvi/a coffee
kahvi (musta) coffee (black)
kahvi ja kerma white coffee with cream
kahviaamiainen continental breakfast
kahvila café
kakku cake
kala- ja äyriäisruokaa seafood
kalaa fish
kalakeitto fish soup
kaljaa home-brewn non-alcoholic beer
kalkkuna turkey
kanaa kermakastikkeessa chicken in
   cream sauce
kanaa riisin kanssa chicken with rice
kanaa sieni- ja valkoviinikastikkeessa
   chicken with mushrooms and wine
kananmaksapasteijaa chicken liver pâté
kania rabbit
karhunpaisti bear steak
katkarapucocktail prawn cocktail
katkarapuja shrimps/prawns
kaurapuuro oatmeal porridge
kebab kebab
keitetty boiled
keitetty muna boiled egg

keitto/a soup
kermajuustoa cream cheese
kermakastikkeessa in cream sauce
kermavaahto whipped cream
keskikypsä medium
kevyt light
kiisseli jellied fruit dessert made of
  wild berries
kinkku ham
kirsikka cherry
kreippi grapefruit
kuha white freshwater fish
kuitti receipt
kuiva dry
kuivattu luumu prune
kukkakaali cauliflower
kuoriaisia shellfish
kuorrutettu ja paistettu meriantura
  sole dipped in flour and fried in
  butter
kuppi cup
kurkku cucumber
kyljys chop
kylkipaisti rib steak
kypsäksi/hyvin paistettu well done
kypsytetty rasvassa deep-fried
lakkalikööri cloudberry liqueur
lammas/ta lamb/mutton
lammaspata vihanneksilla mutton
  stew with vegetables
lampaanniska rack of lamb
lampaanreisi leg of lamb
lasi glass
lasku bill
lasten annos child's portion
lautanen plate
leikkeleitä ham and patés; cold,
  sliced meats
leipä/ä bread
leivos cake
lihaa meat

lihaliemi broth
lihapata beef casserole
lihapullia meatball
likööri liqueur
limonaatia lemonade
lintua poultry
lohi salmon
lounas lunch
lusikka spoon
luumu plum
maito/a milk
maitokahvi white coffee
makaroonia noodles
makea sweet
makkara salami-type sausage, cold
  meats
mansikoita strawberry
manteli almond
marsipaani marzipan
meriantura viini- ja sienikastikkeessa
  sole in white wine and
  mushrooms
mersimarjalikööri arctic bramble
  liqueur
minttuteetä mint tea
munakas omelette
munakokkeli scrambled eggs
munkki doughnut
munuainen kidney
murot cereals
mustaherukka blackcurrant
mustikkapiirakka blueberry tart
mätiä roe
nakki(makkara) frankfurter
näkkileipää crispbread
naudanliha beef
ohukainen pancake
olut beer/ale
omeletti omelette
omena apple
omenapiiras apple pie

osteri oyster
paistettu kana roast chicken
paistettu muna fried egg
paistettu omena baked apple
paisti joint
paistinperunat fried potatoes
palapaisti stew
papuja beans
parsa asparagus
persikka peach
peruna potato
perunamuhennos mashed potatoes
perunoiden ja vihannesten kanssa
    with potatoes and vegetables
pihvi ja ranskalaiset steak and chips
pihvi steak
piimä sour milk
piiras tart, pie
pilsneri lager
pinaattia leaf spinach
piparkakku ginger snap
piparminttu peppermint
pippuri/a pepper
pippuria pepper
polarlikööri cranberry liqueur
poreileva kivennäisvesi sparkling
    mineral water
porkkana carrot
poronliha reindeer
porsaankyljys pork chop
porsasta pork
pulla coffee bread
punakaali red cabbage
punakampela plaice
punapaprika red pepper
punaviiniä red wine
puolikypsä rare
purjosipuli leek
puuro porridge
päivällinen dinner
päivän ruoka dish of the day

päivän ruokalista today's menu
pääruoka main course
päärynä pear
pöytä table
raastettu grated
raavilohi semi-raw salmon
ranskalaiset chips
rapu crayfish
retiisi radish
riisi rice
roquefort blue cheese
roseeviiniä rosé wine
ruis rye
ruispuuro rye porridge
ruokalista menu
rypäle grape
saksanpähkinä walnut
salaatti salad, lettuce
sekasalaatti mixed salad
sekavihannekset with assorted
    vegetables
servietti napkin
sieni mushroom
siideri cider
siika freshwater white fish
silakka Baltic herring (often grilled or
    smoked)
silli salted herring (in various
    sauces)
sillisalaatti root vegetable salad with
    salted herring
simpukoita valkoviinissä mussels in
    white wine
sinappia mustard
sipsit crisps
sipuli onion
sipulikeitto French onion soup
sipulikeitto leivänkuutioiden kanssa
    baked onion soup
sitruuna lemon
sitruunateetä lemon tea

smörgåsbord cold table/starters
sokeri/a sugar
sorsa duck
suola salt
suolakurkku pickled sweet and sour
  gherkins
sämpylä round roll
taimen trout
talon viiniä table wine
tarjoilija waiter
tarjoilijatar waitress
taskurapu crab
tee/tä tea
teelusikka teaspoon
teetä maidon kanssa tea with milk
tomaatti tomato
tomaattikeitto tomato soup
tonnikala tuna
tummaa dark
tuore appelsiinimehu freshly squeezed
  orange juice
turistiruokalista tourist menu
turska cod
tynnyriolut draught beer
vadelmia raspberry
välipala snack
valkoista white
valkokastike white sauce
valkosipuli/a garlic

valkoviiniä white wine
vaniljakastike vanilla custard
vartaassa paistettu roasted on a spit
vasikanmaksaa veal liver
vasikka veal
veitsi knife
veriohukkaat black pudding pancakes
vesi/vettä water
vesihaudutettu muna poached egg
vihanneksia vegetables
vihanneskeitto soup with chopped
  vegetables
vihreä paprika green pepper
vihreä salaatti green salad
viiliä curds (local yoghurt)
viineri Danish pastry
viini/ä wine
viinikastike wine sauce
viinikastikkeessa in red wine sauce
viinilista wine list
vin wine
vispikerma whipped cream
vohveli wafer, waffle
voi/ta butter
voileipä sandwich
voileipäpöytä cold table/starters
vuohenjuusto goat's cheese
vuosikerta viini vintage wine
Wienershcnitzel breaded escalope

FRENCH

CONTENTS

INTRODUCTION

PRONUNCIATION

When reading the imitated pronunciation, the same value should be given to all syllables, since there is hardly any stress in French words. Pronounce each syllable as if it formed part of an English word and you will be understood. Remember the points below, and your pronunciation will be even closer to the correct French.

an represents the nasal sound as in **vin**, **un** and **main** – similar to saying 'an' without sounding the 'n'
g is pronounced hard as in 'get'
i pronounced as 'eye'
j like the 's' sound in 'leisure'
on represents the nasal sound as in **bon**, **en** and **temps** – similar to saying 'on' without sounding the 'n'
oo is how we imitate the French 'u' (say 'seen' with your lips rounded as if you were about to whistle, and the result will be close enough)

USE OF THE FRENCH WORD 'ON'

Phrases involving 'I' or 'we' and impersonal phrases have sometimes been translated with the French word 'on'. For example: **Can I camp here? Est-ce qu'on peut camper ici?** Literally, 'on' means 'one', but is not a formal word like it is in English.

GENDERS AND ARTICLES

French has two genders for nouns – masculine and feminine. We generally give the definite article ('the') – **le** for masculine nouns, **la** for feminine nouns and **les** for plural nouns. Where the indefinite article ('a, an') is more appropriate, we have used **un** for masculine and **une** for feminine nouns or the words for 'some', **du** (masculine), **de la** (feminine) and **des** (plural).

USEFUL PHRASES

Yes, No, OK etc

Yes/no
Oui/non
wee/non

OK
D'accord
dakkor

That's fine
C'est bien
seh byan

That's right
C'est exact
set exakt

Greetings, Introductions

How do you do, pleased to meet you
Enchanté (de faire votre connaissance)
onshontay duh fair vottr konnessonss

Good morning
Bonjour
bonjoor

Good evening/Good night
Bonsoir
bonswahr

Goodbye
Au revoir
oh-rvwahr

How are you?
Comment allez-vous?
kommont allay voo

(familiar form)
Comment ça va?
kommon sa va

My name is …
Je m'appelle …
juh mappell

What's your name?
Comment vous appelez-vous?
kommon vooz appellay voo

(familiar form)
Comment tu t'appelles?
kommon too tappell

This is …
Voici …
vwah-see

Hello/Hi!
Bonjour/Salut!
bonjoor/saloo

PLEASE, THANK YOU, APOLOGIES

Thank you/No, thank you
Merci/Non, merci
mairsee/non mairsee

Please
S'il vous plaît
seel voo pleh

Excuse me!/Sorry!
Pardon!
pardon

WHERE, HOW, ASKING

Excuse me, please
Pardon
pardon

Can you tell me …?
Pouvez-vous me dire …?
poovay voo muh deer

Can I have …?
Est-ce que je pourrais avoir …?
esskuh juh poorray avwah

Would you like a …?
Est-ce que vous voulez un/une …?
esskuh voo voolay <u>an</u>/<u>oon</u>

Would you like to …?
Est-ce que vous voulez …?
esskuh voo voolay

Is there … here?
Est-ce qu'il y a … ici?
esskeel-ya … ee-see

What's that?
Qu'est-ce que c'est?
kesskuh seh

How much is it?
Combien ça coûte?
k<u>on</u>by<u>an</u> sa koot

Where is the …?
Où est le/la …?
oo eh luh/la

Is there wheelchair access?
Y a-t-il un accès pour les personnes à mobilité réduite?
eeahteel onaksay poor lay payrson ah mobeelitay raydooeet

Are guide dogs allowed?
Les chiens guide sont-ils admis?
lay sheean geed sontel admee?

ABOUT ONESELF

I'm from …
Je viens de …
juh vy<u>an</u> duh

I'm … years old
J'ai … ans
jay … on

I'm a …
Je suis …
juh swee

I'm married/single/divorced
Je suis marié/célibataire/divorcé
juh swee maree-ay/sayleebatair/deevorssay

I have … sisters/brothers/children
J'ai … soeurs/frères/enfants
jay … suhr/frair/onfon

HELP, PROBLEMS

Can you help me?
Pouvez-vous m'aider?
poovay voo mayday

I don't understand
Je ne comprends pas
juh nuh konpron pa

Does anyone here speak English?
Est-ce qu'il y a quelqu'un ici qui parle anglais?
esskeel-ya kellkan ee-see kee parl ongleh

I can't speak French
Je ne parle pas français
juh nuh parl pa fronseh

I don't know
Je ne sais pas
juh nuh seh pa

Please speak more slowly
Pouvez-vous parler plus lentement, s'il vous plaît?
poovay voo parlay ploo lontmon seel voo pleh

Please write it down for me
Pouvez-vous me l'écrire, s'il vous plaît?
poovay voo muh laykreer seel voo pleh

I've lost my way
Je me suis perdu
juh me swee pairdoo

Go away!
Allez-vous-en!
allay vooz on

LIKES, DISLIKES, SOCIALIZING

I like/love …
J'aime/j'adore …
jem/jador

I don't like …
Je n'aime pas …
juh nem pa

I hate …
Je déteste …
juh daytest

Do you like …?
Aimez-vous …?
aymay voo

It's delicious/awful!
C'est délicieux/horrible!
seh dayleess-yuh/orreeb-l

I don't drink/smoke
Je ne bois pas/ne fume pas
juh nuh bwah pa/nuh foom pa

Do you mind if I smoke?
Cela ne vous ennuie pas que je fume?
suhla nuh vooz onwee pa kuh juh foom

What would you like to drink?
Qu'est-ce que vous voulez boire?
kesskuh voo voolay bwahr

I would like a …
Je voudrais un/une …
juh voodreh <u>an</u>/<u>oo</u>n

Nothing for me, thanks
Rien pour moi, merci
ry<u>an</u> poor mwah mairsee

Cheers! *(toast)*
Santé!
s<u>on</u>tay

THINGS YOU'LL HEAR

à bientôt	see you later
attention!	look out!
au revoir	goodbye
bien	fine
bon!	right! OK!
bonjour	hello
bon voyage!	have a good trip!
entrez	come in
excusez-moi	excuse me
je vous en prie	don't mention it
papiers, s'il vous plaît	identification papers, please
pardon!/pardon?	sorry!/pardon?
qu'est-ce que vous avez dit?	what did you say?
servez-vous	help yourself
voici	here you are
vraiment?	is that right?

DAYS, MONTHS, SEASONS

Sunday	dimanche	*deemonsh*
Monday	lundi	*landee*
Tuesday	mardi	*mardee*
Wednesday	mercredi	*mairkruhdee*
Thursday	jeudi	*juhdee*
Friday	vendredi	*vondruhdee*
Saturday	samedi	*sammdee*
January	janvier	*jonvee-ay*
February	février	*fayvree-ay*
March	mars	*marss*
April	avril	*ahvreel*
May	mai	*meh*
June	juin	*jwan*
July	juillet	*jwee-ay*
August	août	*oo*
September	septembre	*septonbr*
October	octobre	*oktobr*
November	novembre	*novonbr*
December	décembre	*dayssonbr*
Spring	le printemps	*pranton*
Summer	l'été	*laytay*
Autumn	l'automne	*lohton*
Winter	l'hiver	*leevair*
Christmas	Noël	*noh-el*
Christmas Eve	la veille de Noël	*vay duh noh-el*
Good Friday	Vendredi saint	*vondredee san*
Easter	Pâques	*pak*
New Year	le Nouvel An	*noovel on*
New Year's Eve	la veille du Jour de l'an	*vay doo joor duh lon*
Pentecost	la Pentecôte	*pontkoht*

NUMBERS

0	zéro	*zayro*		
1	un, une	*an*, *oon*		
2	deux	*duh*		
3	trois	*trwah*		
4	quatre	*kattr*		
5	cinq	*sank*		
6	six	*seess*		
7	sept	*set*		
8	huit	*weet*		
9	neuf	*nuhf*		

10	dix	*deess*
11	onze	*onz*
12	douze	*dooz*
13	treize	*trez*
14	quatorze	*kattorz*
15	quinze	*kanz*
16	seize	*sez*
17	dix-sept	*deess-set*
18	dix-huit	*deess-weet*
19	dix-neuf	*deess-nuhf*

20	vingt	*van*
21	vingt et un	*vantay an*
22	vingt-deux	*van duh*
30	trente	*tront*
40	quarante	*karront*
50	cinquante	*sankont*
60	soixante	*swassont*
70	soixante-dix	*swassont-deess*
80	quatre-vingts	*kattruhvan*
90	quatre-vingt-dix	*kattruh-vandeess*
100	cent	*son*
110	cent-dix	*sondeess*
200	deux cents	*duh-son*
1,000	mille	*meel*
10,000	dix mille	*deess meel*
20,000	vingt mille	*van meel*
100,000	cent mille	*son meel*
1,000,000	un million	*meel-ion*

TIME

today	aujourd'hui	*ohjoord-wee*
yesterday	hier	*yair*
tomorrow	demain	*duhman*
this week	cette semaine	*set suhmen*
last week	la semaine dernière	*suhmen dairnee-air*
next week	la semaine prochaine	*suhmen proshen*
this morning	ce matin	*suh mattan*
this afternoon	cet après-midi	*set apreh-meedee*
this evening/ tonight	ce soir	*suh swahr*
in three days	dans trois jours	*don trwah joor*
three days ago	il y a trois jours	*eelya trwah joor*
late	tard	*tar*
early	tôt	*toh*
soon	bientôt	*byantoh*
later on	plus tard	*ploo tar*
at the moment	pour le moment, maintenant	*poor luh momon, mantnon*
second	une seconde	*suhgond*
minute	une minute	*meenoot*
ten minutes	dix minutes	*dee meenoot*
quarter of an hour	un quart d'heure	*kar dur*
half an hour	une demi-heure	*duhmee ur*
three quarters of an hour	trois quarts d'heure	*trwah kar dur*
hour	une heure	*ur*
day	un jour	*joor*
everyday	chaque jour	*shak joor*
all day	toute la journée	*toot la joornay*
week	une semaine	*suhmen*
fortnight	quinze jours, deux semaines	*kanz joor, duh suhmen*
month	un mois	*mwah*
year	une année, un an	*annay, on*

TELLING THE TIME

The 24-hour clock is always used in the written form in timetables and for appointments, and also verbally in enquiry offices and if talking about the times of television and radio programmes. However, in most other situations, people will use the 12-hour clock.

'What time is it?' is **quelle heure est-il?**. 'O'clock' is translated as **heure(s)**, meaning 'hour(s)'. '(It's) one o'clock' is **(il est) une heure**; '(it's) four o'clock' is **(il est) quatre heures** and so on. To denote the half hour use **et demie**, so '5.30' is **cinq heures et demie**.

To express minutes after the hour, state the hour followed by the number of minutes. For example, 'ten past five' is **cinq heures dix**. For minutes to the hour use **moins**, which means 'less'. For example, 'twenty to eleven' is **onze heures moins vingt**.

'Quarter' is **quart**, so 'quarter past three' is **trois heures et quart**, and 'quarter to eight' is **huit heures moins le quart**. The word 'at' in phrases such as 'at quarter past two' can be translated as **à**: **à deux heures et quart**.

am	du matin	_doo matan_
pm (*afternoon*)	de l'après-midi	_duh lapreh-meedee_
(*evening*)	du soir	_doo swahr_
one o'clock	une heure	_oon ur_
ten past one	une heure dix	_oon ur deess_
quarter past one	une heure et quart	_oon ur ay kar_
twenty past two	deux heures vingt	_duhz ur van_
1.30	une heure et demie	_oon ur ay duhmee_
twenty to two	deux heures moins vingt	_duhz ur mwan van_
quarter to two	deux heures moins le quart	_duhz ur mwan luh kar_
two o'clock	deux heures	_duhz ur_
midday	midi	_meedee_
midnight	minuit	_meenwee_

COMMUNICATIONS

Useful Words and Phrases

code	l'indicatif	_andeekateef_
dialling tone	la tonalité	_tonaleetay_
email address	l'adresse électronique	adrays aylayktroneek
enquiries	les renseignements	_ronsen-yuhmon_
extension	le poste, l'extension	_posst, extonss-ion_
fax machine	le fax	_fax_
internet	l'internet	_internet_
mobile phone	le téléphone portable	_taylayfon portabul_
number	le numéro	_noomayroh_
operator	l'opérateur	_opayratur_
(female)	l'opératrice	_opay-ratreess_
phonecard	la télécarte	_taylaykart_
reverse charge	une communication	_kommooneekass-ion_
call	en PCV	_on pay say vay_
telephone	le téléphone	_taylayfon_
telephone box	une cabine	_kabeen_
Web site	le site web	_site web_
wrong number	un faux numéro	_foh noomayroh_

Where is the nearest phone box?
Où se trouve la cabine téléphonique la plus proche?
oo suh troov la kabeen taylay-foneek la ploo prosh

I would like a number in …
Je voudrais un numéro à …
juh voodreh an noomayroh ah

I would like to speak to …
Je voudrais parler à …
juh voodreh parlay ah

My number is …
Mon numéro est le …
mon noomayroh eh luh

Could you leave him/her a message?
Pouvez-vous lui laisser un message?
poovay voo lwee lessay <u>an</u> muhssaj

I'll ring back later
Je rappellerai plus tard
juh rappelray pl<u>oo</u> tar

What's your fax number/email address?
Quel est votre numéro de fax/adresse électronique?
kaylay votr noomayro duh faks/adrays aylayktroneek

Can I send an email/fax from here?
Puis-je envoyer un message électronique/fax d'ici?
pooeej ronvwahiay an maysahj aylayktroneek /faks deesee?

THINGS YOU'LL HEAR

A qui désirez-vous parler?
Who would you like to speak to?

Vous avez un faux numéro
You've got the wrong number

C'est de la part de qui?
May I ask who's calling?

Lui-même/elle-même
Speaking

Ne quittez pas
Hold the line

Pourriez-vous rappeler plus tard?
Could you call back later?

Désolé, il/elle n'est pas là
Sorry, he/she is not in

EMERGENCIES

Useful Words and Phrases

accident	un accident	*ak-seedon*
ambulance	une ambulance	*onboolonss*
breakdown	une panne	*pan*
burglary	un cambriolage	*konbri-olaj*
crash	un accident	*ak-seedon*
emergency	l'urgence	*oorjonss*
fire	le feu	*fuh*
fire brigade	les pompiers	*ponp-yay*
police	la police	*poleess*
police station	le poste de police	*posst duh poleess*

Help!
A l'aide!
ah led

Stop!
Arrêtez!
arretay

Get an ambulance!
Appelez une ambulance!
applay oon onboolonss

Hurry up!
Faites vite!
fet veet

My address is …
Mon adresse est …
mon adress eh

My passport/car has been stolen
On a volé mon passeport/ma voiture
on ah volay mon passpor/ma vwahtoor

HOTELS

USEFUL WORDS AND PHRASES

balcony	un balcon	*balkon*
bathroom	la salle de bain	*sal duh ban*
bed	le lit	*lee*
bed & breakfast	chambre d'hôte	*shonbr doht*
bedroom	la chambre	*shonbr*
bill	la note	*not*
breakfast	le petit déjeuner	*puhtee day-juhnay*
car park	le parking	*par-keeng*
dining room	la salle à manger	*sal ah monjay*
dinner	le dîner	*deenay*
double bed	un grand lit	*gran lee*
double room	une chambre pour deux personnes	*shonbr poor duh pairson*
full board	la pension complète	*ponss-ion konplet*
guesthouse	une pension de famille	*ponss-ion duh famee*
half board	la demi-pension	*duhmee ponss-ion*
hotel	un hôtel	*oh-tell*
key	la clé, la clef	*klay*
lift	l'ascenseur	*assonssur*
lunch	le déjeuner	*day-juhnay*
maid	la femme de chambre	*fam duh shonbr*
manager	le directeur	*deerektur*
receipt	le reçu	*ruh-soo*
reception	la réception	*raysseps-ion*
receptionist	le/la réceptionniste	*raysseps-ioneest*
room	la chambre	*shonbr*
room service	le service en chambre	*sairveess on shonbr*
shower	la douche	*doosh*
single bed	un lit d'une personne	*lee doon pairson*
single room	une chambre pour une personne	*shonbr poor oon pairson*
toilet	les toilettes	*twallet*
twin room	une chambre à deux lits	*shonbr ah duh lee*

Do you have any vacancies?
Avez-vous des chambres de libres?
avay voo day shonbr duh leebr

I have a reservation
J'ai réservé
jay rayzairvay

I'd like a single room
Je voudrais une chambre pour une personne
juh voodreh oon shonbr poor oon pairson

I'd like a room with a bathroom/balcony
Je voudrais une chambre avec salle de bain/balcon
juh voodreh oon shonbr avek sal duh ban/balkon

Is there satellite/cable TV in the rooms?
Les chambres ont-elles la télé par satellite/câblée?
Lay shoombr ontayl la taylay pahr satayleet/kablay

I'd like a room for one night/three nights
Je voudrais une chambre pour une nuit/trois nuits
juh voodreh oon shonbr poor oon nwee/trwah nwee

What is the charge per night?
Quel est le prix pour une nuit?
kell eh luh pree poor oon nwee

When is breakfast/dinner?
A quelle heure servez-vous le petit déjeuner/le dîner?
ah kell ur sairvay voo luh puhtee day-juhnay/luh deenay

Please wake/call me at … o'clock
Réveillez-moi à … heures, s'il vous plaît
rayvay-yay mwah ah … ur seel voo pleh

Can I have breakfast in my room?
Pouvez-vous me servir le petit déjeuner dans la chambre?
poovay voo meh sairveer luh puhtee day-juhnay don la shonbr

My room number is …
Le numéro de ma chambre est le …
luh noomayroh duh ma shonbr eh luh

There is no toilet paper in the bathroom
Il n'y a pas de papier toilette dans la salle de bain
eel nya pa duh papee-ay twalet don la sal duh ban

The window won't open
Pas moyen d'ouvrir la fenêtre
pa mwi-an doovreer la fuhn-ettr

There isn't any hot water
Il n'y a pas d'eau chaude
eel nya pa doh shohd

I'm leaving tomorrow
Je pars demain
juh par duhman

When do I have to vacate the room?
A quelle heure dois-je libérer la chambre?
ah kell ur dwah juh leebayray la shonbr

Can I have the bill, please?
Pouvez-vous préparer ma note, s'il vous plaît?
poovay voo prayparay ma not seel voo pleh

I'll pay by credit card
Je payerai avec une carte de crédit
juh pay-uhray avek oon kart duh kraydee

I'll pay cash
Je payerai comptant
juh pay-uhray konton

Can you get me a taxi?
Pouvez-vous m'appeler un taxi?
poovay voo mapplay an taxee

THINGS YOU'LL SEE

addition	bill
ascenseur	lift
complet	no vacancies
déjeuner	lunch
douche	shower
entrée	entrance
entrée interdite	no admission
escalier	stairs
petit déjeuner	breakfast
poussez	push
privé	private
salle de bain	bathroom
sortie de secours	emergency exit
tirez	pull

THINGS YOU'LL HEAR

Je suis désolé, mais nous sommes complets
I'm sorry, we're full

**Nous n'avons plus de chambres pour deux personnes/
   une personne**
There are no double/single rooms left

Pour combien de nuits?
For how many nights?

Comment payez-vous?
How will you be paying?

Veuillez payer d'avance
Please pay in advance

La chambre doit être libérée à midi
You must vacate the room by noon

SHOPPING

Excuse me, where is/are …?
Pardon, pouvez-vous me dire où se trouve …?
pardon poovay voo muh deer oo suh troov

Do you have …?
Avez-vous …?
avay voo

How much is this?
Ça coûte combien?
sa koot konbyan

Where do I pay?
Où faut-il payer?
oo foh-teel pay-ay

Do you take credit cards?
Acceptez-vous les cartes de crédit?
ak-septay voo lay kart duh kraydee

Can I have a receipt?
Puis-je avoir un reçu?
pweej avwahr an ruhsoo

Have you anything cheaper?
Avez-vous quelque chose de moins cher?
avay voo kellkuh shohz duh mwan shair

Can I have a refund?
Pouvez-vous me rembourser?
poovay voo muh ronboorsay

That's fine. I'll take it
C'est bien. Je le prends
seh byan. juh luh pron

It isn't what I wanted
Ce n'est pas ce que je voulais
suh neh pa suh kuh juh vooleh

EATING OUT

It is not difficult to eat well and inexpensively in France. Since prices have to be displayed, by law, in the window of an eating establishment, you can readily fit your choice of restaurant to your budget. Although service is included in the bill, it is customary to leave a tip for the waiter or waitress. In cafés, even if you have just popped in for coffee or a drink, it is traditional to leave the leftover coins from your change.

Every town has a number of cafés where, at lunchtime, you can order a simple sandwich, a **croque-monsieur** (a grilled ham and cheese sandwich which, with the addition of an egg, becomes a **croque-madame**), the **plat du jour** (dish of the day), **rillettes** (pork or goose meat minced very finely so that it can be spread on bread), pâté or a platter of crudités or cold meats.

Bistros are small bars, often family-run, that also sometimes serve a selection of traditional dishes or snacks at lunchtime and in the evening. The **menu du jour** (today's menu) is usually good value. Regional specialities that you may encounter include: **crêpes** in Brittany; **choucroute** (sauerkraut with sausages and pieces of smoked ham) and onion tart in Alsace; **ratatouille** in Provence; and **bouillabaisse** (fish soup) and **salade niçoise** (mixed salad containing olives, anchovies, tuna, tomatoes and other vegetables) around the Mediterranean coast. House wine is available in carafes, but if you prefer your wine by the bottle, you will find a few listed on the menu.

Brasseries are often large and noisy – not the place to go for an intimate dinner – and offer beer on tap as well as wine. They stay open late, and snacks and full meals are usually available at any time.

French cafés and bars always sell coffee. If you ask for **un café** or **un expresso**, you'll get a small, black coffee. **Un crème** is a small coffee with milk and **un grand crème** is a large coffee with milk. You can also ask for **un café léger** (weak coffee) or **un café bien serré** (very strong coffee).

USEFUL WORDS AND PHRASES

beer	de la bière	*bee-air*
bill	l'addition	*addeess-ion*
bread	du pain	*pan*
butter	du beurre	*bur*
cake	du gâteau	*gattoh*
child's portion	une portion enfant	*porss-ion onfon*
coffee	du café	*kaffay*
cup	une tasse	*tass*
dessert	un dessert	*daissair*
fork	une fourchette	*foorshet*
glass	un verre	*vair*
knife	un couteau	*kootoh*
main course	le plat principal	*pla pranseepal*
menu	le menu	*muhnoo*
milk	du lait	*leh*
napkin	une serviette	*sairvee-et*
pepper	du poivre	*pwahvr*
plate	une assiette	*assee-et*
receipt	le reçu	*ruhssoo*
salt	du sel	*sel*
sandwich	un sandwich	*sondweech*
snack	un snack	*'snack'*
soup	de la soupe	*soop*
spoon	une cuillère	*kwee-air*
starter	une entrée	*ontray*
sugar	du sucre	*sookr*
table	une table	*tabb-l*
tea	du thé	*tay*
teaspoon	une cuillère à café	*kwee-air ah kaffay*
tip	un pourboire	*poorbwahr*
waiter	un serveur	*sairvur*
waitress	une serveuse	*sairvuhz*
water	de l'eau	*oh*
wine	du vin	*van*
wine list	la carte des vins	*kart day van*

A table for one, please
Une table pour une personne, s'il vous plaît
_oo_n tabb-l poor _oo_n pairson seel voo pleh

A table for two/three, please
Une table pour deux/trois personnes, s'il vous plaît
_oo_n tabb-l poor duh/trwah pairson seel voo pleh

Is there a highchair?
Auriez-vous une chaise haute?
oriayvoo oon shayz oht

Can we see the menu/wine list?
Le menu/la carte des vins, s'il vous plaît
luh muhn_oo_/la kart day v_an_ seel voo pleh

What would you recommend?
Que recommandez-vous?
kuh ruhkomm_on_day voo

I'd like …
J'aimerais …
jemmereh

Just a cup of coffee/tea, please
Un café/thé seulement
_an_ kaffay/tay suhlm_on_

I only want a snack
Je voudrais juste manger un snack
juh voodreh _joo_st m_on_jay _an_ snack

Is there a set menu?
Est-ce qu'il y a un menu du jour?
esskeel-ya _an_ muhn_oo_ doo joor

A carafe of house red, please
Une carafe de vin rouge maison, s'il vous plaît
_oo_n karaff duh v_an_ rooj mezz_on_ seel voo pleh

Do you have any vegetarian dishes?
Est-ce que vous servez des plats végétariens?
esskuh voo sairvay day pla vayjaytary<u>an</u>

Could we have some water?
Est-ce que nous pourrions avoir de l'eau?
esskuh noo pooree-<u>on</u> avwahr duh loh

Can you warm this bottle/baby food for me?
Pourriez-vous réchauffer ce biberon/petit pot pour moi?
pooreeay voo rayshohfay suh beebuhron/puhteepoh poor mwah

Waiter/waitress!
Garçon/Mademoiselle!
garss<u>on</u>/madmwazel

We didn't order this
Ce n'est pas ce que nous avons commandé
sneh pa suh kuh nooz av<u>on</u> komm<u>on</u>day

May we have some more …?
Est-ce qu'on peut avoir plus de …?
essk<u>on</u> puh avwahr pl<u>oo</u> duh

Can I have another knife/fork?
Est-ce que je peux avoir un autre couteau/une autre fourchette?
esskuh juh puh avwahr <u>an</u> oht-r kootoh/<u>oon</u> oht-r foorshet

Can we have the bill, please?
L'addition, s'il vous plaît
laddeess-i<u>on</u> seel voo pleh

Could I have a receipt, please?
Est-ce que je peux avoir un reçu, s'il vous plaît?
esskuh juh puh avwahr <u>an</u> ruhss<u>oo</u> seel voo pleh

The meal was very good, thank you
C'était très bon, merci
sayteh treh b<u>on</u> mairsee

MENU GUIDE

à la broche roasted on a spit
à la jardinière with assorted vegetables
à la normande in cream sauce
à point medium
abricot apricot
agneau lamb
ail garlic
ailloli garlic mayonnaise
amande almond
ananas pineapple
anchois anchovies
andouillette spicy sausage
artichaut artichoke
asperge asparagus
au gratin baked in a milk, cream and cheese sauce
avocat avocado
banane banana
bavaroise light mousse
béarnaise with béarnaise sauce (thick sauce made with eggs and butter)
béchamel white sauce, béchamel sauce
beurre butter
beurre noir dark melted butter
bien cuit well done
bière beer
bière à la pression draught beer
bière blonde lager
bifteck steak
bisque de homard lobster soup
blanquette de veau veal stew
bleu rare
bœuf beef
bœuf braisé braised beef
bœuf en daube beef casserole
bouillabaisse fish soup from the Midi
bouilli boiled
bouillon broth

boulette meatball
bouquet rose prawns
bourride fish soup
braisé braised
brioche round roll
brochette kebab
brut very dry
cabillaud cod
café coffee (black)
café au lait white coffee
café complet continental breakfast
café crème white coffee
calamar/calmar squid
calvados apple brandy
canard duck
caneton duckling
carbonnade beef cooked in beer
carotte carrot
carré d'agneau rack of lamb
carrelet plaice
carte menu
carte des vins wine list
casse-croûte snacks
cassis blackcurrant
cassoulet bean, pork and duck casserole
cerise cherry
chambré at room temperature
champignon mushroom
chantilly whipped cream
charcuterie sausages, ham and pâtés; pork products
charlotte dessert consisting of layers of fruit, cream and finger biscuits
chausson aux pommes apple turnover
cheval horse
chèvre goat's cheese
chevreuil venison
chocolat chaud hot chocolate

FRENCH • MENU GUIDE

chou cabbage
chou à la crème cream puff
chou-fleur cauliflower
chou rouge red cabbage
cidre cider
citron lemon
citron pressé fresh lemon juice
cocktail de crevettes prawn cocktail
cœur heart
colin hake
compote stewed fruit, compote
concombre cucumber
confit preserved in fat
confiture jam
consommé clear soup
coq au vin chicken in red wine
côte de porc pork chop
côtelette chop
coupe dessert dish
crabe crab
crème cream, creamy sauce or dessert; white coffee
crème à la vanille vanilla custard
crème anglaise custard
crème chantilly whipped cream
crème pâtissière rich creamy custard
crêpe pancake
crêpes Suzette pancakes flambéed with orange sauce
crevette grise shrimp
crevette rose prawn
croque-madame grilled cheese and ham sandwich with a fried egg
croque-monsieur grilled cheese and ham sandwich
crudités selection of salads, chopped raw vegetables
crustacés shellfish
déjeuner lunch
digestif liqueur
dinde turkey

dîner dinner
doux sweet
eau minérale gazeuse/plate sparkling/still mineral water
entrecôte rib steak
entrée starter
entremets dessert
épinards en branches leaf spinach
escalope de veau milanaise veal escalope with tomato sauce
escalope panée breaded escalope
escargot snail
estouffade de bœuf beef casserole
faisan pheasant
farci stuffed
flageolets kidney beans
flan custard tart
foie de veau veal liver
foie gras goose or duck liver preserve
foies de volaille chicken livers
fonds d'artichaut artichoke hearts
fondue savoyarde cheese fondue
fraise strawberry
framboise raspberry
frit deep-fried
frites chips
fromage cheese
fromage blanc cream cheese
fromage de chèvre goat's cheese
fruits de mer seafood
galette round, flat cake or savoury wholemeal crèpe
garni with potatoes and vegetables
gâteau cake
gaufre wafer; waffle
gigot d'agneau leg of lamb
glace ice cream
grand cru vintage wine
gratin baked cheese dish
gratin dauphinois layers of sliced potatoes baked in milk, cream and cheese

142

gratinée baked onion soup
grillé grilled
haricots beans
haricots beans
homard lobster
hors-d'œuvre starter
huître oyster
jambon ham
julienne soup with chopped vegetables
jus juice
lait milk
langue de bœuf ox tongue
lapin rabbit
léger light
légume vegetable
lièvre hare
limonade lemonade
marchand de vin in red wine sauce
marron chestnut
massepain marzipan
menthe peppermint
menthe à l'eau mint cordial
menu du jour today's menu
menu gastronomique gourmet menu
menu touristique tourist menu
millefeuille custard slice
morue cod
mouclade mussels in creamy sauce with
    saffron, turmeric and white wine
moules marinière mussels in white
    wine
mousseux sparkling
moutarde mustard
mouton mutton
nature plain
navarin mutton stew with vegetables
noisette hazelnut
noix walnut
nouilles noodles
œuf à la coque boiled egg
œuf poché poached egg

œufs à la neige floating islands
    (poached egg whites on top of custard)
œufs brouillés scrambled eggs
œuf sur le plat fried egg
oie goose
oignon onion
omelette omelette
omelette paysanne omelette with
    potatoes and bacon
orange pressée fresh orange juice
pain bread
pain au chocolat chocolate puff pastry
palette de porc shoulder of pork
pamplemousse grapefruit
pastis anise-flavoured alcoholic drink
pâté de canard duck pâté
pâté de foie de volaille chicken liver
    pâté
pâtes pasta
pêche peach
petit déjeuner breakfast
petit pain roll
petit pois peas
petits fours small fancy pastries
petit suisse light, white cream cheese
pistache pistachio
plat du jour dish of the day
plateau de fromages cheese board
poire pear
poire belle Hélène pear in chocolate
    sauce
poireau leek
poisson fish
poivre pepper
poivron red or green pepper
pomme apple
pomme bonne femme baked apple
pomme de terre potato
pommes Dauphine potato fritters
pommes de terre sautées fried potatoes
pommes frites chips

porc pork
potage soup
potage printanier vegetable soup
pot-au-feu beef and vegetable stew
potée vegetable and meat stew
poule au pot chicken and vegetable stew
poule au riz chicken with rice
poulet chasseur chicken with mushrooms and white wine
poulet rôti roast chicken
provençale with tomatoes, garlic and herbs
prune plum
pruneau prune
purée mashed potatoes
purée de marrons chestnut purée
radis radish
ragoût stew
raisin grape
râpé grated
riz rice
rognon kidney
roquefort blue cheese
rôti joint
rouille sauce accompanying **bouillabaisse**
saint-honoré cream puff cake
salade salad, lettuce
salade composée mixed salad
salade verte green salad
sanglier wild boar
sauce aurore white sauce with tomato
sauce béarnaise thick sauce with eggs and butter
sauce blanche white sauce
sauce matelote wine sauce
sauce suprême creamy sauce
sauce vinot wine sauce
saucisse sausage
saucisson salami-type sausage

saumon salmon
saumon fumé smoked salmon
sec dry
sel salt
sirop cordial
sole bonne femme sole in white wine and mushrooms
sole meunière sole dipped in flour and fried in butter
soupe à l'oignon French onion soup
soupe aux tomates tomato soup
soupe de poisson fish soup
steak frites steak and chips
steak haché minced meat, minced beef
sucre sugar
suprême de volaille chicken in cream sauce
tarte tart, pie
tarte frangipane almond cream tart
tarte Tatin baked apple dish
terrine pâté
thé tea
thé à la menthe mint tea
thé au lait tea with milk
thé citron lemon tea
thon tuna
tomate tomato
tourte covered pie
truite trout
veau veal
velouté de tomate cream of tomato soup
viande meat
vin wine
vin blanc white wine
vin de pays local wine
vin de table table wine
vin rosé rosé wine
vin rouge red wine
volaille poultry
yaourt yoghurt

GERMAN

CONTENTS

INTRODUCTION

PRONUNCIATION

When reading the imitated pronunciation, stress the part that is underlined. Pronounce each syllable as if it formed part of an English word, and you will be understood sufficiently well. Remember the points below, and your pronunciation will be even closer to the correct German.

g   is pronounced hard as in 'get'.

KH   represents the guttural German 'ch' and should sound like the Scottish 'loch' (which *isn't* 'lock').

oo   represents the long German 'u'; make this an English 'oo' as in 'food' (*not* short as in 'foot').

oo   represents the shorter German 'u', as in English 'took', 'book'.

(v)   is how we imitate the German 'ü', which sounds like the 'ee' in 'seen' if you pronounce it with rounded lips (or like the French 'u').

ow   should sound like the 'ow' in 'cow' (*not* as in 'low').

'YOU' AND 'I'

In most cases we have given the polite form for 'you' – which is **Sie** (*zee*). The familiar form **du** (*doo*) can also be used, but normally only if you are talking to someone you know well and would regard as a personal friend.

Questions involving 'I' have sometimes been translated with **man**, for example 'Can I …?' **Kann man …?**. Literally **man** means 'one' but is not a formal word as it is in English.

USEFUL PHRASES

Yes, No, OK etc

Yes/No
Ja/Nein
ya/nine

OK
Okay
ok<u>ay</u>

That's fine
In Ordnung
in <u>o</u>rtnoong

That's right
Stimmt
shtimmt

Greetings, Introductions

How do you do, pleased to meet you
Guten Tag, freut mich
g<u>oo</u>ten tahk froyt mich

Good morning/good afternoon/good evening
Guten Morgen/Guten Tag/Guten Abend
g<u>oo</u>ten morgen/g<u>oo</u>ten tahk/g<u>oo</u>ten ahbent

Good night (*going to bed*)
Gute Nacht
g<u>oo</u>tuh n<u>a</u>кнt

(*leaving late at night*)
Auf Wiedersehen
owf v<u>ee</u>der-zayn

Goodbye
Auf Wiedersehen
owf v<u>ee</u>der-zayn

How are you?
Wie geht es Ihnen?
vee gayt ess <u>ee</u>nen

(*familiar form*)
Wie geht es dir?
vee gayt ess deer

My name's ...
Ich heiße ...
ish hice-uh

What's your name? (*familiar form*)
Wie heißen Sie? Wie heißt du?
vee hice-en zee *vee hice-t doo*

This is ...
Das ist ...
dass ist

Hello/Hi
Hallo
hallo

PLEASE, THANK YOU, APOLOGIES

Thank you/No, thank you
Danke/Nein, danke
dankuh/nine dankuh

Please
Bitte
bittuh

Sorry!
Entschuldigung!
ent-shooldigoong

WHERE, HOW, ASKING

Excuse me, please
Entschuldigen Sie bitte
ent-shooldigen zee bittuh

Can you tell me ...?
Können Sie mir sagen ...?
kurnen zee meer zahgen

Can I have …?
Kann ich … haben?
kan ish … h<u>ah</u>ben

Would you like a …?
Möchten Sie einen/eine/ein …?
m<u>ur</u>shten zee <u>ine</u>-en/<u>ine</u>-uh/ine

Would you like to …?
Möchten Sie …?
m<u>ur</u>shten zee

Is there … here?
Gibt es hier …?
geept ess heer

What's that?
Was ist das?
vass ist dass

How much is it?
Was kostet das?
vass k<u>o</u>stet dass

Where is the …?
Wo ist der/die/das …?
vo ist dair/dee/dass

Is there wheelchair access?
Kann man dort mit einem Rollstuhl hinein?
kan man dohrt mit ine-nem rollst<u>uh</u>l hin-ine

Are guide dogs allowed?
Sind Blindenhunde erlaubt?
zint blindenhoonduh airlowpt

ABOUT **O**NESELF

I'm from …
Ich bin aus …
ish bin owss

I'm … years old
Ich bin … Jahre alt
ish bin … yaruh allt

I'm a …
Ich bin …
ish bin

I'm married/single/divorced
Ich bin verheiratet/single/geschieden
ish bin fairhyrahtet/single/gusheeden

I have … sisters/brothers/children
Ich habe … Schwestern/Brüder/Kinder
ish hahbuh … shvestern/brooder/kinder

HELP, PROBLEMS

Can you help me?
Können Sie mir helfen?
kurnen zee meer helfen

I don't understand
Ich verstehe nicht
ish fairshtayuh nisht

Do you speak English/French?
Sprechen Sie Englisch/Französisch?
shprechen zee eng-lish/frantsur-zish

Does anyone here speak English?
Spricht hier jemand Englisch?
shprisht heer yaymant eng-lish

I can't speak German
Ich spreche kein Deutsch
ish shpreshuh kine doytsh

I don't know
Ich weiß nicht
ish vice nisht

Please speak more slowly
Sprechen Sie bitte etwas langsamer
shpreshen zee bittuh etvass langzahmer

Please write it down for me
Könnten Sie es mir bitte aufschreiben?
kurnten zee ess meer bittuh owf-shryben

I've lost my way   (driving)
Ich habe mich verlaufen   Ich habe mich verfahren
ish hahbuh mish fairlowfen   *ish hahbuh mish fairfaren*

LIKES, DISLIKES, SOCIALIZING

I like …
Ich möchte … gern
ish murshtuh … gairn

I love …
Ich liebe …
ish leebuh

I don't like …
Ich möchte … nicht gern
ish murshtuh … nisht gairn

Do you like …?
Möchten Sie …?
murshten zee

It's delicious/awful!
Es ist köstlich/furchtbar!
ess ist kurstlish/foorshtbar

I don't drink/smoke
Ich trinke/rauche nicht
ish trinkuh/rowкниh nisht

Do you mind if I smoke?
Haben Sie etwas dagegen, wenn ich rauche?
hahben zee etvass dagaygen ven ish rowкниh

What would you like (to drink)?
Was möchten Sie (trinken)?
vass murshten zee (trinken)

I would like a …
Ich möchte gern einen/eine/ein …
ish murshtuh gairn ine-en/ine-uh/ine

Nothing for me, thanks
Nichts für mich, danke
nishts foor mish dankuh

Cheers!
Prost!
prohst

THINGS YOU'LL HEAR

Achtung!	attention, look out!
bedienen Sie sich	help yourself
bis später	see you later
bitte?	pardon?
bitte (schön/sehr)	here you are, you're welcome
danke gleichfalls	the same to you
Entschuldigung	excuse me
gut	good
gute Reise	have a good trip
ich verstehe nicht	I don't understand
ich weiß nicht	I don't know
timmt	that's right
Verzeihung	excuse me
vielen Dank	thank you very much
wie bitte?	what did you say?
wie geht es Ihnen?	how are you?
wie geht's?	how are things?
wirklich?	is that so?
	really?

DAYS, MONTHS, SEASONS

Sunday	Sonntag	*zontahk*
Monday	Montag	*mohntahk*
Tuesday	Dienstag	*deenstahk*
Wednesday	Mittwoch	*mitvoкн*
Thursday	Donnerstag	*donnerstahk*
Friday	Freitag	*frytahk*
Saturday	Samstag,	*zamstahk,*
	Sonnabend	*zonnahbent*
January	Januar	*yanooar*
February	Februar	*faybrooar*
March	März	*mairts*
April	April	*april*
May	Mai	*my*
June	Juni	*yoonee*
July	Juli	*yoolee*
August	August	*owgoost*
September	September	*zeptember*
October	Oktober	*oktober*
November	November	*november*
December	Dezember	*daytsember*
Spring	Frühling	*frooling*
Summer	Sommer	*zommer*
Autumn	Herbst	*hairpst*
Winter	Winter	*vinter*
Christmas	Weihnachten	*vynaкнten*
Christmas Eve	Heiligabend	*hylish-ahbent*
New Year	Neujahr	*noy-yar*
New Year's Eve	Silvester	*zilvester*
Easter	Ostern	*ohstern*
Good Friday	Karfreitag	*karfrytahk*
Whitsun	Pfingsten	*pfingsten*

NUMBERS

0 null *nool*	10 zehn *tsayn*
1 eins *ine-ss*	11 elf *elf*
2 zwei *tsvy*	12 zwölf *tsvurlf*
3 drei *dry*	13 dreizehn *dry-tsayn*
4 vier *feer*	14 vierzehn *veer-tsayn*
5 fünf *fOOnf*	15 fünfzehn *fOOnf-tsayn*
6 sechs *zex*	16 sechzehn *zesh-tsayn*
7 sieben *zeeben*	17 siebzehn *zeep-tsayn*
8 acht *аКНt*	18 achtzehn *аКНt-tsayn*
9 neun *noyn*	19 neunzehn *noyn-tsayn*

20 zwanzig *tsvantsish*
21 einundzwanzig *ine-oont-tsvantsish*
22 zweiundzwanzig *tsvy-oont-tsvantsish*
30 dreißig *drysish*
40 vierzig *feertsish*
50 fünfzig *fOOnftsish*
60 sechzig *zeshtsish*
70 siebzig *zeeptsish*
80 achtzig *аКНtsish*
90 neunzig *noyntsish*
100 hundert *hoondert*
110 hundertzehn *hoondert-tsayn*
200 zweihundert *tsvy-hoondert*
1,000 tausend *towzent*
10,000 zehntausend *tsayn-towzent*
100,000 hunderttausend *hoondert-towzent*
1,000,000 eine Million *ine-uh mill-yohn*

Ordinal numbers are formed by adding **-te**, or **-ste** if the number ends in **-ig**. For example, **fünfte** (*fOOnftuh*, 'fifth'), **zwanzigste** (*tsvantsishstuh*, 'twentieth'). Exceptions are: **erste** (*airstuh*, 'first'), **dritte** (*drittuh*, 'third') and **siebte** (*zeeptuh*, 'seventh').

TIME

TELLING THE TIME

To say the hour in German use the word **Uhr** (*oor*) preceded by the appropriate number, for example: **neun Uhr** (*noyn oor*) is 'nine o'clock'. The 24-hour clock is used much more commonly in Germany.

The word for 'past' is **nach** (*nahкн*). So **zehn nach neun** (*tsayn nahкн noyn*) is 'ten past nine'. The word for 'to' is **vor** (*for*). So **zehn vor neun** (*tsayn for noyn*) is 'ten to nine'. The word for '(a) quarter' is **viertel** (*feertel*). So **viertel nach/vor neun** (*feertel nahкн/for noyn*) is '(a) quarter past/to nine'.

The important thing to remember when telling the time is that, when talking about the half hour, Germans count back from the next full hour, so that, for example, 'half past nine' is said in German as 'half ten'. So **es ist halb zehn** (*ess ist halp tsayn*) means 'it's half past nine'. Think 'half to' instead of 'half past'.

USEFUL WORDS AND PHRASES

today	heute	*hoytuh*
yesterday	gestern	*gestern*
tomorrow	morgen	*morgen*
this week	diese Woche	*deezuh voкнuh*
last week	letzte Woche	*letstuh voкнuh*
next week	nächste Woche	*naykstuh voкнuh*
this morning	heute morgen	*hoytuh morgen*
this afternoon	heute nachmittag	*hoytuh nahкнmit-tahk*
this evening	heute abend	*hoytuh ahbent*
tonight	heute abend	*hoytuh ahbent*
last night		
(*last evening*)	gestern Abend	*gestern ahbent*
(*late at night*)	gestern Nacht	*gestern naкнt*
in three days	in drei Tagen	*in dry tahgen*
three days ago	vor drei Tagen	*for dry tahgen*

late	spät	shpayt
early	früh	frш
soon	bald	balt
later on	später	shpayter
at the moment	im Moment	im moment
second	die Sekunde	zekoonduh
minute	die Minute	minootuh
one minute	eine Minute	ine-uh minootuh
two minutes	zwei Minuten	tsvy minooten
quarter of an hour	eine Viertelstunde	feertelshtoonduh
half an hour	eine halbe Stunde	halbuh shtoonduh
three quarters of an hour	eine Dreiviertel- stunde	dryfeertel-shtoonduh
hour	die Stunde	shtoonduh
day	der Tag	tahk
every day	jeden Tag	yayden tahk
all day	den ganzen Tag	dayn gantsen tahk
the next day	am nächsten Tag	am nayksten tahk
week	die Woche	voкнuh
fortnight	zwei Wochen	tsvy voкнen
month	der Monat	mohnaht
year	das Jahr	yar
what time is it?	wie spät ist es?	vee shpayt ist ess
am	morgens	morgens
pm	nachmittags	nahкнmittahks
(in the evening)	abends	ahbents
one o'clock	ein Uhr	ine oor
ten past one	zehn nach eins	tsayn nahкн ine-ss
quarter past one	viertel nach eins	feertel nahкн ine-ss
half past one	halb zwei	halp tsvy
twenty to two	zwanzig vor zwei	tsvantsish for tsvy
quarter to two	viertel vor zwei	feertel for tsvy
13.00	dreizehn Uhr	dry-tsayn oor
16.30	sechzehn Uhr dreißig	zesh-tsayn oor drysish
at half past five	um halb sechs	oom halp zex

COMMUNICATIONS

Useful Words and Phrases

code	die Vorwahl	_forvahl_
dialling tone	das Amtszeichen	_amts-tsyshen_
email address	die E-mail Adresse	_ee-mail adressuh_
enquiries	die Auskunft	_owsskoonft_
extension	der Nebenanschluß	_nayben-anshlooss_
fax	das Fax	_fax_
internet	das Internet	_'internet'_
mobile phone	das Mobiltelefon	_mohbeeltelefohn_
payphone	das Münztelefon	_mawnts-telefohn_
phonecard	die Telefonkarte	_telefohn-kartuh_
reverse charge call	das R-Gespräch	_air-gushpraysh_
telephone	das Telefon	_telefohn_
Web site	die Webseite	_'website'_
wrong number	die falsche Nummer	_falshuh noommer_

Where is the nearest phone box?
Wo ist die nächste Telefonzelle?
vo ist dee naykstuh telefohn-tselluh

I would like a number in …
Ich hätte gern eine Nummer in …
ish hettuh gairn ine-uh noommer in

I would like to speak to …
Kann ich bitte … sprechen?
kan ish bittuh … shpreshen

Hello, this is … speaking
Hallo, hier spricht …
hallo heer shprisht

Could you leave him/her a message?
Können Sie ihm/ihr etwas ausrichten?
kurnen zee eem/eer etvass owssrishten

I'll ring back later
Ich rufe später zurück
ish roofuh shpayter tsoorvk

Sorry, (I've got the) wrong number
Tut mir leid, ich habe mich verwählt
toot meer lite ish hahbuh mish fairvaylt

What's your fax number/email address?
Wie ist ihre Faxnummer/E-mail Adresse?
vee isst eeruh faxnummer/ee-mail adressuh

Can I send an email/fax from here?
Kann ich von hier eine E-mail/ein Fax senden?
kan ish von hear ine-nuh ee-mail/ine fax senden

THINGS YOU'LL HEAR

Am Apparat
Speaking

Wen möchten Sie sprechen?
Who would you like to speak to?

Sie sind falsch verbunden
You've got the wrong number

Wer spricht bitte?
Who's speaking?

Welche Nummer haben Sie?
What is your number?

Tut mir leid, er ist nicht im Hause
Sorry, he's not here

Ich werde ihm/ihr sagen, daß Sie angerufen haben
I'll tell him/her you called

Bitte warten
Please hold

EMERGENCIES

Useful Words and Phrases

accident	der Unfall	_oonfal_
ambulance	der Krankenwagen	_kranken-vahgen_
breakdown	die Panne	_pannuh_
burglary	der Einbruch	_ine-brookн_
crash	der Zusammenstoß	_tsoozammen-shtohss_
emergency	der Notfall	_nohtfal_
fire	das Feuer	_foyer_
fire brigade	die Feuerwehr	_foyer-vayr_
police	die Polizei	_poli-tsy_
police station	die Polizeiwache	_poli-tsy-vaкнuh_

Help!
Hilfe!
hilfuh

Stop!
Halt!
halt

Get an ambulance!
Rufen Sie einen Krankenwagen!
roofen zee ine-en kranken-vahgen

Hurry up!
Beeilen Sie sich!
buh-ile-en zee zish

My address is …
Meine Adresse ist …
mine-uh adressuh ist

My passport/car has been stolen
Mein Paß/Auto ist gestohlen worden
mine pas/owto ist gushtohlen vorden

HOTELS

bath *(tub)*	die Badewanne	*bahduh-vannuh*
bathroom	das Bad	*baht*
bed	das Bett	*bet*
bed and breakfast	Übernachtung mit Frühstück	*wbernaкнtoong mit frwshtwk*
bedroom	das (Schlaf)zimmer	*(shlahf)tsimmer*
bill	die Rechnung	*reshnoong*
breakfast	das Frühstück	*frwshtwk*
dining room	der Speisesaal	*shpyzuh-zahl*
dinner *(evening)*	das Abendessen	*ahbentessen*
double bed	das Doppelbett	*doppelbet*
double room	das Doppelzimmer	*doppeltsimmer*
foyer	das Foyer	*fwa-yay*
full board	Vollpension	*follpangz-yohn*
hotel	das Hotel	*hotel*
key	der Schlüssel	*shlwssel*
lift	der Aufzug, der Lift	*owf-tsook, lift*
lounge	der Aufenthaltsraum	*owfenthaltsrowm*
lunch	das Mittagessen	*mittahkessen*
maid	das Zimmermädchen	*tsimmer-maydshen*
manager	der Geschäftsführer	*gushefts-fwrer*
receipt	die Quittung	*kvittoong*
reception	der Empfang	*empfang*
receptionist	der Empfangschef	*empfangs-shef*
(woman)	die Empfangsdame	*empfangs-dahmuh*
room	das Zimmer	*tsimmer*
room service	der Zimmerservice	*tsimmer-'service'*
shower	die Dusche	*dooshuh*
single bed	das Einzelbett	*ine-tselbet*
single room	das Einzelzimmer	*ine-tsel-tsimmer*
toilet	die Toilette	*twalettuh*
twin room	das Zweibettzimmer	*tsvybet-tsimmer*
washbasin	das Waschbecken	*vashbecken*

Do you have any vacancies?
Haben Sie Zimmer frei?
h*ah*ben zee ts*i*mmer fry

I have a reservation
Ich habe ein Zimmer reserviert
ish h*ah*buh ine ts*i*mmer rezerv*ee*rt

I'd like a single room
Ich möchte ein Einzelzimmer
ish m*u*rshtuh ine *ine*-tsel-tsimmer

I'd like a room with a bathroom/balcony
Ich möchte ein Zimmer mit Bad/Balkon
ish m*u*rshtuh ine ts*i*mmer mit baht/balk*o*ng

Is there satellite/cable TV in the rooms?
Gibt es Satelliten/Kabel fernsehen in den Zimmern?
gipt as zatel*ee*ten/k*ah*bel fairnzayhen in den tsimmen

I'd like a room for one night/three nights
Ich möchte ein Zimmer für eine Nacht/drei Nächte
ish m*u*rshtuh ine ts*i*mmer fωr *ine*-uh naкнt/dry n*e*shtuh

What is the charge per night?
Was kostet es pro Nacht?
vass k*o*stet ess pro naкнt

When is breakfast/dinner?
Wann wird das Frühstück/Abendessen serviert?
vann veert dass frωhsht(ω)k/*ah*bentessen zairv*ee*rt

Please wake/call me at … o'clock
Bitte wecken Sie mich um … Uhr
b*i*ttuh v*e*cken zee mish oom … oor

Can I have breakfast in my room?
Können Sie mir das Frühstück auf mein Zimmer bringen?
k*u*rnen zee meer dass frωsht(ω)k owf mine ts*i*mmer br*i*ng-en

My room number is …
Meine Zimmernummer ist …
mine-uh tsimmer-noommer ist

There is no toilet paper in the bathroom
Im Badezimmer ist kein Toilettenpapier
im bahduh-tsimmer ist kine twaletten-papeer

The window won't open
Das Fenster geht nicht auf
dass fenster gayt nisht owf

There isn't any hot water
Es gibt kein warmes Wasser
ess geept kine varmess vasser

I'm leaving tomorrow
Ich reise morgen ab
ish ryzuh morgen ap

When do I have to vacate the room?
Bis wann muß ich das Zimmer räumen?
biss van mooss ish dass tsimmer roymen

Can I have the bill, please?
Kann ich bitte die Rechnung haben?
kan ish bittuh dee reshnoong hahben

I'll pay by credit card
Ich zahle mit Kreditkarte
ish tsahluh mit kredeetkartuh

I'll pay cash
Ich zahle in bar
ish tsahluh in bar

Can you get me a taxi?
Können Sie mir ein Taxi bestellen?
kurnen zee meer ine taxi bushtellen

THINGS YOU'LL SEE

Aufzug	lift
Bad	bath
belegt	no vacancies
drücken	push
Dusche	shower
Eingang	entrance
Empfang	reception
Frühstück	breakfast
kein Zutritt	no admission
Mittagessen	lunch
Notausgang	emergency exit
Parkplatz	car park
Rechnung	bill
Speisesaal	restaurant, dining room
ziehen	pull

THINGS YOU'LL HEAR

Tut mir leid, wir sind voll belegt
I'm sorry, we're full

Es sind keine Einzelzimmer/Doppelzimmer mehr frei
There are no single/double rooms left

Für wie lange?
For how long?

Wie möchten Sie zahlen?
How would you like to pay?

Könnten Sie bitte im voraus bezahlen
Could you please pay in advance

Sie müssen das Zimmer bis zwölf Uhr räumen
You must vacate the room by noon

SHOPPING

Excuse me, where is/are …?
Entschuldigung, wo finde ich …?
ent-shooldigoong vo finduh ish

Do you have …?
Haben Sie …?
hahben zee

How much is this?
Was kostet das?
vass kostet dass

Where do I pay?
Wo ist die Kasse?
vo ist dee kassuh

Do you take credit cards?
Akzeptieren Sie Kreditkarten?
aktsepteeren zee kredeetkarten

Can I have a receipt?
Kann ich eine Quittung bekommen?
kan ish ine-uh kvittoong bukommen

Do you have anything cheaper?
Haben Sie etwas Billigeres?
hahben zee etvass billigeress

Can I have a refund?
Kann ich mein Geld zurückbekommen?
kan ish mine gelt tsoorvk-bukommen

That's fine. I'll take it
In Ordnung. Ich nehme es
in ortnoong ish naymuh ess

It isn't what I wanted
Es ist nicht das, was ich wollte
ess ist nisht dass vass ish volltuh

EATING OUT

In Germany you'll find a wide range of places to eat, from the gourmet restaurant to the sausage and chips kiosk on the pavement. Fast food outlets, Chinese, Italian and Greek restaurants will be familiar. Not so perhaps the **Balkangrill**, serving spicy dishes from the Balkan countries.

If you want something typically German you could do a lot worse than try a small **Gasthaus** (_gast-howss_), or inn. Some dishes vary from region to region, but one shared characteristic you'll find is that German portions are not skimpy. Germans tend to eat a lot of meat; vegetarians might have to make a special request.

Ask for a small beer (**ein kleines Bier**, _ine kline-ess beer_) and you'll normally get a glass of around 0.2 litres. A large beer (**ein großes Bier**, _ine grohss-ess beer_) will normally be 0.4 or 0.5 litres, although in Bavaria you may well get a litre, which is known as **eine Maß** (_ine-uh mahss_). German beer is usually **Pils**. In some areas you might try **Alt**, which is a darker beer. German wine is either **süß** (_süss_, 'sweet'), **trocken** (_trocken_, 'dry') or, if you like it dry and a little sharper, **herb** (_hairp_). If you'd like to try a local wine, ask for **einen Wein aus dieser Gegend** (_ine-en vine owss deezer gaygent_).

If you're having a drink in a pub or bar you don't pay when ordering. Instead, the barman or barmaid will keep a tally of what you've bought, often ticking it off on your beer mat. If you sit at a table, you can expect table service (for no extra charge). There are no restrictions on taking children into pubs.

Useful Words and Phrases

beer	das Bier	_beer_
bill	die Rechnung	_reshnoong_
bottle	die Flasche	_flashuh_
bread	das Brot	_broht_
butter	die Butter	_bootter_
café	das Café	_kaffay_

cake	der Kuchen	_kOOKHen_
carafe	die Karaffe	_karaffuh_
children's portion	der Kinderteller	_kinderteller_
coffee	der Kaffee	_kaffay_
cup	die Tasse	_tassuh_
dessert	das Dessert	_dessair_
fork	die Gabel	_gahbel_
glass	das Glas	_glahss_
half-litre	der halbe Liter	_halbuh leeter_
knife	das Messer	_messer_
main course	das Hauptgericht	_howpt-gurisht_
menu	die Speisekarte	_shpyzuh-kartuh_
milk	die Milch	_milsh_
pepper	der Pfeffer	_pfeffer_
plate	der Teller	_teller_
receipt	die Quittung	_kvittoong_
restaurant	das Restaurant	_restorong_
salt	das Salz	_zalts_
sandwich	das belegte Brot	_bulayktuh broht_
serviette	die Serviette	_zairvee-ettuh_
snack	der Imbiß	_imbiss_
soup	die Suppe	_zooppuh_
spoon	der Löffel	_lurfel_
starter	die Vorspeise	_forshpyzuh_
sugar	der Zucker	_tsooker_
table	der Tisch	_tish_
tea	der Tee	_tay_
teaspoon	der Teelöffel	_taylurfel_
tip	das Trinkgeld	_trinkgelt_
waiter	der Ober	_ohber_
waitress	die Bedienung	_budeenoong_
water	das Wasser	_vasser_
wine	der Wein	_vine_
wine list	die Weinkarte	_vine-kartuh_

A table for one/two/three, please
Einen Tisch für eine Person/zwei/drei Personen, bitte
ine-en tish fœr ine-uh pairzohn/tsvy/dry pairzohnen bittuh

Can I see the menu/wine list?
Könnte ich bitte die Speisekarte/Weinkarte haben?
kurntuh ish bittuh dee shpyzuh-kartuh/vine-kartuh hahben

What would you recommend?
Was könnten Sie empfehlen?
vass kurnten zee empfaylen

I'd like …
Ich hätte gern …
ish hettuh gairn

Just a cup of coffee, please
Nur eine Tasse Kaffee, bitte
noor ine-uh tassuh kaffay bittuh

I only want a snack
Ich möchte nur eine Kleinigkeit
ish murshtuh noor ine-uh kline-ishkite

Is there a set menu?
Gibt es ein Tagesgericht?
geept ess ine tahges-gurisht

A litre carafe of house red, please
Einen Liter roten Tafelwein, bitte
ine-en leeter rohten tahfel-vine bittuh

Do you have any vegetarian dishes?
Haben Sie vegetarische Gerichte?
hahben zee vegetarishuh gurishtuh

Could we have some water, please?
Könnten Sie uns ein Glas Wasser geben?
kurnten zee oonss ine glas vasser gayben

Do you do children's portions?
Gibt es auch Kinderteller?
geept ess owкн kinderteller

Is there a highchair/baby changing room?
Gibt es dort einen Hochstuhl/einen Wickelraum?
gipt as dohrt ine-nen hoкнshtuhl/ine-nen vikkelrowm

Can you warm this bottle/baby food for me?
Können Sie diese Flasche/Babynahrung für mich aufwärmen?
kurnnen zee deezuh flahshuh/baibee-nahrunk fʊr mish owf-vayrmen

Waiter/Waitress!
Herr Ober!/Fräulein!
hair ohber/froyline

We didn't order this
Das haben wir nicht bestellt
dass hahben veer nisht bushtellt

May we have some more …?
Könnten wir noch etwas … haben?
kurnten veer noкн etvass … hahben

Can we have the bill, please?
Zahlen, bitte
tsahlen bittuh

Could I have a receipt, please?
Könnte ich bitte eine Quittung bekommen?
kurntuh ish bittuh ine-uh kvittoong bukommen

Can we pay separately?
Können wir getrennt bezahlen?
kurnen veer gutrennt butsahlen

The meal was very good, thank you
Es hat sehr gut geschmeckt, vielen Dank
es hat zair goot gushmeckt feelen dank

MENU GUIDE

Äpfel apples
Apfelkompott stewed apples
Apfelmus apple purée
Apfelsaft apple juice
Apfelsinen oranges
Apfelstrudel apple strudel
Apfeltasche apple turnover
Apfelwein cider
Aprikosen apricots
Artischocken artichokes
Auflauf (baked) pudding or omelette
Aufschnitt sliced cold meats, cold cuts
Austern oysters
Backpflaume prune
Baiser meringue
Balkansalat cabbage and pepper salad
Bananen bananas
Bandnudeln ribbon noodles
Bedienung service
Beilagen side dishes
Berliner jam doughnut
Bier beer
Birnen pears
Biskuit sponge cake
Biskuitrolle Swiss roll
Bismarckhering filleted pickled herring
Blätterteig puff pastry
blau boiled
Blaukraut red cabbage
Blumenkohl cauliflower
blutig rare
Blutwurst black pudding
Bockwurst large frankfurter
Bohnen beans
Bouillon clear soup
Bouletten meatballs
Braten roast meat
Bratensoße gravy

Bratkartoffeln fried potatoes
Bratwurst grilled pork sausage
Brot bread
Brötchen roll
Brühwurst large frankfurter
Buttercremetorte cream cake
Buttermilch buttermilk
Champignons mushrooms
Dampfnudeln sweet yeast dumpling
Dicke Bohnen broad beans
Dillsoße dill sauce
durchgebraten well-done
durchwachsen with fat
durchwachsener Speck streaky bacon
Eier eggs
Eierauflauf omelette
Eierkuchen, Eierpfannkuchen pancake
Eierspeise egg dish
eingelegt pickled
Eintopf stew
Eintopfgericht stew
Eis ice
Eisbecher sundae
Eisbein knuckles of pork
englisch rare
Entenbraten roast duck
Erbsen peas
Erdbeertorte strawberry cake
Essig vinegar
Falscher Hase meat loaf
Fenchel fennel
Fisch fish
Fischfrikadellen fishcakes
Fischstäbchen fish fingers
Fleischkäse meat loaf
Fleischklößchen meatball(s)
Fleischwurst pork sausage
Forelle trout

Frikadelle rissole
Frikassee fricassee
Fruchtsaft fruit juice
Gans goose
Gebäck pastries, cakes
gebacken baked
gebraten roast
gedünstet steamed
Geflügel poultry, chicken
gefüllt stuffed
gekocht boiled
gemischter Salat mixed salad
Gemüse vegetable(s)
gepökelt salted, pickled
geräuchert smoked
Geschnetzeltes strips of meat in sauce
Geselchtes salted and smoked meat
Getränke beverages
Gewürze spices
Gewürzgurken gherkins
gratiniert au gratin
Grieß semolina
grüne Bohnen French beans
grüne Nudeln green pasta
Gulasch goulash
Gurkensalat cucumber salad
Hackfleisch mince
Hähnchen chicken
Hähnchenkeule chicken leg
Hammelfleisch mutton
Hartkäse hard cheese
Hauptspeisen main courses
Hausfrauenart, Hausmacher home-made
Hecht pike
Heidelbeeren bilberries, blueberries
Heilbutt halibut
Herz heart
Himbeeren raspberries
Himmel und Erde potato and apple purée
  with black pudding or liver sausage
Honig honey

Honigkuchen honey cake
Huhn chicken
Hühnersuppe chicken soup
Hummer lobster
Kabeljau cod
Kaffee coffee
Kalbfleisch veal
Kalbsbraten roast veal
kaltes Büfett cold buffet
Kaninchen rabbit
Karotten carrots
Karpfen carp
Kartoffelknödel potato dumplings
Kartoffeln potatoes
Kartoffelpüree potato purée
Käse cheese
Käsekuchen cheesecake
Käseplatte selection of cheeses
Kasserolle casserole
Kassler smoked and braised pork chop
Kastanien chestnuts
Katenrauchwurst smoked sausage
Keule leg, haunch
Kirschen cherries
klare Brühe clear soup
Klöße dumplings
Knäckebrot crispbread
Knackwurst frankfurter
Knoblauch garlic
Knochen bone
Knödel dumplings
Kohl cabbage
Konfitüre jam
Königskuchen type of fruit cake
Kopfsalat lettuce
Kotelett chop
Krabben shrimps; prawns
Kraftbrühe beef consommé
Kräuter herbs
Krautsalat coleslaw
Kroketten croquettes

Kuchen cake
Kürbis pumpkin
Labskaus meat, fish and potato stew
Lachs salmon
Lachsforelle sea trout
Lamm lamb
Lauch leek
Leber liver
Leberkäse baked pork and beef loaf
Leipziger Allerlei mixed vegetables
Linseneintopf lentil stew
Linsensuppe lentil soup
Mandeln almonds
mariniert marinaded, pickled
Marmelade jam
Meeresfrüchte seafood
Meerrettich horseradish
Meerrettichsoße horseradish sauce
Melone melon
Miesmuscheln mussels
Milch milk
Milchmixgetränk milk shake
Milchreis rice pudding
Mineralwasser (sparkling) mineral water
Möhren, Mohrrüben carrots
Mus purée
Muscheln mussels
Muskat(nuß) nutmeg
Nachspeisen desserts
Nieren kidneys
Nüsse nuts
Obstsalat fruit salad
Ochsenschwanzsuppe oxtail soup
Öl oil
Oliven olives
Olivenöl olive oil
Omelett omelette
Orangen oranges
Orangensaft orange juice
Palatschinken stuffed pancakes

Paprika peppers
Paradiesäpfel tomatoes
Pastete vol-au-vent
Petersilie parsley
Pfannkuchen pancake(s)
Pfeffer pepper
Pfirsiche peaches
Pflaumen plums
Pflaumenkuchen plum tart
pikant spicy
Pilze mushrooms
Platte selection
pochiert poached
Pökelfleisch salt meat
Porree leek
Potthast braised beef with sauce
Poularde young chicken
Preiselbeeren cranberries
Prinzeßbohnen unsliced runner beans
Pumpernickel black rye bread
Püree (potato) purée
püriert puréed
Puter turkey
Radieschen radishes
Rahm (sour) cream
Räucheraal smoked eel
Räucherhering kipper, smoked herring
Räucherlachs smoked salmon
Räucherspeck smoked bacon
Reibekuchen potato waffles
Reis rice
Reisauflauf rice pudding
Renke whitefish
Rettich radish
Rhabarber rhubarb
Rindfleisch beef
Risi-Pisi rice and peas
Rohkostplatte selection of salads
rosa rare to medium
Rosenkohl Brussels sprouts
Rosinen raisins

Rostbraten roast
Rösti fried potatoes and onions
Röstkartoffeln fried potatoes
Rote Bete beetroot
rote Grütze red fruit jelly
Rotkohl, Rotkraut red cabbage
Rühreier scrambled eggs
Sahne cream
Salate salads
Salatsoße salad dressing
Salz salt
Salzburger Nockerln sweet soufflés
Salzkartoffeln boiled potatoes
sauer sour
Sauerbraten marinaded pot roast
Sauerkraut white cabbage, finely chopped and pickled
Sauerrahm sour cream
Schaschlik (shish-)kebab
Schellfisch haddock
Schinken ham
Schinkenröllchen rolled ham
Schinkenwurst ham sausage
Schlagsahne whipped cream
Schmorbraten pot roast
Scholle plaice
Schulterstück slice of shoulder
Schwarzbrot brown rye bread
Schwarzwälder Kirschtorte Black Forest cherry gâteau
Schweinefleisch pork
Schweinshaxe knuckle of pork
Seezunge sole
Semmel bread roll
Semmelknödel bread dumplings
Senf mustard
Spargel asparagus
Spätzle home-made noodles
Speck fatty bacon
Speisekarte menu
Spiegeleier fried eggs

Spinat spinach
Spitzkohl white cabbage
Sprudel(wasser) mineral water
Streuselkuchen cake with crumble topping
Suppen soups
süß sweet
süß-sauer sweet-and-sour
Tafelwasser (still) mineral water
Tagesgericht dish of the day
Tageskarte menu of the day
Taube pigeon
Tee tea
Thunfisch tuna
Tintenfisch squid
Tomaten tomatoes
Törtchen tart(s)
Torte gâteau
Truthahn turkey
überbacken au gratin
verlorene Eier poached eggs
Vollkornbrot dark whole grain bread
Vorspeisen hors d'oeuvres, starters
Waffeln waffles
Wasser water
Weichkäse soft cheese
Weincreme pudding with wine
Weintrauben grapes
Weißbrot white bread
Weißwein white wine
Wild game
Windbeutel cream puff
Wirsing savoy cabbage
Wurst sausage
Würstchen frankfurter(s)
Wurstplatte selection of sausages
Zitrone lemon
Zucker sugar
Zunge tongue
Zwiebeln onions
Zwischengerichte entrées

GREEK

CONTENTS

INTRODUCTION

Pronunciation

When reading the imitated pronunciation, stress the part that is underlined. Pronounce each syllable as if it formed part of an English word, and you will be understood sufficiently well. Remember the points below, and your pronunciation will be even closer to the correct Greek.

e   is always short, as in 'bed'

i   is always long, as in 'Lolita'

     (So when you see the imitation *ine*, remember to make this two syllables 'ee-ne'. Similarly, *ne* and *me* should be kept short – *don't* say 'nee' or 'mee'.)

g   should be a rolled, guttural sound at the back of the throat.

h   is a guttural 'ch', as in the Scottish 'loch'
     (*Don't* pronounce this as 'lock'.)

oo   long, as in 'moon'

th   as in 'then' or 'the' (Notice this particularly, and *don't* confuse it with TH in small capitals.)

TH   as in 'theatre' or 'thin'

The Greek Alphabet

To help you read signs or notices printed in capital letters (which are sometimes quite unlike their lower-case counterparts), the Greek alphabet is given below. Alongside each letter is its name and a guide to its pronunciation.

letter		*name*	*pronunciation*
A	α	alfa	*a* as in 'father'
B	β	vita	*v* as in 'victory'
Γ	γ	ghamma	before *a*, *o* and *u*, it is a guttural *gh*; before *e* and *i* sounds, it is like *y* in 'yes'

Δ	δ	dhelta	*th* as in 'then'
E	ε	epsilon	*e* as in 'end'
Z	ζ	zita	*z* as in 'zest'
H	η	ita	*i* as in 'Maria'
Θ	θ	thita	*th* as in 'theatre' (TH in the imitated pronunciation system)
I	ι	yiota	before *a* and *o* sounds, like *y* in 'yes'; otherwise like *i* in 'Maria'
K	κ	kapa	like *k* in 'king', but softer
Λ	λ	lamdha	*l* as in 'love'
M	μ	mi	*m* as in 'mother'
N	ν	ni	*n* as in 'no'
Ξ	ξ	ksi	*x* as in 'box', or *ks* as in 'books'
O	o	omikron	*o* as in 'orange'
Π	π	pi	like *p* in 'Peter', but softer
P	ρ	ro	*r* as in 'Rome', trilled or rolled
Σ	σ, ς	sighma	*s* as in 'sing'. The alternative small letter ς is used only at the end of a word
T	τ	taf	like *t* in 'tea', but softer
Y	υ	ipsilon	*i* as in 'Maria'
Φ	φ	fi	*f* as in 'friend'
X	χ	hi	*ch* as in the Scottish 'loch'. But before *e* or *i* sounds, it is like *h* in 'hue'
Ψ	ψ	psi	like *ps* in 'lapse'
Ω	ω	omegha	*o* as in 'orange'

Note that the Greek question mark is a semicolon (;). Stress is indicated by an accent above the Greek letter and an underline in the pronuciation.

USEFUL PHRASES

Yes/No
Ναι/Όχι
ne/ohi

Thank you
Ευχαριστώ
efharisto

No, thank you
Όχι, ευχαριστώ
ohi efharisto

Please
Παρακαλώ
parakalo

I don't understand
Δεν καταλαβαίνω
then katalaveno

Do you speak English/French/German?
Μιλάτε Αγγλικά/Γαλλικά/Γερμανικά;
milate Anglika/Galika/Yermanika

I can't speak Greek
Δέν μιλάω Ελληνικά
then milao elinika

Please speak more slowly
Παρακαλώ, μιλάτε πιό αργά;
parakalo, milate pio arga

Please write it down for me
Μου το γράφετε, παρακαλώ;
moo to grafete, parakalo

Good morning/good afternoon/good night
Καλημέρα/καλησπέρα/καληνύχτα
kalimera/kalispera/kalinihta

Goodbye
Αντίο
andio

How are you?
Τι κάνεις;
ti kanis

Excuse me, please
Συγγνώμη, παρακαλώ
singnomi, parakalo

Sorry!
Συγγνώμη!
singnomi

I'm really sorry
Ειλικρινά, λυπάμαι
ilikrina, lipame

Can you help me?
Μπορείς να με βοηθήσεις;
boris na me voiTHisis

Can you tell me ...?
Μου λέτε ...;
moo lete

Can I have …?
Μπορώ να έχω …;
boro na eho

I would like …
Θα ήθελα …
THa iTHela

Is there … here?
Υπάρχει … εδώ;
iparhi … etho

Where are the toilets?
Που είναι οι τουαλέτες;
poo ine i tooaletes

Where can I get …?
Που μπορώ να πάρω …;
poo boro na paro

Is there wheelchair access?
Υπάρχει πρόσβαση για αναπηρικό καροτσάκι;
iparhi prosvasi ya anapiriko karotsaki

How much is it?
Πόσο κάνει;
poso kani

Do you take credit cards?
Δέχεστε πιστωτικές κάρτες;
theheste pistotikes kartes

Can I pay by cheque?
Μπορώ να πληρώσω με επιταγή;
boro na pliroso me epitayi

What time is it?
Τι ώρα είναι;
ti ora ine

I must go now
Πρέπει να πηγαίνω τώρα
prepi na piyeno tora

Cheers!
Εις υγείαν!
is iyian

Go away!
Παράτα με!
paratame

THINGS YOU'LL SEE OR HEAR

ανακοίνωση	*anakinosi*	announcement
ΑΝΑΧΩΡΗΣΕΙΣ/	*anahorisis*	departures
αναχωρήσεις		
ΑΝΟΙΚΤΑ/ανοικτά	*anikta*	open
ΑΝΟΙΚΤΟΝ/ανοικτόν	*anikton*	open
ΑΣΑΝΣΕΡ/ασανσέρ	*asanser*	lift
αντίο	*andio*	goodbye
απαγορεύεται	*apagorevete*	no smoking
το κάπνισμα	*to kapnisma*	
αργά	*arga*	slow
αριστερά	*aristera*	left
ΑΦΙΞΕΙΣ/αφίξεις	*afixis*	arrivals
βιβλιοθήκη	*vivlioTHiki*	library
ΓΥΝΑΙΚΩΝ/γυναικών	*yinekon*	women
ΔΕΝ ΛΕΙΤΟΥΡΓΕΙ/	*then litooryi*	out of order
δεν λειτουργεί		
δεξιά	*thexia*	right

⟶

διάλειμμα	thialima	interval
ΕΙΣΟΔΟΣ/είσοδος	isothos	way in, entrance
έκθεση	ekTHesi	exhibition, show room
έλεγχος	elenhos	check, inspection
ελεύθερος	elefTHeros	free
ΕΞΟΔΟΣ/έξοδος	exothos	way out
ευχαριστώ	efharisto	thank you
καλώς ήρθατε	kalos irTHate	welcome
ΚΑΠΝΙΖΟΝΤΕΣ/καπνίζοντες	kapnizodes	smokers
ΚΑΤΗΛΗΜΜΕΝΟΣ/ κατηλημμένος	katilimenos	engaged
ΚΙΝΔΥΝΟΣ/κίνδυνος	kinthinos	danger
ΚΛΕΙΣΤΑ/κλειστά	klista	closed
ΚΛΕΙΣΤΟΝ/κλειστόν	kliston	closed
μέχρι	mehri	until
μη	mi	do not
ναί	ne	yes
ορίστε;	oriste?	can I help you?
όχι	ohi	no
παρακαλώ	parakalo	please; can I help you?
πεζοί	pezi	pedestrians
προσοχή παρακαλώ	prosohi parakalo	attention, please
ΠΡΟΣΟΧΗ!/προσοχή!	prosohi	caution!
ΣΥΡΑΤΕ/σύρατε	sirate	pull
ΣΤΟΠ/στόπ	stop	stop
στρίψατε	stripsate	turn
ΣΧΟΛΕΙΟ/σχολείο	s-holio	school
ΤΑΜΕΙΟ/ταμείο	tamio	till, cash desk
ΤΕΛΩΝΕΙΟ/Τελωνείο	Telonio	Customs
ΤΟΥΡΙΣΤΙΚΗ ΑΣΤΥΝΟΜΙΑ/ Τουριστική Αστυνομία	Tooristiki Astinomia	Tourist Police
χαίρετε	herete	hello
ωθήσατε	oTHisate	push
ώρες λειτουργίας	ores litooryias	opening hours

DAYS, MONTHS, SEASONS

Sunday	Κυριακή	*kiriaki*
Monday	Δευτέρα	*theftera*
Tuesday	Τρίτη	*triti*
Wednesday	Τετάρτη	*tetarti*
Thursday	Πέμπτη	*pembti*
Friday	Παρασκευή	*paraskevi*
Saturday	Σάββατο	*savato*
January	Ιανουάριος	*ianooarios*
February	Φεβρουάριος	*fevrooarios*
March	Μάρτιος	*martios*
April	Απρίλιος	*aprilios*
May	Μάιος	*maios*
June	Ιούνιος	*ioonios*
July	Ιούλιος	*ioolios*
August	Αύγουστος	*avgoostos*
September	Σεπτέμβριος	*septemvrios*
October	Οκτώβριος	*oktovrios*
November	Νοέμβριος	*noemvrios*
December	Δεκέμβριος	*thekemvrios*
Spring	άνοιξη	*anixi*
Summer	καλοκαίρι	*kalokeri*
Autumn	φθινόπωρο	*fтнinoporo*
Winter	χειμώνας	*himonas*
Christmas	Χριστούγεννα	*hristooyena*
Christmas Eve	παραμονή	*paramoni*
	Χριστουγέννων	*hristooyenon*
Good Friday	Μεγάλη	*megali*
	Παρασκευή	*paraskevi*
Easter	Πάσχα	*pas-ha*
New Year	Πρωτοχρονιά	*protohronia*
New Year's Eve	Παραμονή	*paramoni*
	Πρωτοχρονιάς	*protohronias*

NUMBERS

0	μηδέν *mithen*	5	πέντε *pende*
1	ένα *ena*	6	έξι *exi*
2	δύο *thio*	7	επτά *epta*
3	τρία *tria*	8	οχτώ *ohto*
4	τέσσερα *tesera*	9	εννιά *enia*

10	δέκα	*theka*
11	έντεκα	*edeka*
12	δώδεκα	*thotheka*
13	δεκατρία	*theka-tria*
14	δεκατέσσερα	*theka-tesera*
15	δεκαπέντε	*theka-pende*
16	δεκαέξι	*theka-exi*
17	δεκαεπτά	*theka-epta*
18	δεκαοκτώ	*theka-ohto*
19	δεκαεννιά	*theka-enia*
20	είκοσι	*ikosi*
21	εικοσιένα	*ikosi-ena*
22	εικοσιδύο	*ikosi-thio*
30	τριάντα	*trianda*
31	τριανταένα	*trianda-ena*
32	τριανταδύο	*trianda-thio*
40	σαράντα	*saranda*
50	πενήντα	*peninda*
60	εξήντα	*exinda*
70	εβδομήντα	*evthomida*
80	ογδόντα	*ogthonda*
90	ενενήντα	*eneninda*
100	εκατό	*ekato*
110	εκατόν δέκα	*ekaton theka*
200	διακόσια	*thiakosia*
1,000	χίλια	*hilia*
1,000,000	ένα εκατομμύριο	*ena ekatomirio*

TIME

today	σήμερα	si̱mera
yesterday	χτες	htes
tomorrow	αύριο	a̱vrio
the day before yesterday	προχτές	prohte̱s
the day after tomorrow	μεθαύριο	meTHa̱vrio
this week	αυτή την εβδομάδα	afti̱ tin evthoma̱tha
last week	την περασμένη εβδομάδα	tin perasme̱ni evthoma̱tha
next week	την επόμενη εβδομάδα	tin epo̱meni evthoma̱tha
this morning	το πρωί	to proi̱
this afternoon	το απόγευμα	to apo̱yevma
this evening	το βράδυ	to vra̱thi
tonight	απόψε	apo̱pse
yesterday afternoon	χτες το απόγευμα	htes t'apo̱yevma
last night	χτες τη νύχτα	htes ti ni̱hta
tomorrow morning	αύριο το πρωί	a̱vrio to proi̱
tomorrow night	αύριο το βράδυ	a̱vrio to vra̱thi
in three days	σε τρεις μέρες	se tris me̱res
three days ago	πριν τρεις μέρες	prin tris me̱res
late	αργά	arga̱
early	νωρίς	nori̱s
soon	σύντομα	si̱ndoma
later on	αργότερα	argo̱tera
at the moment	προς το παρόν	pros to paro̱n
second	το δευτερόλεπτο	to theftero̱lepto
minute	το λεπτό	to lepto̱
ten minutes	δέκα λεπτά	the̱ka lepta̱
quarter of an hour	ένα τέταρτο	e̱na te̱tarto
half an hour	μισή ώρα	misi̱ o̱ra

183

three quarters of an hour	τρία τέταρτα της ώρας	*tria tetarta tis oras*
hour	ώρα	*ora*
day	μέρα	*mera*
week	εβδομάδα	*evthomatha*
fortnight	σε δύο εβδομάδες	*se thio evthomathes*
month	μήνας	*minas*
year	χρόνος	*hronos*

TELLING THE TIME

In Greek you always put the hour first and then use the word **ke** (και) to denote the minutes 'past' the hour and **para** (παρά) for the minutes 'to' the hour (eg 'five-twenty' = **5 ke 20**; 'five-forty' = **6 para 20**). The 24-hour clock is used officially in timetables and enquiry offices. Don't forget that Greek Standard Time is always two hours ahead of Greenwich Mean Time.

one o'clock	μία η ώρα	*mia i ora*
ten past one	μία και δέκα	*mia ke theka*
quarter past one	μία και τέταρτο	*mia ke tetarto*
twenty past one	μία και είκοσι	*mia ke ikosi*
half past one	μία και μισή	*mia ke misi*
twenty to two	δύο παρά είκοσι	*thio para ikosi*
quarter to two	δύο παρά τέταρτο	*thio para tetarto*
ten to two	δύο παρά δέκα	*thio para theka*
two o'clock	δύο η ώρα	*thio i ora*
13.00 (1 pm)	δεκατρείς	*theka-tris*
16.30 (4.30 pm)	δεκαέξι και τριάντα	*theka-exi ke trianda*
20.10 (8.10 pm)	είκοσι και δέκα	*ikosi ke theka*
at half past five	στις πέντε και μισή	*stis pede ke misi*
at seven o'clock	στις επτά	*stis epta*
noon	το μεσημέρι	*to mesimeri*
midnight	τα μεσάνυχτα	*ta mesanihta*

COMMUNICATIONS

Useful Words and Phrases

code	ο κωδικός	o kothik_os_
to dial	καλώ	kal_o_
emergency	η επείγουσα ανάγκη	i epig_oo_sa an_ag_i
enquiries	οι πληροφορίες	i pliror_ie_s
extension	το εσωτερικό	to esoterik_o_
mobile phone	το κινητό τηλέφωνο	tokinit_o_ tilefono
number	ο αριθμός	o ariTHm_o_s
phonecard	η τηλεφωνική κάρτα	i tilefonik_i_ karta,
reverse charge call	το τηλεφώνημα κολέκτ	to tilef_o_nima kol_e_kt
telephone	το τηλέφωνο	to tilefono
telephone box	ο τηλεφωνικός θάλαμος	o tilefonik_os_ THa_l_amos
wrong number	λάθος νούμερο	l_a_THos n_oo_mero

Where is the nearest phone box?
Που είναι ο πλησιέστερος τηλεφωνικός θάλαμος;
poo i_ne o plisi-_e_steros tilefonik_os_ THa_l_amos

Hello, this is … speaking
Χαίρετε, είμαι ο/η …
h_e_rete, i_me o/i

Is that …?
Ο/η …;
o/i

Speaking
ο ίδιος
o i_thios

I would like to speak to …
Θα ήθελα να μιλήσω στον …
THα i_THela na mil_i_so ston

185

Please tell him … called
Παρακαλώ του λέτε ότι τηλεφώνησε ο/η …
parakalo too lete oti tilefonise o/i

Ask him to call me back, please
Πέστε του να με ξαναπάρει παρακαλώ
peste too na me xanapari parakalo

My number is …
το τηλέφωνό μου είναι …
to tilefono moo ine

Do you know where he is?
Ξέρετε που είναι;
xerete poo ine

Could you leave him a message?
Μπορείτε να του αφήσετε ένα μήνυμα;
borite na too afisete ena minimas

I'll ring back later
Θα σε ξαναπάρω αργότερα
THa se xanaparo argotera

Sorry, wrong number
Πήρατε λάθος αριθμό
pirate laTHos ariTHmo

How much is a call to …?
Πόσο στοιχίζει ένα τηλεφώνημα στο …;
poso sti-hizi ena tilefonima sto

I would like to reverse the charges
Θα ήθελα τα έξοδα να πληρωθούν εκεί
THa iTHela ta exotha na pliroTHoon eki

I would like a number in …
Θέλω ένα αριθμό στην …
THelo ena ariTHmo stin

What's your fax number/What's your email address?
Ποιός είναι ο αριθμός του φαξ/Ποιά είναι η διεύθυνση (email);
pios ine o arithmos too fax/pia ine i thiefTHinsi 'email'

Can I send a fax/email from here?
Μπορώ να στείλω φαξ/email από εδώ;
boro na stilo fax/'email' apo etho

THINGS YOU'LL SEE OR HEAR

ακουστικό	*akoostiko*	receiver
άμεσος δράσις	*amesos thrasis*	emergencies, police
αριθμός	*ariTHmos*	number
δεν λειτουργεί	*then litooryi*	out of order
καλεί	*kali*	ringing
καλέσατε	*kalesate*	dial
κέρματα	*kermata*	coins
κωδικός	*kothikos*	code
λάθος νούμερο	*laTHos noomero*	wrong number
μιλάει	*milai*	engaged
μονάδες	*monathes*	units
νούμερο	*noomero*	number
πυροσβεστική	*pirosvestiki*	fire brigade
σηκώσατε	*sikosate*	pick up
τηλεφώνημα	*tilefonima*	call
τηλεφωνώ	*tilefono*	to call
τοπικό	*topiko*	local call
χαίρετε	*herete*	Hello
χρυσός οδηγός	*hrisos othigos*	Yellow Pages
υπεραστικό	*iperastiko*	long-distance call, international call

HOTELS

Useful Words and Phrases

balcony	το μπαλκόνι	*to balkoni*
bathroom	το λουτρό	*to lootro*
bed	το κρεβάτι	*to krevati*
bedroom	το υπνοδωμάτιο	*to ipnothomatio*
bill	ο λογαριασμός	*o logariasmos*
breakfast	το πρωινό	*to proino*
dining room	η τραπεζαρία	*i trapezaria*
dinner	το δείπνο	*to thipno*
double room	το διπλό δωμάτιο	*to thiplo thomatio*
foyer	το φουαγέ	*to fooaye*
full board	η φουλ-πανσιόν	*i fool-pansion*
half board	η ντεμί-πανσιόν	*i demi-pansion*
hotel	το ξενοδοχείο	*to xenothohio*
key	το κλειδί	*to klithi*
lift	το ασανσέρ	*to asanser*
lounge	το σαλόνι	*to saloni*
lunch	το γεύμα	*to yevma*
manager	ο διευθυντής	*o thi-eftHindis*
receipt	η απόδειξη	*i apothixi*
reception	η ρεσεψιόν	*i resepsion*
receptionist	ο ρεσεψιονίστας	*o resepsionistas*
restaurant	το εστιατόριο	*to estiatorio*
room	το δωμάτιο	*to thomatio*
room service	το σέρβις δωματίου	*to servis thomatioo*
shower	το ντους	*to doos*
single room	το μονό δωμάτιο	*to mono thomatio*
toilet	η τουαλέτα	*i tooaleta*
twin room	το δωμάτιο με δύο κρεβάτια	*to thomatio me thio krevatia*

Have you any vacancies?
Εχετε κενά δωμάτια;
ehete kena thomatia

I have a reservation
Εχω κλείσει δωμάτιο
eho klisi thomatio

I'd like a single room
Θα ήθελα ένα μονό δωμάτιο
THa itHela ena mono thomatio

I'd like a double room
Θα ήθελα ένα δωμάτιο με διπλό κρεβάτι
THa itHela ena thomatio me thiplo krevati

I'd like a twin room
Θα ήθελα ένα δωμάτιο με δύο κρεβάτια
THa itHela ena thomatio me thio krevatia

I'd like a room with a bathroom/balcony
Θα ήθελα ένα δωμάτιο με μπάνιο/μπαλκόνι
THa itHela ena thomatio me banio/balkoni

Is there satellite/cable TV in the rooms?
Τα δωμάτια έχουν δορυφοκή/καλωδιακή τηλεόραση;
ta thomatia ehoon thoriforiki/kalothiaki tileorasi

I'd like a room for one night/three nights
Θα ήθελα ένα δωμάτιο για μία νύχτα/τρεις νύχτες
THa itHela ena thomatio ya mia nihta/tris nihtes

What is the charge per night?
Πόσο στοιχίζει η διανυκτέρευση;
poso stihizi i thianihterefsi

When is breakfast/dinner?
Πότε έχει πρωινό/δείπνο;
pote ehi proino/thipno

Would you have my luggage brought up?
Θα μου φέρετε τις βαλίτσες μου;
THa moo ferete tis valitses moo

Please call me at ... o'clock
Παρακαλώ ειδοποιήστε με στις ...
parakalo ithopi-isteme stis

Can I have breakfast in my room?
Μπορώ να πάρω το πρωινό στο δωματιό μου;
boro na paro to proino sto thomatio moo

I'll be back at ... o'clock
Θα επιστρέψω στις ...
THa epistrepso stis

My room number is ...
Ο αριθμός του δωματιού μου είναι ...
o ariTHmos too thomatioo moo ine

I'm leaving tomorrow
Φεύγω αύριο
fevgo avrio

Can I have the bill, please?
Τον λογαριασμό παρακαλώ
ton logariasmo parakalo

Can you get me a taxi?
Μου καλείτε ένα ταξί;
moo kalite ena taxi

THINGS YOU'LL SEE

ασανσέρ	*asanser*	lift, elevator
δείπνο	*thipno*	dinner
δωμάτια	*thomatia*	rooms
είσοδος	*isothos*	entrance
έξοδος κινδύνου	*exothos kinthinoo*	emergency exit
εστιατόριο	*estiatorio*	restaurant
λογαριασμός	*logariasmos*	bill
λουτρό	*lootro*	bathroom
ντους	*doos*	shower
ξενοδοχείο	*xenothohio*	hotel
πρωινό	*proino*	breakfast
ρεσεψιόν	*resepsion*	reception
σκάλες	*skales*	stairs
σύρατε	*sirate*	pull
τουαλέτες	*tooaletes*	toilets
υπόγειο	*ipoyio*	basement
φαγητό	*fayito*	meal, lunch
ωθήσατε	*oTHisate*	push

THINGS YOU'LL HEAR

Then iparhoon mona/thipla thomatia kena
There are no single/double rooms left

Imaste yemati
No vacancies

Parakalo, plironete prokatavolika
Please pay in advance

Parakalo, afinete to thiavatsrio sas etho
Please leave your passport here

SHOPPING

Where is the … department?
Που είναι το τμήμα των …;
poo ine to tmima ton

Do you have …?
Εχετε …;
ehete

How much is this?
Πόσο κάνει αυτό;
poso kani afto

Where do I pay?
Πού πληρώνω;
poo plirono

Have you anything cheaper?
Έχετε τίποτα φτηνότερο;
ehete tipota ftinotero

Could you wrap it for me?
Μου το τυλίγετε;
moo to tiliyete

Can I have a receipt?
Μου δίνετε μία απόδειξη;
moo thinete mia apothixi

I'd like to change this, please
Θα ήθελα να το αλλάξω αυτό, παρακαλώ
THa iTHela na to alaxo afto, parakalo

I'm just looking
Απλώς κοιτάζω
aplos kitazo

I'll come back later
Θα επιστρέψω αργότερα
THa epistrepso argotera

EATING OUT

Some examples of places to eat and drink are shown below (notice that signs in Greek capital letters often look different from the same words in lower-case).

ΕΣΤΙΑΤΟΡΙΟΝ Εστιατόριον *estiatorion* (restaurant)
In all tourist places you will find the menu printed in English as well as in Greek, and the staff will almost certainly speak English. If you feel more adventurous, you might prefer to try some of the many Greek delicacies available, and in smaller places you will be welcomed into the kitchen to see what's cooking. The menu will usually give you two prices for each item – the higher one includes a service charge.

ΤΑΒΕΡΝΑ Ταβέρνα *taverna*
A typical Greek restaurant, where draught wine is available.

ΨΑΡΟΤΑΒΕΡΝΑ Ψαροταβέρνα *psarotaverna*
A restaurant specializing in seafood.

ΨΗΣΤΑΡΙΑ Ψησταριά *psistaria*
A restaurant specializing in charcoal-grilled food.

ΟΥΖΕΡΙ Ουζερί *oozeri*
A bar that serves ouzo (a strong, aniseed-flavoured spirit) and beer with snacks (**mezethes**) which could be savouries or sometimes, especially in the islands, octopus or local seafood.

ΖΑΧΑΡΟΠΛΑΣΤΕΙΟ Ζαχαροπλαστείο *zaharoplastio*
A pastry shop or café that serves cakes and soft drinks and is also an ideal place to have breakfast.

ΚΑΦΕΝΕΙΟ Καφενείο *kafenio*
A coffee house, where Greek coffee is served with traditional sweets. Here you can play a game of cards or backgammon.

Useful Words and Phrases

beer	η μπύρα	i bira
bill	ο λογαριασμός	o logariasmos
bottle	το μπουκάλι	to bookali
cake	το γλυκό	to gliko
chef	ο μάγειρας	o mayiras
coffee	ο καφές	o kafes
cup	το φλυτζάνι	to flitzani
fork	το πιρούνι	to pirooni
glass	το ποτήρι	to potiri
knife	το μαχαίρι	to maheri
menu	το μενού	to menoo
milk	το γάλα	to gala
napkin	η χαρτοπετσέτα	i hartopetseta
plate	το πιάτο	to piato
receipt	η απόδειξη	i apothixi
sandwich	το σάντουιτς	to sandooits
soup	η σούπα	i soopa
spoon	το κουτάλι	to kootali
sugar	η ζάχαρη	i zahari
table	το τραπέζι	to trapezi
tea	το τσάι	to tsai
teaspoon	το κουταλάκι	to kootalaki
tip	το πουρμπουάρ	to poorbooar
waiter	ο σερβιτόρος	o servitoros
waitress	η σερβιτόρα	i servitora
water	το νερό	to nero
wine	το κρασί	to krasi
wine list	ο κατάλογος κρασιών	o katalogos krasion

A table for 1/2/3, please
Ένα τραπέζι για ένα/δύο/τρία άτομα, παρακαλώ
ena trapezi ya ena/thio/tria atoma, parakalo

Can we see the menu?
Μπορούμε να δούμε το μενού;
bor<u>oo</u>me na th<u>oo</u>me to men<u>oo</u>

Is there a highchair?
Υπάρχει παιδιχή καρέκλα;
ip<u>a</u>rhi pethik<u>i</u> kar<u>e</u>kla

What would you recommend?
Τι θα προτείνατε;
ti THA prot<u>i</u>nate

Is this suitable for vegetarians?
Είναι για χορτοφάγους;
<u>I</u>ne y<u>a</u> hortof<u>a</u>goos

I'd like …
Θα ήθελα …
THA <u>i</u>THela

Waiter!
Γκαρσόν!
gars<u>o</u>n

Can we have the bill, please?
Μας φέρνετε τον λογαριασμό, παρακαλώ;
mas f<u>e</u>rnete ton logariasm<u>o</u>, parakal<u>o</u>

I didn't order this
Δεν παράγγειλα αυτό
then par<u>a</u>ngila aft<u>o</u>

The meal was very good, thank you
Το φαγητό ήταν πολύ καλό, ευχαριστούμε
to fayit<u>o</u> <u>i</u>tan pol<u>i</u> kal<u>o</u>, efharist<u>oo</u>me

MENU GUIDE

αλάτι *alati* salt

αλλαντικά *alandika* sausages, salami, meats

αμύγδαλα *amigthala* almonds

ανανάς *ananas* pineapple

ανθότυρο *anthotiro* kind of cottage cheese

αντζούγιες *antsooyies* anchovies

αρακάς λαδερός *arakas* peas

αρνί lamb

αρνί κοκκινιστό *arni kokkinisto* lamb in tomato sauce

αρνί μπριζόλες *arni brizoles* lamb chops

αρνί της σούβλας *arni tis soovlas* spit-roast lamb

αστακός lobster

αυγά *avga* eggs

αυγά μάτια *avga matia* fried eggs

αυγά ομελέτα *avga omeleta* omelette

αυγοτάραχο *avgotaraho* roe

αχλάδι χυμός *ahlathi himos* pear juice

αχλαδιά *ahlathia* pears

βερύκοκκα *verikoka* apricots

βούτυρο *vootiro* butter

βρασμένος, βραστός *vrasmenos, vrastos* boiled

βύσσινο *visino* cherries

βοδινό *vothino* beef

γάβρος τηγανιτός *gavros tiganitos* fried small fish

γάλα *gala* milk

γαλακτομπούρεκο *galaktobooreko* cream pie with honey

γαλλικός καφές *galikos kafes* French (filtered) coffee

γαλοπούλα *galopoola* turkey

γαρίδες *garithes* prawns

γαρνιτούρα με *garnitoora* sautéed

γιαλατζή ντολμάδες *yalantzi dolmathes* vine leaves stuffed with rice

γιαούρτι *yaoorti* yoghurt

γιαούρτι πρόβειο *yaoorti provio* sheep's yoghurt

γιουβαρλάκια *yioovarlakia* meatballs

γιουβέτσι *yoovetsi* oven-cooked lamb with a kind of pasta

γκοφρέττα *gofreta* chocolate wafer

γκρέϊπ φρουτ 'grapefruit' grapefruit

γλυκό *gliko* preserve in syrup

γλυκό μαστίχα *gliko mastiha* fudge

γλώσσα *glosa* sole

γόπα τηγανητή *gopa tiganiti* type of fried fish

γραβιέρα τυρί *graviera tiri* kind of savoury cheese

γρανίτα *granita* sorbet

δαμάσκηνα *thamaskina* prunes

δίπλες, τηγανητές *thiples, tiganites* pancakes

ελαιόλαδο *eleolatho* olive oil

ελιές *elies* olives

ελληνικός καφές *elinikos kafes* Greek coffee

εσκαλόπ *eskalop* escalope

ζαμπόν *zabon* ham

ζάχαρη *zahari* sugar

ζελέ *zele* jelly

ζυμαρικά *zimarika* pasta

ηλιέλαιο *ilieleo* sunflower oil

θαλασσινά *thalassina* seafood

καβούρια ψητά *kavooria psita* grilled crab

κακαβιά *kakavia* fish soup

κακάο *kakao* cocoa

κακάο ρόφημα *kakao rofima* hot chocolate

καλαμαράκια kalamarakia squid
καλαμποκέλαιο kalabokeleo corn oil
καλαμπόκι kalaboki corn
κανάπε kanape canapés
καπαμάς αρνί kapamas arni lamb cooked in spices and tomato sauce
καραβίδες karavithes prawns
καραμέλες karameles sweets
καρμπονάρα karbonara spaghetti carbonara
καρότα karota carrots
καρπούζι karpoozi watermelon
καρύδα karitha coconut
καρύδια karithia walnuts
καρυδόπιττα karithopita cake with nuts and syrup
κασέρι kaseri type of Greek cheese
κάστανα kastana chestnuts
καταΐφι kataifi sweet with honey and nuts
καφές βαρύς γλυκός kafes varis glikos sweet Greek coffee
καφές με γάλα kafes me gala coffee with milk
κέϊκ keik cake
κεράσια kerasia cherries
κέτσαπ ketsap ketchup
κέφαλος kefalos mullet
κεφαλοτύρι kefalotiri type of Greek parmesan-style cheese
κεφτέδες keftethes meatballs
κόλα kola cola
κολιοί koli-i mackerel
κολοκυθάκια kolokiTHakia courgette
κολοκυθοτυρόπιττα kolokiTHotiropita courgette and cheese pie
κομπόστα komposta compôte
κορν φλέϊκς korn fleiks corn flakes
κότα kota chicken
κότα κοκκινιστή kota kokkinisti chicken in tomato sauce

κότα ψητή σούβλας kota psiti soovlas spit-roast chicken
κοτολέτες kotolete cutlets
κοτόπιττα kotopita chicken pie
κοτόπουλο kotopoolo chicken
κοτόσουπα kotosoopa chicken soup
κουκιά λαδερά kookia lathera broad beans in tomato sauce
κουνέλι kooneli rabbit
κρασί krasi wine
κρασί άσπρο krasi aspro white wine
κρασί κόκκινο krasi kokino red wine
κρασί ρετσίνα krasi retsina dry white Greek wine
κρασί ροζέ krasi roze rosé
κρέας kreas beef
κρεατόπιττες kreatopites ground meat pies
κρέμα καραμελέ krema karamele crème caramel
κρέμα krema cream
κρεμμύδια kremithia onions
κροκέτες kroketes croquettes
κρουασάν krooasan croissants
κυδωνόπαστο kithonopasto thick quince jelly
κωκ kok cream cake with chocolate topping
λαγός lagos hare
λάδι lathi oil
λαχανάκια μικτά lahanakia mikta mixed vegetables
λάχανο lahano cabbage
λάχανο ντολμάδες με σάλτσα ντομάτας lahano dolmathes me saltsa domatas stuffed vine leaves in tomato sauce
λαχανοσαλάτα lahanosalata cabbage salad
λεμόνι lemoni lemon
λιθρίνι ψητό liTHrini psito grilled mullet

λουκάνικα *lookanika* sausages
λουκουμάδες *lookoomathes* doughnuts
λουκούμια *lookoomia* Turkish delight
μαγιά *mayia* yeast
μαγιονέζα *mayoneza* mayonnaise
μαϊντανός *maidanos* parsley
μακαρόνια *makaronia*
   spaghetti/macaroni
μανιτάρια *manitaria* mushrooms
μανταρίνι *madarini* tangerine
μαργαρίνη *margarini* margarine
μαρίδες τηγανητές *marithes tiganites*
   small fried fish
μαρμελάδα *marmelatha* jam
μαρούλια σαλάτα *maroolia salata*
   lettuce salad
μέλι *meli* honey
μελιτζάνες *melitzanes* aubergine
μελιτζάνοσαλάτα *melitzanosalata*
   aubergine salad
μελομακάρονα *melomakarona* sweet
   cakes with cinnamon, nuts and syrup
μήλα *mila* apples
μηλόπιττα *milopita* apple pie
μηλοχυμός *milohimos* apple juice
μοσχάρι κοκκινιστό *mos-hari* veal
μοσχαρίσιος κιμάς *mos-harisios kimas*
   ground beef
μουσακά *moosaka* moussaka
μουστοκούλουρα *moostokooloora* kind of
   Greek biscuit
μουστάρδα *moostartha* mustard
μπακαλιάρος πλακί *bakaliaros* salt cod
μπακλαβάς *baclavas* layers of filo pastry
   with nuts and syrup
μπάμιες *bamies* okra
μπανάνα *banana* banana
μπαρμπούνια πανέ *barboonia pane*
   breaded red mullet
μπεσαμέλ σάλτσα *besamel saltsa*
   béchamel sauce

μπισκότα σοκολάτας *biskota sokolatas*
   chocolate biscuits
μπισκοτάκια αλμυρά *biskotakia almira*
   savoury biscuits
μπιφτέκι *bifteki* grilled meatballs
μπον φιλέ *bon file* fillet steak
μπουγάτσα γλυκιά *boogatsa glikia* puff
   pastry with cream filling
μπουρεκάκια *boorekakia* cheese or
   mince pies
μπριάμι με κολοκυθάκια *briami me
   kolokiTHakia* courgette cooked with
   potatoes in the oven
μπριζόλες στο τηγάνι *brizoles sto tigani*
   fried T-bone steak
μπριζόλες χοιρινές *brizoles hirines* pork
   chops
μπρόκολο *brokolo* broccoli
μπύρα *bira* beer
μυαλά πανέ *miala pane* breaded cow's
   brains
μύδια τηγανητά *mithia tiganita* fried
   mussels
νες καφέ *nes kafe* any instant coffee
ντολμάδες γιαλαντζή *dolmathes
   yialantzi* stuffed vine leaves with rice
ντοματόσουπα *domatosoopa* tomato
   soup
ντοματοσαλάτα *domatosalata* tomato
   salad
ντομάτα *domata* tomato
ντόνατς *donats* doughnuts
ξηροί καρποί *xiri karpi* all types of nuts
ξιφίας *xifias* sword fish
ξύδι *xithi* vinegar
ομελέτα *omeleta* omelette
ορεκτικά *orektika* hors d'oeuvres
ούζο *oozo* ouzo
παγωτό *pagoto* ice cream
παγωτό κρέμα *pagoto krema* vanilla ice
   cream

παγωτό με σαντυγί *pagoto me sandiyi* ice cream with whipped cream

πάπρικα *paprika* paprika

πάστα *pasta* gâteau

παστίτσιο λαζάνια *pastitsio lazania* lasagne

πατάτες *patates* potatoes

πατάτες πουρέ *patates poore* mashed potatoes

πατάτες σουφλέ *patates soofle* potato soufflé

πατάτες τηγανητές *patates tiganites* chips

πατάτες τσιπς *patates tsips* crisps

πατατοσαλάτα *patatosalata* potato salad

πατζάρια *patzaria* beets

πατσάς σούπα *patsas soopa* tripe soup

πεπόνι *peponi* melon

πέστροφα *pestrofa* trout

πηχτή *pihti* headcheese

πιλάφι με σάλτσα ντομάτα *pilafi me saltsa domata* rice with tomato sauce

πιπέρι *piperi* pepper

πιπεριές πράσινες/κόκκινες *piperies prasines/kokines* green/red peppers

πιροσκί *piroski* mince or sausage rolls

πίτσα *pitsa* pizza

πίττα με κιμά *pita me kima* ground meat pie

πορτοκαλάδα *portokalatha* orange juice

πορτοκάλι *portokali* orange

πουτίγκα με ανανά *pootiga me anana* pineapple pudding

πουτίγκα με καρύδια *pootiga me karithia* pudding with walnuts

πουτίγκα με σταφίδες *pootiga me stafithes* sultana pudding

πρασσόπιττα *prasopita* leek pie

πράσα *prasa* leeks

παρμεζάνα *parmezana* parmesan cheese

ραβανί *ravani* very sweet sponge cake

ρίγανη *rigani* oregano

ροδάκινα *rothakina* peaches

ροσμπίφ αρνί μοσχάρι *rozbif arni mos-hari* roast beef, veal or lamb

ρυζόγαλο *rizogalo* rice pudding

ρώσικη σαλάτα *rosiki salata* vegetable salad

σαλάμι *salami* salami

σαλάτα *salata* salad

σαλάτα με σπαράγγια *salata me sparagia* asparagus salad

σαλάτα χωριάτικη *salata horiatiki* Greek salad—tomatoes, cucumber, feta cheese, peppers, and olives

σαλιγκάρια *saligaria* snails

σάλτσα *saltsa* sauce

σάλτσα ντομάτα *saltsa domata* tomato sauce

σαμάλι *samali* semolina cake with honey

σαντιγή *sandiyi* whipped cream

σαρδέλλες *sartheles* sardines

σέλινο *selino* celery

σιμιγδάλη *simigthali* semolina

σιρόπι *siropi* syrup

σκορδαλιά με ψωμί *skorthalia me psomi* thick garlic sauce with bread

σκόρδο *skortho* garlic

σοκολάτα *sokolata* chocolate

σολομός καπνιστός *solomos kapnistos* smoked salmon

σουβλάκι καλαμάκι *soovlaki kalamaki* shish kebab

σουβλάκι ντονέρ με *soovlaki doner* doner kebab

σούπα ρεβύθια *soopa revithia* chickpea soup

σούπα τραχανάς *soopa trahanas* milk broth with flour

σούπα φακές *soopa fakes* lentil soup

σουπιές τηγανητές *soopies tiganites* fried cuttlefish

σουσάμι *soosami* sesame

σουτζουκάκια *sootzookakia* spicy meatballs in red sauce

σπαγέτο *spageto* spaghetti

σπαράγγια σαλάτα *sparangia salata* asparagus salad

σταφίδες *stafithes* raisins

σταφιδόψωμο *stafithopsomo* bread with raisins

σταφύλι χυμός *stafili himos* grape juice

σταφύλια *stafilia* grapes

στιφάδο *stifatho* chopped meat in onions

στρείδια *strithia* oysters

σύκα *sika* figs

συκωτάκια *sikotakia* liver

συναγρίδα *sinagritha* sea bream

σφυρίδα *sfiritha* pike

ταραμοκεφτέδες *taramokeftethes* roe pâté balls with spices

ταραμοσαλάτα *taramosalata* roe pâté

τάρτα *tarta* tart

τας-κεμπάπ *tas kebab* spicy lamb cutlets

τζατζίκι *tzatziki* yogurt, cucumber, garlic, dried mint, and olive oil

τηγανητός *tiganitos* fried

τηγανήτες *tiganites* pancakes

τόνος *tonos* tuna

τοστ *tost* toasted sandwich

τούρτα *toorta* gâteau

τρουφάκια *troofakia* small chocolate balls

τσάι *tsai* tea

τσιπούρες *tsipoores* flatfish

τσίπουρο *tsipooro* kind of ouzo

τσουρέκια *tsoorekia* sweet Easter bread with fresh butter

τυρί *tiri* cheese

τυρόπιττα *tiropita* cheese pie

τυροπιττάκια *tiropitakia* small cheese pies

φάβα *fava* continental lentils

φασολάδα *fasolatha* thick bean soup

φασολάκια *fasolakia* green beans

φέτα *feta* feta cheese

φιλέτο *fileto* fillet steak

φοντάν *fodan* sweets

φουντούκι *foodooki* hazelnut

φράουλες *fraooles* strawberries

φρουί-γκλασέ *frooi-glase* dried assorted fruits with sugar

φρουτοσαλάτα *frootosalata* fruit salad

φρυγανιές *friganies* French toast

φύλλο πίττας *filo pitas* thin pastry

φυστίκια *fistikia* peanuts

φυστίκια Αιγίνης *fistikia eyinis* pistachios

χαβιάρι *haviari* caviar

χαλβάς *halvas* halva, sweet made from sesame seeds and nuts

χάμπουργκερ *hamboorger* hamburger

χοιρινό *hirino* pork

χοιρινό σούβλας *hirino soovlas* pork on the spit

χορτόσουπα *hortosoopa* vegetable soup

χταπόδι *htapothi* octopus

χυλοπίττες *hilopites* tagliatelle

χυμός *himos* juice

χωριάτικη σαλάτα *horiatiki salata* Greek salad—tomatoes, cucumber, feta cheese, peppers, and olives

ψάρι βραστό μαγιονέζα *psari vrasto mayoneza* steamed fish with mayonnaise

ψάρια μαρινάτα *psaria marinata* marinated fish

ψάρια τηγανητά *psaria tiganita* fried fish

ψαρόσουπα *psarosoopa* fish soup

ψητός *psitos* grilled

ψωμί άσπρο/μαύρο *psomi aspro/mavro* white/brown bread

HUNGARIAN

CONTENTS

INTRODUCTION

Pronunciation

When reading the imitated pronunciation, pronounce each syllable as if it formed part of an English word, and you will be understood sufficiently well. Remember the points below, and your pronunciation will be even closer to correct Hungarian. The first syllable of each word should be stressed and double consonants should be pronounced (eg as in Ben Nevis).

a	as the long 'a' in father
ay	as in 'pay'
e	as in 'Ted'
ew	similar to the sound in 'hew'
g	always as in 'goat'
i	as in 'bit'
o	as in the 'ou' in 'ought'
u	as in 'tuck'
y	always as in 'yes' (except as in *ay* above)
yuh	as the 'yu' in 'yucca' but only slightly sounded
zh	like the 's' in leisure

Summary of Special Characteristics in Hungarian

In Hungarian, every vowel forms a syllable, so all vowels must be pronounced individually, even when several follow each other. The acute accent is often only an indication of length, as in the pairs **o/ó**, **u/ú**, **ö/ő** and **ü/ű** (yes, you have to look closely to see the difference in the last two pairs!). However, this is not the case with **a/á** and **e/é**; here, each letter has a completely different sound – as also happens with **o/ö** and **u/ü**. It is very important, therefore, to distinguish between these sounds, as failure to do so may result in lack of comprehension. The sounds of Hungarian vowels (**a, e, i, o, u**) as modified by various accents are approximated below, together with those consonants that are not pronounced as in English.

a	is similar to the 'u' in 'tuck'
á	is a long 'a' as in 'father'
c	'ts' as in 'lots'
cs	'ch' as in 'church'
é	'ay' as in 'pay'
gy	is similar to the 'de' in 'dew' or the 'du' in 'duration'
í	as 'ee' in 'weed'
j	as the 'y' in 'yet' or 'yawn'
ly	as the 'y' in 'yet' or 'yawn'
ny	is similar to the 'nu' in 'tenure' or the 'ni' in 'onion'
o	is similar to the 'ou' in 'ought'
ó	as the word 'awe'
ö	similar to the 'ur' in 'fur'
ő	similar to the 'ur' in 'fur' but longer
s	'sh' as in 'shop'
sz	's' as in 'soap'
ty	as the 'tu' in 'tune' or 'Tuesday'
u	as the 'oo' in 'look'
ú	as the 'oo' in 'moon'
ü	similar to the 'ew' in 'hew'
ű	similar to the 'ew' in 'hew' but longer
zs	similar to the 's' in 'vision' or 'measure'

There are three words for 'you' in Hungarian: **te** *teh* (informal), **maga** *muguh* (commonly used) and **ön** *urn* (formal). **Te** (or **ti**, in the plural) is only appropriate with children, close friends and acquaintances of your own age. Although the more general **maga** is widely used in addressing all types of people, it may be considered impolite by some Hungarians. To be on the safe side, we recommend that you use the polite form **ön** (plural **önök** *urnurk*) in all cases.

USEFUL PHRASES

Yes/no
Igen/nem
igen/nem

Thank you/no, thank you
Köszönöm/köszönöm nem
kurssurnurm/kurssurnurm nem

Please *(offering)*   *(asking for something)*
Tessék   Kérem
teshayk   *kayrem*

I don't understand
Nem értem
nem ayrtem

Do you speak English/French/German?
Beszél angolul/franciául/németül?
bessayl ungolool/fruntsia-ool/naymet-ewl

I can't speak Hungarian
Nem beszélek magyarul
nem bessaylek mud-yarool

I don't know
Nem tudom
nem toodom

Please speak more slowly
Tessék lassabban beszélni
teshayk lushubbun bessaylni

Please write it down for me
Legyen szíves leírni
led-yen sseevesh leh-eerni

My name is …
A nevem …
uh nevem

How do you do, pleased to meet you
Örülök hogy megismerhettem
ur-rewlurk hod-yuh megishmerhettem

Good morning
Jó reggelt kívánok
yawreggelt keevanok

Good afternoon/good evening
Jó napot/jó estét
yawnupot/yaw-eshtayt

Good night
Jó éjszakát/jó éjt
yaw-ayssukat/yaw-ayt

Goodbye
Viszontlátásra
vissontlatashruh

How are you? *(formal)*   *(informal)*
Hogy van?   Hogy vagy?
hod-yuh vun   *hod-yuh vud-yuh*

Excuse me, please
Bocsánatot kérek
bochanutot kayrek

Sorry!
Elnézést!
elnayzaysht

I'm really sorry
Igazán nagyon sajnálom
iguzan nud-yon shuh-ynalom

Can you help me?
Kérhetem a segítségét?
kayrhetem uh shegeechaygayt

Can you tell me …?
Meg tudná mondani, hogy …?
meg toodnah monduni hod-yuh

Can I have …?
Kaphatnék egy …?
kuphutnayk ed-yuh

I would like …
Szeretnék egy …
seretnayk ed-yuh

Is there … here?
Van itt …?
vun itt

Where can I get …?
Hol kaphatok …-t?
hol kuphutok …-t

How much is it?
Mennyibe kerül?
menn-yibeh kerewl

What time is it?
Hány óra van?
han-yuh awruh vun

I must go now
Mennem kell
vmennem kell

I'll be late
Elkések
elkayshek

I've lost my way
Eltévedtem
eltayved-tem

Cheers! *(formal)*   *(informal)*
Egészségére!   Egészségedre!
egayss-shaygayreh   *egayss-shaygedreh*

Do you take credit cards?
Elfogadják a hitelkártyákat?
elfogud-yak uh hitelkart-yakut

Where is the toilet?
Hol van a WC?
hol vun uh vaytsay

Where is the US/British embassy?
Merre van az amerikai nagykövetség?
merre vun az amerikai nad-ykurvetshayg

I've lost my passport/money/key/credit cards
Elvesztettem az útlevelem/pénzem/szobakulcsom/hitelkártyáim
elvestettem az ootlevelem/paynzem/sobuh-kulchom/hitelkart-yaim

Go away!
Hagyjon békén!
hud-yon baykayn

Excellent!
Nagyszerű!
nud-yusserew

THINGS YOU'LL HEAR

bocsánat!	sorry!
bocsánatot kérek!	excuse me!
elnézést (kérek)!	sorry!
helló!	hey!
hogy van?	how are you?
igaza van	you're right, he is right
kezitcsókolom	hello (literally 'kiss-the-hand', a polite greeting used by children, and to women by men)
kösz	thanks
köszönöm nagyon jól – és ön?	very well, thank you – and you?
nem értem	I don't understand
nem tudom	I don't know
pardon	excuse me
örvendek	how do you do, nice to meet you
szevasz!/szia!	hi!
szívesen	you're welcome
tényleg?	is that so?
tessék?	pardon?
tessék (parancsolni)	Can I help you?
tessék befáradni	come straight in
tessék vigyázni!	look out!
úgy van	that's right
vigyázz/vigyázzon	look out!

DAYS, MONTHS, SEASONS

Sunday	vasárnap	*vusharnup*
Monday	hétfő	*haytfur*
Tuesday	kedd	*kedd*
Wednesday	szerda	*serduh*
Thursday	csütörtök	*chewturturk*
Friday	péntek	*payntek*
Saturday	szombat	*sombut*
January	január	*yunoo-ar*
February	február	*febroo-ar*
March	március	*martsi-oosh*
April	április	*aprilish*
May	május	*mah-yoosh*
June	június	*yooni-oosh*
July	július	*yooli-oosh*
August	augusztus	*owgoosstoosh*
September	szeptember	*september*
October	október	*oktawber*
November	november	*november*
December	december	*detsember*
Spring	tavasz	*tuvuss*
Summer	nyár	*n-yar*
Autumn	ősz	*urss*
Winter	tél	*tayl*
Christmas	karácsony	*kurachon-yuh*
Christmas Eve	szenteste	*senteshteh*
Good Friday	nagypéntek	*nud-yupayntek*
Easter	húsvét	*hooshvayt*
Whitsun	pünkösd	*pewnkurshd*
New Year	újév	*oo-yayv*
New Year's Eve	szilvester	*silvester*

NUMBERS

0	nulla *noolluh*	10	tíz *teez*
1	egy *ed-yuh*	11	tizenegy *tizened-yuh*
2	kettő, két *kettur, kayt*	12	tizenkettő *tizenkettur*
3	három *harom*	13	tizenhárom *tizenharom*
4	négy *nayd-yuh*	14	tizennégy *tizen-nayd-yuh*
5	öt *urt*	15	tizenöt *tizenurt*
6	hat *hut*	16	tizenhat *tizenhut*
7	hét *hayt*	17	tizenhét *tizenhayt*
8	nyolc *n-yolts*	18	tizennyolc *tizenn-yolts*
9	kilenc *kilents*	19	tizenkilenc *tizenkilents*

20 húsz *hooss*
21 huszonegy *hoossoned-yuh*
22 huszonkettő *hoossonkettur*
30 harminc *hurmints*
40 negyven *ned-yuven*
50 ötven *urtven*
60 hatvan *hutvun*
70 hetven *hetven*
80 nyolcvan *n-yoltsvun*
90 kilencven *kilentsven*
100 száz *saz*
110 száztíz *sazteez*
200 kétszáz *kayt-saz*
300 háromszáz *haromssaz*
400 négyszáz *nayd-yussaz*
500 ötszáz *urt-saz*
600 hatszáz *hut-saz*
700 hétszáz *hayt-saz*
800 nyolcszáz *n-yolts-saz*
900 kilencszáz *kilents-saz*
1000 ezer *ezer*
100,000 százezer *sazezer*
1,000,000 millió *milliaw*

TIME

today	ma	*muh*
yesterday	tegnap	*tegnup*
tomorrow	holnap	*holnup*
this week	a héten	*uh hayten*
last week	múlt héten	*moolt hayten*
next week	jövő héten	*yurvur hayten*
this morning		
(4 to 9 am)	ma reggel	*muh reggel*
(9 am to noon)	délelőtt	*daylelurt*
(midnight to	ma éjjel	*muh ay-yel*
4 am)		
this afternoon	ma délután	*muh daylootan*
this evening	ma este	*muh eshteh*
tonight	ma éjjel	*muh ay-yel*
in three days	három nap múlva	*harom nup moolvuh*
three days ago	három nappal ezelőtt	*harom nuppul ezelurt*
this year	idén	*idayn*
last year	tavaly	*tuvuh-yuh*
next year	jövőre	*yurvur-reh*
late	késő	*kayshur*
early	korán	*koran*
soon	nemsokára	*nemshokaruh*
later on	később	*kayshurb*
at the moment	pillanatnyilag	*pillunutn-yilug*
second	másodperc	*mashodperts*
minute	perc	*perts*
quarter of an hour	negyedóra	*ned-yedawruh*
half an hour	félóra	*faylawruh*
three quarters	háromnegyedóra	*haromned-yedawruh*
of an hour		
hour	óra	*awruh*
that day	aznap	*uznup*
every day	mindennap	*mindennup*
the next day	másnap	*mashnup*

TELLING THE TIME

Minutes past the hour are expressed by ... **perccel múlt** ... (*pertsel moolt*), so 'ten past three' is **tíz perccel múlt három** (*teez pertsel moolt harom*). For minutes to the hour, the expression ... **perc múlva** ... (*perts moolvuh*) is used, so 'ten to three' is **tíz perc múlva három** (*teez perts moolvuh harom*).

Half past and quarter hours are referred to the hour approaching, so 'half past three' becomes **fél négy** (*fayl nayd-yuh*), literally 'half four'; 'quarter past three' is **negyed négy** (*ned-yed nayd-yuh*), literally 'quarter four'; and 'quarter to four' is **háromnegyed négy** (*haromned-yed nayd-yuh*), literally 'three quarters four'.

In the simplest, though not quite as common, way of telling the time, the word for the hours comes first, followed by **óra** (*awruh*) 'hour' and the number of the minutes; thus 'three ten' can also be expressed as **három óra tíz** (*harom awruh teez*); 'three fifty' as **három óra ötven** (*harom awruh urtven*); 'three fifteen' as **három óra tizenöt** (*harom awruh tizenurt*); 'three thirty' as **három óra harminc** (*harom awruh harmints*) and 'three forty five' as **három óra negyvenöt** (*harom awruh nedyuvenurt*).

am	d.e./délelőtt	*daylelurt*
pm	d.u./délután	*daylootan*
one o'clock	egy óra	*ed-yuh awruh*
ten past one	tíz perccel múlt egy	*teez pertsel moolt ed-yuh*
quarter past one	negyed kettő	*ned-yed kettur*
half past one	fél kettő	*fayl kettur*
twenty to two	húsz perc múlva kettő	*hooss perts moolvuh kettur*
quarter to two	háromnegyed kettő	*haromned-yed kettur*
two o'clock	két óra	*kayt awruh*
at half past five	fél hatkor	*fayl hutkor*
at seven o'clock	hét órakor	*hayt awrukor*
noon	dél	*dayl*
midnight	éjfél	*ayfayl*

COMMUNICATIONS

Useful Words and Phrases

code	körzethívószám	*kur-rzetheevawssam*
dialling tone	tárcsahang	*tarchuh-hung*
email address	e-mail cím	*eemayl tseem*
enquiries	tudakozó	*toodukozaw*
extension	mellék	*mellayk*
fax machine	faxkészülék	*foks-kaysewlaykut*
internet	internet	*'internet'*
mobile phone	mobiltelefon, bunkó	*mobiltelefon, bunkaw*
number	szám	*sam*
operator	telefonközpont	*telefonkurzpont*
phone card	telefonkártya	*telefonkartya*
reverse charge call	R-beszélgetés	*er bessaylgetaysh*
telephone	telefon	*telefon*
telephone box	telefonfülke	*telefonfewlkeh*
Web site	hálószem	*halawsem*
wrong number	téves kapcsolás	*tayvesh kupcholash*

Where is the nearest phone box?
Hol van a legközelebbi telefonfülke?
hol van uh legkurzelebbi telefonfewlkeh

I would like a number in …
Egy …-i telefonszámra lenne szükségem
ed-yuh …-i telefonssamruh lenneh sewkshaygem

I would like to speak to …
Szeretnék …-val beszélni
seretnayk …-vul bessaylni

My number is …
A telefonszámon …
un telefonssamom

Could you leave him a message?
Hagyhatnék egy üzenetet?
hud-yuhutnayk ed-yuh ewzenetet

Sorry, wrong number
Sajnálom, téves kapcsolás
shuh-yunalom tayvesh kupcholash

What's your fax number/email address?
Faxszáma/e-mail címe van?
fokssama/ee-mayl tseemeh vun

Can I send a fax/email from here?
Küldhetnék innen e-mailt/faxot?
kewldhetnayk innen ee-maylt/foksot

THINGS YOU'LL HEAR

Téves számot hívott
You've got the wrong number

Kivel beszélek?
Who's speaking?

Sajnos a vonal foglalt
Unfortunately the line is busy

Sajnálom, nincs benn
Sorry, he's not in

Mi az ön telefonszáma?
What is your number?

Tessék holnap újra hívni
Please call again tomorrow

Megmondom, hogy ön kereste
I'll tell him you called

Tessék talán kés≤bb újra megpróbálni
Perhaps you can try a little later

Things You'll See

a hívott fél fizet	reverse charge call
ár	price
azonnali beszélgetés	immediate call
belföldi távhívás	domestic long-distance call
díj	charges
helyi beszélgetés	local call
hibaelhárító szolgálat	faults service
hitelkártyával fizetett beszélgetés	call paid by credit card
igen sürgős beszélgetés	very urgent call
interurbán hívás	long-distance call
kézi kapcsolással	through the operator
körzethívószám	code
közvetlen tárcsázás	direct dialling
nem működik	out of order
nemzetközi hívás	international call
R-beszélgetés	reverse charge call
sürgős beszélgetés	urgent call
távbeszélő	telephone (box)
távhívás	long-distance call
távolsági beszélgetés	long-distance call
telefonfülke	telephone box
telefonközpont	operator
tudakozó	enquiries
balesetbejelentés	emergency call

HOTELS

Useful Words and Phrases

balcony	erkély	*erkay*
bath	fürdő	*fewrdur*
bathroom	fürdőszoba	*fewrdurssobuh*
bed	ágy	*ad-yuh*
bedroom	hálószoba	*halawssobuh*
bill	számla	*samluh*
breakfast	reggeli	*reggeli*
dining room	étterem	*aytterem*
dinner	vacsora	*vuchoruh*
double room	duplaágyas szoba	*doopluh-ad-yush sobuh*
foyer	hall	*hull*
full board	teljes ellátás	*tel-yesh ellatash*
half board	fél panzió	*fayl punzi-aw*
hotel	szálloda	*salloduh*
key	kulcs	*koolch*
lift	lift	*lift*
lounge	szalon	*sulon*
lunch	ebéd	*ebayd*
manager	igazgató	*iguzgutaw*
reception	recepció	*retseptsi-aw*
receptionist	recepciós, portás	*retseptsi-awsh, portash*
restaurant	étterem	*aytterem*
room	szoba	*sobuh*
room service	szobaszervíz	*sobusserveez*
shower	zuhany	*zoohun-yuh*
shower room	zuhanyozó	*zoohun-yozaw*
single room	egyágyas szoba	*ed-yad-yush sobuh*
suite	lakosztály	*lukossta-yuh*
toilet	WC	*vaytsay*
TV	tévé	*tayvay*
twin room	kétágyas szoba	*kaytad-yush sobuh*

Have you any vacancies?
Van kiadó szobájuk?
vun ki-udaw soba-yook

I have a reservation
Foglaltam egy szobát
foglultum ed-yuh sobat

I'd like a single/double room
Szeretnék egy egyágyas/duplaágyas szobát kivenni
seretnayk ed-yuh ed-yad-yush/doopluh-ad-yush sobat kivenni

I'd like a room with a bathroom/balcony
Fürdőszobás/erkélyes szobát szeretnék
fewrdurssobash/erkay-yesh sobat seretnayk

I'd like a room for one night/three nights
Egy/három éjszakára szeretnék egy szobát kivenni
ed-yuh/harom ayssukaruh seretnayk ed-yuh sobat kivenni

What is the charge per night?
Mennyibe kerül a szoba egy éjszakára?
menn-yibeh kerewl uh sobuh ed-yuh ayssukaruh

Is there satellite/cable TV in the rooms?
A szobákban fogható-e kábel/műholdas tv?
a sobakban foghato-eh kabel/mewholdash tayvay

Is there a reduction for children?
Adnak engedményt gyerek számára?
odnok engedmaynt d-yerek samaruh

Is there wheelchair access?
Tolószékkel hozzáférhető?
tolowsaykkul hozzafayrhetew

Can you warm this bottle/baby food for me?
Felmelegítené ezt a cuclisüveget/babapempőt?
felmelegeetenay est o tsutslish-ewveget/bobopempurt

Please call me at … o'clock
Legyen szíves … órakor felhívni
led-yen ssivesh … awrukor felheevni

Can I have breakfast in my room?
Kérem a reggelit a szobámban felszolgálni
kayrem uh reggelit uh sobambun felssolgalni

My room number is …
Szobaszámom …
sobussamom

I'm leaving tomorrow
Holnap elutazom
holnup elootuzom

Can I have the bill, please?
Legyen szíves elkészíteni a számlát?
led-yen ssivesh elkaysseeteni uh samlat

I'll pay by credit card
Hitelkártyával fizetek
hitelkart-yavul fizetek

I'll pay cash
Készpénzzel fizetek
kaysspaynzel fizetek

Can you get me a taxi?
Rendeljen kérem egy taxit
rendel-yen kayrem ed-yuh tuxit

THINGS YOU'LL SEE

ebéd	lunch
étterem	restaurant
felvonó	lift
fürdőszoba	bathroom
hölgyek	women
húzni	pull
megtelt	no vacancies
mosdók	lavatories
porta	reception
reggeli	breakfast
számla	bill
tolni	push
vacsora	dinner, supper
vészkijárat	emergency exit

THINGS YOU'LL HEAR

Sajnálom, megtelt
I'm sorry, we're full

Nincs több egyágyas szobánk
There are no single rooms left

Nincs több duplaágyas szobánk
There are no double rooms left

Hány éjszakára?
For how many nights?

Hogyan szándékozik fizetni?
How will you be paying?

Előre kell fizetni
Please pay in advance

SHOPPING

Where is the … department?
Hol találom a … osztályt?
hol tulalom uh … ossta-yut

Do you have …?
Kapható önöknél …?
kuphutaw urnurknayl

How much is this?
Ez mennyibe kerül?
ez menn-yibeh kerewl

Where do I pay?
Hol lehet fizetni?
hol lehet fizetni

Have you anything cheaper?
Ennél olcsóbb nincs?
ennayl olchawb ninch

Could you wrap it for me?
Legyen szíves becsomagolni
led-yen ssivesh bechomugolni

Can I have a receipt?
Kaphatnék róla számlát?
kuphutnayk rawluh samlat

Can I have a refund?
Visszakaphatnám a pénzemet?
vissukuphutnam uh paynzemet

I'm just looking
Csak körülnézek
chuk kur-rewlnayzek

I'll come back later
Később visszajövök
kayshurb vissuh-yurvurk

EATING OUT

Most savoury dishes are cooked with pork-fat and seasoned with paprika, but the food in Hungary is not exclusively Hungarian: you may find dishes of Austrian, Slovakian, Serbian, Italian and even French origin in local restaurants.

Although there are a few dishes without meat (primarily made with pasta **tészta** (*taysstuh*) or mushrooms **gomba** (*gombuh*), vegetarians will find most menus rather forbidding: Hungarians eat various forms of meat from early morning to late evening. The main type of meat is pork. Poultry and beef are also popular, but a proper beefsteak is something of a rarity. You will see many dishes prepared with a variety of freshwater fish: do not miss **halászlé** (*hulasslay*) – a thick fish soup flavoured with paprika.

Hungarians are fond of soups and, traditionally, meals always start with a bowl of soup. The variety is astonishing – some are even made from fruit. Even the famous Hungarian goulash started life as (an admittedly very rich) soup, as **gulyásleves** (*goo-yashlevesh*), its local name, bears witness. Meat stews are the most popular main courses and there are three main variations: **pörkölt** (*purkurlt*) – stewed, diced meat with paprika; **paprikás** (*puprikash*), similar to **pörkölt** but with more paprika, and with sour cream added; and **tokány** (*tokan-yuh*) where the meat is sliced very thinly and stewed in its own juices.

Pastry (**sütemény** *shewtemayn-yuh*) is simply wonderful in Hungary. Visit a **cukrászda** – a type of teashop which sells its own cakes and pastries, freshly baked on the premises. Local sweets are enhanced by Viennese patisserie, many recipes for which originated in Hungary anyway. Particularly enticing are the various fillings used for Hungarian pancakes (**palacsinta** *puluchintuh*) which can be sweet or savoury: jam, cottage cheese, chocolate, cream, ham, cheese or mushrooms.

There are various categories of restaurant: an **étterem** is generally a quite smart restaurant, while a **vendéglő** is more mundane, even sober. A **csárda** is a country inn with regional specialities, and a **sörkert** or **söröző** is a cross between a pub and a restaurant. Self-service (**önkiszolgáló**) and fast-food (**ételbár, snack-bár, bisztró, büfé**) establishments are also common in most towns and holiday resorts. The opening hours vary but, in general, restaurants are open from 11.30 am to 11 pm or later. Some restaurants have gypsy music from about 6 pm onwards. A tip of about 15 per cent is customary.

Between meals, look out for small kiosks on street corners, where you can buy hamburgers and hot dogs. Around Lake Balaton similar kiosks offer more local food, such as a variety of grilled meats (**lacikonyha** *lutsikon-yuhuh*), fried fish (**sült hal** *shewlt hul*) or fried crispy doughnuts called **lángos** (*langosh*).

Traditionally a wine-growing region, Hungary's wines are quite outstanding. Between the world-famous Tokay and the fiery red Bull's Blood, there's a whole range of excellent whites and reds ready to be explored – go to a **borkostoló** (wine cellar) or **borozó** (wine bar) to sample these. If beer is more to your taste, try the local **söröző** (*shururzur*).

USEFUL WORDS AND PHRASES

beer	sör	*shur*
bill	számla	*samluh*
bottle	üveg	*ewveg*
bread	kenyér	*ken-yayr*
cake	sütemény	*shewtemayn-yuh*
chef	szakács	*sukach*
coffee	kávé	*kavay*
cup	csésze	*chaysseh*
fork	villa	*villuh*
glass	pohár	*pohar*
knife	kés	*kaysh*
menu	étlap	*aytlup*
milk	tej	*tay*
pepper	bors	*borsh*
plate	tányér	*tan-yayr*
receipt	nyugta	*n-yoogtuh*
red wine	vörösbor	*vurrurshbor*

salt	só	*shaw*
sandwich	szendvics	*sendvich*
serviette	kéztörlő, szalvéta	*kayzturlur, sulvaytuh*
soup	leves	*levesh*
spoon	kanál	*kunal*
sugar	cukor	*tsookor*
table	asztal	*usstul*
tea	tea	*teh-uh*
teaspoon	kávéskanál	*kavayshkunal*
tip	borravaló	*borruvulaw*
waiter	pincér	*pintsayr*
waitress	pincérnő	*pintsayrnur*
water	víz	*veez*
white wine	fehérbor	*fehayrbor*
wine	bor	*bor*
wine list	itallap	*itullup*

A table for one/two/four, please
Egy asztalt szeretnék egy/két/négy személyre
ed-yuh usstult seretnayk ed-yuh/kayt/nayd-yuh semayreh

Can I see the menu/wine list?
Az étlapot/itallapot, legyen szíves?
uz aytlupot/itullupot led-yen ssivesh

What would you recommend?
Mit tud ajánlani?
mit tood uh-yanluni

I'd like …
Szeretnék egy …-t
seretnayk ed-yuh …-t

Just a cup of coffee, please
Csak egy csésze kávét kérek
chuk ed-yuh chaysseh kavayt kayrek

Waiter!/Waitress!
Főúr!/Kisasszony! Legyen szíves!
fur-oor/kishusson-yuh led-yen ssivesh

Is this suitable for vegetarians?
Ezt vegetáriánus eheti?
est vegetarianush eheti

Do you do children's portions?
Gyerekadag is kapható?
d-yerekodog ish kophotaw

I didn't order this
Én nem ezt rendeltem
ayn nem ezt rendeltem

May we have some more …?
Kaphatnánk még …-t?
kuphutnank mayg …-t

The meal was very good, thank you
Nagyon finom volt az étel, köszönöm szépen
nud-yon finom volt uz aytel kurssurnurm saypen

Can we have the bill, please?
Legyen szíves elkészíteni a számlát?
led-yen ssivesh elkaysseeteni uh samlat

THINGS YOU'LL HEAR

Jó étvágyat (kívánok)!
Enjoy your meal!

Mit parancsolnak az urak/hölgyek?
What would the gentlemen/ladies like to order?

MENU GUIDE

alma apple
almás rétes apple strudel
ásványvíz mineral water
bab beans
banán banana
barack apricot
barackosfánk apricot doughnut
bárány lamb
bécsi szelet veal cutlet in breadcrumbs
bélszínfilé boneless tenderloin steak
besamelmártás white cream sauce
betyárleves 'outlaw' ragoût – a thick
  spicy broth with vegetables
birka mutton
bográcsgulyás goulash soup – thick
  spicy meat and vegetable soup
bor wine
borjú(lús) veal
bors pepper
borsostokány beef casserole
buggyantott tojás poached eggs
bukta jam-filled sweet roll
bundás alma apple fritter
burgonya potatoes
burgonyapüré mashed potatoes
cékla beetroots
citrom lemon
cukkini courgettes
cseresznye cherry
csikóstokány beef casserole with diced
  bacon, onions, tomatoes and peppers
csirke chicken
csirke becsinált chicken ragoût
csontleves clear meat soup
csuka pike
daragaluska small cornmeal dumplings
daragombóc cornmeal dumpling
datolya dates

derelye parcels of pasta filled with jam,
  cheese or meat
dió walnuts
disznóhús pork
disznócsülök káposztával smoked
  knuckle of pork with sauerkraut
édességek sweets, desserts
egres gooseberry
előételek starters
eper strawberries
erdélyi tokány Transylvanian beef
  casserole with bacon
erőleves broth
fácán pheasant
fánk jam doughnut
fehérbab dried white beans
fejes saláta lettuce
felfújt soufflé
felvágott salami, cold meats
finommetélt thin egg noodles
fokhagyma garlic
főételek main courses
főtt boiled
füge figs
fürjtojás quail's egg
galuska small soft dumplings
gesztenye chestnuts
gomba mushrooms
gombóc ball, dumpling
göngyölt felsál beef olive
görögdinnye watermelon
gulyásleves goulash soup
gyömbér ginger
gyümölcs fruit
gyümölcslé fruit juice
hab mousse
habosszilva plum and chocolate mousse
hagyma onions

hal fish
halászlé fish soup
harcsa catfish
hideg előételek cold starters
hús meat
húsleves broth
húspástétom meat pie
ízestekercs jam roll
joghurt yoghurt
kacsa duck
kapor dill
káposzta cabbage
karfiol cauliflower
kávé coffee
kelbimbó Brussels sprouts
keménytojás hard-boiled egg
kenyér bread
képviselőfánk custard-filled doughnut
  sometimes with chocolate icing
keszeg bream
kifli crescent-shaped roll
kókusz coconut
kókusztekercs coconut roll
kolbász spicy paprika sausage
kolozsvári gulyás Transylvanian goulash
  stew with cabbage
kovászos uborka pickled gherkins
körömpörkölt pork knuckle casserole
kőrözött ewe's cheese spread
körte pears
krumpli potatoes
kukorica sweetcorn
lágy sajt soft cheese
lágytojás soft-boiled egg
lángos savoury doughnuts
lé juice
lecsó green pepper and tomato stew
lekvár jam
lencse lentils
lepény pie
leves soup

liba goose
libapecsenye roast goose
limonádé lemonade
magyaros hidegtál assorted cold meats
máj liver
májgaluska small liver dumplings
majonézmártás mayonnaise
mák poppy seed
malac sucking pig
málna raspberry
mandula almonds
marha beef
marhapörkölt beef casserole
mártás sauce
meggy morello cherry
meggyes rétes morello cherry strudel
melegszendvics toasted sandwiches
metélt sweet pasta
menü menu
méz honey
mogyorótorta hazelnut gâteau
mustár mustard
napi ajánlatunk today's special
narancs orange
nyúl rabbit, hare
olaj oil
omlett omelette
orjaleves pork broth
őszibarack peaches
őzhúsleves venison soup
padlizsán aubergines
padlizsánpástétom aubergine purée
palacsinta pancakes
palócgulyás lamb goulash stew
paprikás diced meat stewed in paprika
  and sour cream
paradicsom tomatoes
paradicsomos tökfőzelék marrows in
  thick tomato sauce
paradicsomsaláta tomato salad
paraj spinach

párolt braised
pászkagombóc dumpling made of bread
pirítós toast
pirított burgonya roast potatoes
pirított máj sautéed liver
pirospaprika paprika
piskóta sponge cake
piskótatekercs jam roll
ponty carp
pogácsa savoury scone
pörkölt casserole made with diced meat
puliszka cornmeal porridge
pulyka turkey
puncstorta rich rum-flavoured gâteau
rablóhús mixed kebab
rakott layered
rántott breaded
retek radish
rétes strudel
ribizli redcurrant
ringló greengages
rizibizi rice mixed with peas
rizsfelfújt rice soufflé
rizsköret rice garnish
rostélyos braised steak
roston/rostonsült grilled
rozmaring rosemary
sajt cheese
saláta salad
sárgabarack apricot
sárgaborsó dried peas
sárgadinnye honeydew melon
sárgarépa carrots
savanyú káposzta sauerkraut
savanyúság pickles
sertés pork
sertéshúspogácsa minced pork balls
só salt
sonka ham
sós sütemény savoury cakes made from thin flaky pastry

sör beer
spárga asparagus
specialitások specialities
spenót spinach
spenótbomba spinach fritters
süllő pike/perch
sült fried, roast
sült burgonya chips
sütemények pastry
svájci sajtfondue cheese fondue
szalmakrumpli crisps
szalonna fat bacon
szamóca wild strawberries
szárazbableves haricot bean soup
szárnyas poultry, fowl
szárnyaskrémleves cream of fowl soup
szarvasgomba truffles
szarvas magyarosan haunch of venison in paprika and sour cream sauce
szegedi gulyás beef goulash with bacon and sauerkraut
szegfűszeg cloves
székelygulyás Transylvanian sauerkraut and pork stew with sour cream
szendvicsek sandwiches
szerb gulyás Serbian goulash stew with cabbage
szerecsendió nutmeg
szódavíz soda water
szőlő grapes
szörp fruit squash
szűzpecsenye roast tenderloin of pork
tarhonya fine grains of pasta made from eggs and barley
tárkony tarragon
tartármártás tartar sauce
tavaszi saláta spring salad – cucumbers, tomatoes, turnips, radish and lettuce
tea tea
tej milk
tejberizs rice pudding

tejeskávé coffee with milk

tejföl sour cream

tejfölös bableves bean soup with sour cream

tejszín cream

tejszínhab whipped cream

téliszalámi Hungarian salami

tengeri hal saltwater fish

tészták pastry, sweet pasta dish

tojás egg

tokány casserole made with onions and diced meat

tonhal Orly módra tuna fried in batter and served with tomato sauce

torta gâteau

tök marrow

tökfőzelék marrow in thick sour cream sauce

töltött stuffed

töltött fasírozott meat loaf stuffed with hard-boiled eggs

töltött paprika stuffed green peppers in tomato sauce

töpörtyű pork or goose crackling

tüdő cow's lungs

túró cottage cheese

túrós metélt pasta with soft white cheese, bacon and sour cream

túrós palacsinta pancakes with sweet cottage cheese and raisin filling

túrós pite sweet cottage cheese pie

túróspogácsa scone containing soft white cheese

túrós puliszka cornmeal porridge with cottage cheese

túrós rétes cheese strudel

tüzdelt fehérpecsenye larded tenderloin steak

tüzdelt nyúlgerinc larded saddle of hare

tyúkhúsleves chicken broth

uborka cucumbers

uborkasaláta cucumber salad

ürü mutton

ürüborda mutton chop

ürücomb leg of mutton

vadas sauce served with game or beef, made from lemon juice, mustard, sour cream and diced vegetables

vadasan meat braised with red onions, vegetables and spices, and served with game sauce

vaddisznó erdész módra haunch of wild boar with mushrooms, bacon and potatoes

vadszárnyas fowl

vagdalt libamelle goose meat loaf

vaj butter

vanília vanilla

vargabéles cake made with curd, vanilla and raisins

vegyes saláta mixed salad

velő brains

véres hurka fried black pudding

virsli frankfurters

vitaminsaláta grated cabbage, carrot, radish and onion salad

vörösbor red wine

vöröshagyma purple onions

zabpehely oat flakes

zeller celery

zellerkrémleves cream of celery soup

zöldbab green beans

zöldborsó peas

zöldpaprika green pepper

zöldségleves mixed vegetable broth

zsemle bread roll

zsemlegombóc potato and bread dumplings

zserbószelet cake with chocolate icing, made up of alternate layers of apricot jam, nuts and chocolate cream

zsiványpecsenye mixed meat roast

ITALIAN

CONTENTS

INTRODUCTION

PRONUNCIATION

The pronunciation of an Italian word is very similar to the way it is written. When reading the imitated pronunciation, stress the part that is underlined. Pronounce each syllable as if it formed part of an English word and you will be understood. Remember the points below, and your pronunciation will be even closer to the correct Italian.

ai	as in 'fair'
ay	as in 'pay'
e	as in 'bed'
	(pronounced as a separate syllable at the end of a word)
g	always hard as in 'get'
I	as in 'I'
ow	as in 'cow'
r	always strongly pronounced
y	always pronounced as in 'yet,' except in *ay* as above

Note that when there are two identical consonants separated by a hyphen, eg **vorrei** – *vor-ray*, both consonants must be pronounced as if you were pronouncing two separate English words: eg 'jus_t t_wo', 'fu_ll l_ength'.

GENDERS AND ARTICLES

Italian has two genders for nouns – masculine and feminine. In the vocabulary sections, we generally give the definite article ('the'). For masculine nouns, the definite article is **il** (plural **i**) before nouns beginning with a consonant, **lo** (plural **gli**) before nouns beginning with **s** + consonant or with **z**, and **l'** (plural **gli**) before nouns beginning with a vowel.
For feminine nouns, use **la** before a noun beginning with a consonant and **l'** before a vowel (plural **le**).

The masculine indefinite article ('a/an') is **uno** before a noun beginning with a consonant and **un** before a vowel. The feminine is **una** before a consonant and **un'** before a vowel.

USEFUL PHRASES

Yes, No, OK, etc.

Yes/No
Si/No
see/no

OK
OK
'ok'

That's fine
Va bene
va bene

That's right
È vero
eh vayro

Greetings, Introductions

How do you do, pleased to meet you
Piacere di conoscerla
pee-achaire dee konoshairla

Good morning/Good evening/Good night
Buon giorno/Buona sera/Buona notte
bwon jorno/bwona saira/bwona not-te

Goodbye
Arrivederci
ar-reevedairchee

How are you?   (familiar)
Come sta?   Come stai?
kome sta   *kome sti*

My name is …
Mi chiamo …
mee k-yamo

What's your name?   *(familiar)*
Come si chiama?   Come ti chiami?
kome see k-yama   *kome tee k-yamee*

This is … *(introducing male/female)*
Questo è …/Questa è …
kwesto eh/kwesta eh

Hello/Hi!
Ciao/Salve!
chow/salve

PLEASE, THANK YOU, APOLOGIES

Thank you/No, thank you
Grazie/No grazie
gratzee-e/no gratzee-e

Please *(offering)*   *(asking for something)*
Prego   Per favore/per piacere
prego   *pair favore/pair pee-achaire*

Sorry!/Excuse me!   *(familiar)*
Scusi!   Scusa!
skoozee   *skooza*

WHERE, HOW, ASKING

Excuse me, please *(to get past etc)*
Permesso
pairmesso

Can you tell me …?
Potrebbe dirmi …?
potreb-be deermee

Can I have …?
Potrei avere …?
potray avaire

Would you like a …?
Vorrebbe un/una …?
vor-reb-be oon/oona

Would you like to …?
Le piacerebbe …?
le pee-achaireb-be

Is there … here?
C'è …?
cheh

What's that?
Che cos'è?
ke kozeh

How much is it?
Quanto costa?
kwanto kosta

Where is the …?
Dov'è il/la …?
doveh eel/la

Is there wheelchair access?
È possibile l'accesso con la sedia a rotelle?
eh pos-see-bee-leh l'aches-so kon la saidee-a rotail-le

Are guide dogs allowed?
È permesso portare i cani guida?
eh pairmes-so portarai ee kanee gweeda

ABOUT ONESELF

I'm from …
Sono di …
sono dee

I'm … years old
Ho … anni
o … an-nee

I'm a ... *(occupation)*
Faccio il/la ...
facho eel/la

I'm married/single/divorced *(said by a man)*
Sono sposato/celibe/divorziato
sono spozato/cheleebe/deevortz-yato

(said by a woman)
Sono sposata/nubile/divorziata
sono spozata/noobeele/deevortz-yata

I have ... sisters/brothers/children
Ho ... sorelle/fratelli/bambini
o ... sorel-le/fratel-lee/bambeenee

HELP, PROBLEMS

Can you help me?
Può aiutarmi?
pwo i-ootarmee

I don't understand
Non capisco
non kapeesko

Does anyone here speak English?
C'è qualcuno che parla inglese?
cheh kwalkoono ke parla eengleze

I can't speak Italian
Non parlo italiano
non parlo eetal-yano

I don't know
Non so
non so

Please speak more slowly
Per favore, parli più lentamente
pair favore parlee p-yoo lentamente

Please write it down for me
Me lo scriva, per favore
me lo skreeva pair favore

I'm lost *(said by a man/woman)*
Mi sono perso/persa
mee sono pairso/pairsa

Go away!   *(familiar)*
Se ne vada!   Vattene!
se ne vada   *vat-tene*

LIKES, DISLIKES, SOCIALIZING

I like/love …
Mi piace …
mee pee-ache

I don't like …
Non mi piace …
non mee pee-ache

Do you like …?
Le piace …?
le pee-ache

It's delicious/awful!
È buonissimo/terribile!
eh bwoneess-seemo/ter-reebeele

I don't drink/smoke
Non bevo/fumo
non bevo/foomo

Do you mind if I smoke?
Le dispiace se fumo?
le deespee-ache se foomo

What would you like (to drink)?
Cosa desidera (da bere)?
koza dezeedaira da baire

I would like a …
Vorrei un/una …
vor-re oon/oona

Nothing for me, thanks
Per me niente, grazie
pair me nee-ente gratzee-e

Cheers! *(toast)*
Alla salute!/Cin cin!
al-la saloote/cheen cheen

THINGS YOU'LL HEAR

a più tardi	see you later
arrivederci	goodbye
attenzione!	look out! pay attention!
avanti!	come in!
bene	good, fine
buon viaggio!	have a good trip!
cosa hai/ha detto?	what did you say?
ecco-ti qua!	here you are!
mi dispiace tanto!	I'm so sorry!
mi scusi	excuse me
molte grazie	thank you very much
non capisco	I don't understand
prego	you're welcome, don't mention it
prego?	pardon?
serviti/si serva/servitevi	help yourself
scusi?, come?	excuse me?
va bene	that's right

DAYS, MONTHS, SEASONS

Sunday	domenica	*domeneeka*
Monday	lunedì	*loonedee*
Tuesday	martedì	*martedee*
Wednesday	mercoledì	*mairkoledee*
Thursday	giovedì	*jovedee*
Friday	venerdì	*venairdee*
Saturday	sabato	*sabato*
January	gennaio	*jen-na-yo*
February	febbraio	*feb-bra-yo*
March	marzo	*martzo*
April	aprile	*apreele*
May	maggio	*maj-jo*
June	giugno	*joon-yo*
July	luglio	*lool-yo*
August	agosto	*agosto*
September	settembre	*set-tembre*
October	ottobre	*ot-tobre*
November	novembre	*novembre*
December	dicembre	*deechembre*
Spring	primavera	*preemavaira*
Summer	estate	*estate*
Autumn	autunno	*owtoon-no*
Winter	inverno	*eenvairno*
Christmas	Natale	*natale*
Christmas Eve	la Vigilia di Natale	*veejeel-ya dee natale*
Good Friday	Venerdì Santo	*venairdee santo*
Easter	Pasqua	*paskwa*
New Year	Capodanno	*kapodan-no*
New Year's Eve	San Silvestro	*san seelvestro*
Pentecost	Pentecoste	*pentekoste*

NUMBERS

0	zero *tzairo*	10	dieci *dee-echee*
1	uno *oono*	11	undici *oon-deechee*
2	due *doo-e*	12	dodici *doh-deechee*
3	tre *tre*	13	tredici *tre-deechee*
4	quattro *kwat-tro*	14	quattordici *kwat-tor-deechee*
5	cinque *cheenkwe*	15	quindici *kween-deechee*
6	sei *say*	16	sedici *say-deechee*
7	sette *set-te*	17	diciassette *deechas-set-te*
8	otto *ot-to*	18	diciotto *deechot-to*
9	nove *no-ve*	19	diciannove *deechan-no-ve*

20	venti *ventee*	
21	ventuno *vent-oono*	
22	ventidue *ventee-doo-e*	
30	trenta *trenta*	
31	trentuno *trentoono*	
32	trentadue *trentadoo-e*	
40	quaranta *kwaranta*	
50	cinquanta *cheenkwanta*	
60	sessanta *ses-santa*	
70	settanta *set-tanta*	
80	ottanta *ot-tanta*	
90	novanta *novanta*	
100	cento *chento*	
110	centodieci *chento-dee-echee*	
200	duecento *doo-e-chento*	
1,000	mille *meele*	
10,000	diecimila *dee-echeemeela*	
20,000	ventimila *venteemeela*	
50,000	cinquantamila *cheenkwantameela*	
100,000	centomila *chentomeela*	
1,000,000	un milione *oon meel-yone*	

Note that thousands are written 1.000, 10.000, etc, in Italian.

TIME

today	oggi	*oj-jee*
yesterday	ieri	*yairee*
tomorrow	domani	*domanee*
this week	questa settimana	*kwesta set-teemana*
last week	la settimana scorsa	*set-teemana skorsa*
next week	la settimana prossima	*set-teemana pros-seema*
this morning	stamattina	*stamat-teena*
this afternoon	questo pomeriggio	*kwesto pomereej-jo*
this evening	stasera	*stasaira*
tonight	stanotte	*stanot-te*
in three days	tra tre giorni	*tra tre jornee*
three days ago	tre giorni fa	*tre jornee fa*
late	tardi	*tardee*
early	presto	*presto*
soon	presto	*presto*
later on	più tardi	*p-yoo tardee*
at the moment	in questo momento	*een kwesto momento*
second	un secondo	*sekondo*
minute	un minuto	*meenooto*
two minutes	due minuti	*doo-e meenootee*
quarter of an hour	un quarto d'ora	*kwarto dora*
half an hour	mezz'ora	*medzora*
three quarters of an hour	tre quarti d'ora	*tre kwartee dora*
hour	un'ora	*ora*
day	un giorno	*jorno*
week	una settimana	*set-teemana*
fortnight	quindici giorni	*kween-deechee jornee*
month	un mese	*meze*
year	un anno	*an-no*
that day	quel giorno	*kwel jorno*
every day	ogni giorno	*on-yee jorno*
the next day	il giorno dopo	*jorno dopo*

TELLING THE TIME

The hour is expressed in Italian by the ordinal number only:
sono le due 'it's two o'clock', **alle due** 'at two o'clock'. There is
no equivalent of 'o'clock'. To denote the half hour, add **e mezza**
after the hour: **sono le due e mezza** 'it's 2.30'. To say 'quarter
past', add **e un quarto** 'and a quarter' to the hour: **sono le tre e
un quarto** is 'it's a quarter past three'.

Quarter to the hour is expressed either by adding **e tre quarti**
'and three quarters' to the hour, or adding **meno un quarto**
'less a quarter' to the next hour. 'It's a quarter to eight' is **sono
le sette e tre quarti** or **sono le otto meno un quarto**.

To express minutes after the hour, add the minutes to the
hour: **sono le sette e quaranta** 'it's seven forty'. For minutes to
the hour use **meno** followed by the number of minutes to the
next hour: **sono le otto meno venti** 'it's twenty to eight'.

There are no equivalents of am and pm, although you can use
di mattina/del mattino 'in the morning,' **di/del pomeriggio** 'in
the afternoon,' **di sera** 'in the evening,' and **di notte** 'at night'.

what time is it?	che ore sono?	*ke ore sono?*
it's one o'clock	è l'una	*eh loona*
it's two/three/four o'clock	sono le due/tre/ quattro	*sono le doo-e/tre/ kwat-tro*
ten past one	l'una e dieci	*loona ay dee-echee*
quarter past one	l'una e un quarto	*loona ay oon kwarto*
1.30	l'una e mezza	*loona ay medza*
twenty to two	le due meno venti	*lay doo-e meno ventee*
quarter to two	le due meno un quarto	*le doo-e meno oon kwarto*
two o'clock	le due	*le doo-e*
at 5.30	alle cinque e mezza	*al-le cheenkwe ay medza*
at seven o'clock	alle sette	*al-le set-te*
noon	mezzogiorno	*medzojorno*
midnight	mezzanotte	*medzanot-te*

COMMUNICATIONS

Useful Words and Phrases

code	il prefisso	_prefees-so_
dialling tone	il segnale di libero	_sen-yale dee leebairo_
email	la posta elettronica	_posta ai-lait-tronee-ka_
emergency	l'emergenza	_emairjentza_
extension	l'interno	_eentairno_
fax machine	il fax	_'fax'_
internet	l'internet	_'internet'_
mobile phone	il telefonino	_telefonino_
number	il numero	_noomairo_
operator	l'operatore	_opairatore_
payphone	il telefono a gettoni	_telefono a jet-tonee_
phonecard	la scheda telefonica	_skeda telefoneeka_
reverse charge call	la chiamata a carico del destinatario	_k-yamata a kareeko del desteenataree-o_
telephone	il telefono	_telefono_
telephone box	la cabina telefonica	_kabeena telefoneeka_
Web site	il sito internet	_seeto 'internet'_
wrong number	il numero sbagliato	_noomairo zbal-yato_

Where is the nearest telephone box?
Dov'è la cabina telefonica più vicina?
doveh la kabeena telefoneeka p-yoo veecheena

I would like a number in …
Ho bisogno del numero di un abbonato di …
o beezon-yo del noomairo dee oon ab-bonato dee

I would like to speak to …
Vorrei parlare con …
vor-ray parlare kon

My number is …
Il mio numero è …
eel mee-o noomairo eh

Could you leave him/her a message?
Potrebbe lasciargli/lasciarle un messaggio?
potrebbe lasharl-yee/lasharle oon mes-saj-jo

I'll call back later
Richiamerò più tardi
reekeeah-mayro p-yoo tardee

What's your fax number/email address?
Qual'è il suo numero di fax/posta elettronica?
kwal-ai eel soo-o noo-mairo dee fax/posta ai-lait-tronee-ka

Can I send an email/fax from here?
Posso inviare della posta elettronica/un fax da qui?
pos-so eenvee-arai del-la posta ai-lait-tronee-ka/oon fax da kwee

---

THINGS YOU'LL HEAR

Pronto
Hello

Sono io/pronto
Speaking

Con chi vuole parlare?
Who would you like to speak to?

Ha sbagliato numero
You've got the wrong number

Chi parla?
Who's calling?

Attenda in linea, prego
Hold, please

Mi dispiace, non c'è
I'm sorry, he/she's not in

Gli dirò che ha chiamato
I'll tell him you called

EMERGENCIES

USEFUL WORDS AND PHRASES

accident	l'incidente	*eencheedente*
ambulance	l'ambulanza	*amboolantza*
breakdown	il guasto	*gwasto*
burglary	il furto	*foorto*
crash	l'incidente	*eencheedente*
emergency	l'emergenza	*emairjentza*
fire	il fuoco	*fwoko*
fire brigade	i vigili del fuoco	*veejeelee del fwoko*
police	la polizia	*poleetzee-a*
police station	il commissariato	*kom-mees-sar-yato*
	di polizia	*dee poleetzee-a*

Help!
Aiuto!
I-ooto

Stop!
Si fermi!
see fairmee

Get an ambulance!
Chiami un'ambulanza!
k-yamee oon amboolantza

Hurry up!
Presto!
presto

My address is …
Il mio indirizzo è …
eel mee-o eendeereetzo eh

My passport/car has been stolen
Mi hanno rubato il passaporto/la macchina
mee an-no roobato eel pas-saporto/la mak-keena

243

HOTELS

Useful Words and Phrases

balcony	il balcone	*bal-kone*
bathroom	il bagno	*ban-yo*
bed	il letto	*let-to*
bed and breakfast	camera con colazione	*kamaira kon kolatz-yone*
bedroom	la camera da letto	*kamaira da let-to*
bill	il conto	*konto*
breakfast	la prima colazione	*preema kolatz-yone*
car park	il parcheggio	*parkej-jo*
dining room	la sala da pranzo	*sala da prantzo*
dinner	la cena	*chena*
double bed	il letto matrimoniale	*let-to matreemonyale*
double room	la stanza doppia	*stantza doppee-a*
full board	la pensione completa	*pens-yone kompleta*
guesthouse	la pensione, la locanda	*pens-yone, lokanda*
half board	la mezza pensione	*medza pens-yone,*
hotel	l'albergo, l'hotel	*albairgo, oh-tel*
key	la chiave	*k-yave*
lift	l'ascensore	*ashen-sore*
maid	la cameriera	*kamair-yaira*
manager	il direttore	*deeret-tore*
receipt	la ricevuta	*reechevoota*
reception	la reception	*'reception'*
receptionist	il/la receptionist	*'receptionist'*
room	la camera, la stanza	*kamaira, stantza*
room service	il servizio in camera	*serveetz-yo een kamaira*
shower	la doccia	*docha*
single bed	il letto singolo	*let-to seengolo*
single room	la stanza singola	*stantza seengola*
toilet	la toilette	*twalet*

Have you any vacancies?
Avete una stanza libera?
avete oona stantza leebaira

I have a reservation
Ho prenotato una stanza
o prenotato oona stantza

I'd like a single room
Vorrei una stanza singola
vor-ray oona stantza seengola

I'd like a room with a bathroom/balcony
Vorrei una stanza con bagno/con il balcone
vor-ray oona stantza kon ban-yo/kon eel bal-kone

Is there satellite/cable TV in the rooms?
C'è la TV satellite/cavo in queste stanze?
Cheh la tee-vee satail-lee-te/kavo een kwaiste stantze

I'd like a room for one night/three nights
Vorrei una stanza per una notte/tre notti
vor-ray oona stantza pair oona not-te/tre not-tee

What is the charge per night?
Quanto si paga per notte?
kwanto see paga pair not-te

When is breakfast/dinner?
A che ora viene servita la colazione/la cena?
a ke ora v-yene serveeta la kolatz-yone/la chena

Please wake me at … o'clock
Mi svegli, per favore, alle …
mee zvel-yee pair favore al-le

Can I have breakfast in my room?
Potrei avere la colazione in camera?
potray avaire la kolatz-yone een kamaira

My room number is …
Il mio numero di stanza è …
eel mee-o noomero dee stantza eh

There is no toilet paper in the bathroom
Non c'è carta igienica in bagno
non cheh karta eej-yeneeka een ban-yo

The window won't open
La finestra non si apre
la feenestra non see apre

There isn't any hot water
Non c'è acqua calda
non cheh akwa kalda

I'm leaving tomorrow
Parto domani
parto domanee

When do I have to vacate the room?
Entro che ora devo liberare la camera?
entro ke ora devo leebairare la kamaira

Can I have the bill, please?
Mi da il conto, per favore?
mee da eel konto pair favore

I'll pay by credit card
Pago con la carta di credito
pago kon la karta dee kredeeto

I'll pay cash
Pago in contanti
pago een kontantee

Can you get me a taxi, please?
Potrebbe chiamarmi un taxi, per favore?
potreb-be k-yamarmee oon 'taxi' pair favore

THINGS YOU'LL SEE

ascensore	lift
bagno	bathroom
cena	dinner
colazione	breakfast
completo	no vacancies
conto	bill
entrata	entrance
parcheggio	car park
pranzo	lunch
prenotazione	reservation
scale	stairs
spingere	push
tirare	pull
uscita d'emergenza	emergency exit

THINGS YOU'LL HEAR

Mi spiace, siamo al completo
I'm sorry, we're full

Non ci sono più camere singole/doppie
There are no single/double rooms left

Per quante notti?
For how many nights?

Come vuole pagare?
How will you be paying?

Pagamento anticipato, per favore
Please pay in advance

Dovete liberare la stanza entro mezzogiorno
You must vacate the room by midday

SHOPPING

Excuse me, where is/where are …?
Mi scusi, dov'è/dove sono …?
mee sk<u>oo</u>zee dov<u>eh</u>/d<u>o</u>ve s<u>o</u>no

Do you have …?
Avete …?
av<u>e</u>te

How much is this?
Quanto costa questo?
kw<u>a</u>nto k<u>o</u>sta kw<u>e</u>sto

Where do I pay?
Dove si paga?
d<u>o</u>ve see p<u>a</u>ga

Do you take credit cards?
Accettate carte di credito?
ach-chet-t<u>a</u>te k<u>a</u>rte dee kr<u>e</u>deeto

Can I have a receipt/a bag, please?
Potrebbe darmi lo scontrino/un sacchetto?
potr<u>e</u>b-be d<u>a</u>rmee lo skontr<u>ee</u>no/oon sak-k<u>e</u>t-to

Have you anything cheaper?
Non ha niente di più economico?
non a n-y<u>e</u>nte dee p-yoo ekon<u>o</u>meeko

Can I have a refund?
Posso riavere indietro i soldi?
p<u>o</u>s-so ree-av<u>ai</u>re endee-<u>e</u>tro ee s<u>o</u>ldee

That's fine. I'll take it!
Va bene. Lo prendo!
va b<u>e</u>ne. lo pr<u>e</u>ndo

It isn't what I wanted
Non è quello che volevo
non eh kw<u>e</u>l-lo ke vol<u>e</u>vo

EATING OUT

There are various types of places to eat in Italy. For snacks, the most common is the bar. These are open all day from early morning until about 10 pm. They are all licensed to sell alcohol and usually offer a variety of sandwiches, rolls, cakes, and hot and cold drinks. In most bars you are required to first go to the cashier, place your order, pay and get a receipt (**scontrino**). Then hand the receipt to the bartender and repeat your order. You will notice that most Italians stand up in bars – sitting down costs extra. The sign **tavola calda** means that hot dishes are also served.

For full meals there are **osteria**, **pizzeria**, **trattoria**, **taverna** and **ristorante**. Wherever possible, it's a good idea to choose the **menu turistico** (tourist menu) or the **menu fisso** (set menu). Although the variety is more restricted, the food is of the same standard and you get a good deal more for your money, without having to face any service charge shocks at the end of the meal. Always ask for the local culinary specialities and local wine. These are generally excellent, and wine is less expensive and of superior quality in its place of origin.

In Italy, you can order the following types of coffee: **espresso** (small, strong, black coffee), **caffè macchiato** (espresso with a dash of milk), **cappuccino** (frothy, milky coffee sprinkled with cocoa), **caffelatte** (coffee with milk). These are the most common, but there is also **caffè corretto** (espresso with a liqueur), **caffè decaffeinato** (decaffeinated coffee), **caffè lungo** (weak espresso) and **caffè ristretto** (strong espresso). Remember that if you ask for 'Un caffè, per favore', you will be served an **espresso**.

Useful Words and Phrases

beer	la birra	_beer_-ra
bill	il conto	_konto_
bottle	la bottiglia	bot-_teel_-ya
bread	il pane	_pane_
butter	il burro	_boor_-ro

café	il bar	*bar*
cake	la torta	*torta*
carafe	la caraffa	*karaf-fa*
child's portion	una porzione per bambini	*portz-yone pair bambeenee*
coffee	il caffè	*kaf-feh*
cup	la tazza	*tatza*
dessert	il dessert	*desser*
fork	la forchetta	*forket-ta*
glass	il bicchiere	*beek-yaire*
half litre	da mezzo litro	*da metzo leetro*
knife	il coltello	*koltel-lo*
litre	un litro	*leetro*
main course	il piatto principale	*p-yat-to preencheepale*
menu	il menù	*menoo*
milk	il latte	*lat-te*
napkin	il tovagliolo	*toval-yolo*
pepper	il pepe	*pepey*
plate	il piatto	*p-yat-to*
restaurant	il ristorante	*reestorante*
salt	il sale	*sale*
sandwich	il panino	*paneeno*
snack	lo spuntino	*spoonteeno*
soup	la minestra	*meenestra*
spoon	il cucchiaio	*kook-ya-yo*
starter	l'antipasto	*anteepasto*
sugar	lo zucchero	*dzookairo*
table	il tavolo	*tavolo*
tea	il tè	*teh*
teaspoon	il cucchiaino	*kook-ya-eeno*
tip	la mancia	*mancha*
waiter	il cameriere	*kamair-yaire*
waitress	la cameriera	*kamair-yaira*
water	l'acqua	*akwa*
wine	il vino	*veeno*
wine list	la lista dei vini	*leesta day veenee*

A table for one/two/three, please
Un tavolo per una persona/per due/per tre, per favore
oon tavolo pair oona pairsona/pair doo-e/pair tray pair favore

Is there a highchair?
Si può avere un seggiolone?
see pwo avaire oon seg-gee-olone

Can I see the menu/wine list?
Potrei vedere il menu/la lista dei vini?
potray vedaire eel menoo/la leesta day veenee

What would you recommend?
Cosa ci consiglia?
koza chee konseel-ya

I'd like …
Vorrei …
vor-ray

Just an espresso/cappuccino/coffee with milk, please
Solo un caffè/un cappuccino/un caffelatte, per favore
solo oon kaf-feh/oon kap-poocheeno/oon kaf-felat-te pair favore

I only want a snack
Vorrei solo uno spuntino
vor-ray solo oono spoonteeno

Is there a set menu?
C'è un menù fisso?
cheh oon menoo fees-so

A litre of house red, please
Un litro di vino rosso della casa, per favore
oon leetro dee veeno ros-so del-la kaza pair favore

Do you have any vegetarian dishes?
Avete piatti vegetariani?
avete p-yat-tee vejetar-yanee

I'm allergic to nuts/shellfish
Sono allergico/a alle noci/ai frutti di mare
sono al-lairjeeko/a al-lai nochee/aee froot-tee dee marai

Could we have some water?
Potremmo avere un po' d'acqua?
potrem-mo avaire oon po dakwa

Do you do children's portions?
Fate porzioni per bambini?
fatai porzeeonee pair bambeenee

Can you warm this bottle/baby food for me?
Mi può riscaldare il biberon/il pasto del bambino?
mee pwo reeskaldarai eel bee-bairon/eel pazto del bambeeno

Waiter/waitress!
Cameriere/cameriera!
kamair-yaire/kamair-yaira

We didn't order this!
Non lo abbiamo ordinato!
non lo abb-yamo ordeenato

May we have some more …?
Potremmo avere ancora un po' di …?
potrem-mo avaire ankora oon po dee

Can I have another knife/spoon?
Potrei avere un altro coltello/cucchiaio?
potray avaire oon altro koltel-lo/kook-ya-yo

Can we have the bill, please?
Può portarci il conto, per favore?
pwo portarchee eel konto pair favore

Could I have a receipt, please?
Potrei avere la ricevuta/lo scontrino, per favore?
potray avaire la reechevoota/lo skontreeno pair favore

MENU GUIDE

acqua water
acqua minerale gassata sparkling mineral water
acqua minerale non gassata still mineral water
aglio garlic
agnello lamb
albicocche apricots
anatra duck
anguria watermelon
antipasti starters
antipasti misti variety of starters
aragosta lobster
arancia orange
aranciata orangeade
aringa herring
arrosto di … roast …
baccalà dried cod
bavarese ice-cream cake with cream
besciamella white sauce
bistecca (di manzo) steak
braciola di maiale pork steak
branzino al forno baked sea bass
brasato braised beef with herbs
bresaola dried, salted beef sliced thinly, and eaten cold with oil and lemon
brodo clear broth
brodo di pollo chicken broth
brodo vegetale clear vegetable broth
budino pudding
burro butter
caffè coffee
caffè corretto espresso with a dash of liqueur
caffè lungo weak espresso
caffè macchiato espresso with a dash of milk
caffè ristretto strong espresso

caffelatte half coffee, half hot milk
calamaro squid
calzone folded pizza with tomato and mozzarella or ricotta inside
cannella cinnamon
capretto al forno roast kid
carciofi artichokes
carne meat
carote carrots
cassata siciliana Sicilian ice-cream cake with glacé fruit, chocolate and ricotta
castagne chestnuts
cavoletti di Bruxelles Brussels sprouts
cavolfiore cauliflower
cavolo cabbage
cefalo mullet
cicoria chicory
ciliege cherries
cioccolata chocolate
cipolle onions
coniglio rabbit
contorni vegetables
cotechino spiced pork sausage
cotoletta veal, pork or lamb chop
cozze mussels
crema custard dessert
crema di funghi cream of mushroom soup
crema di piselli cream of pea soup
crema pasticciera confectioner's custard
crespelle type of savoury pancake filled with white sauce and other fillings
dolci sweets, desserts, cakes
fagiano pheasant
fagioli beans
fagiolini long, green beans
fegato liver
fettuccine ribbon-shaped pasta

fichi figs
filetti di pesce persico fillets of perch
filetti di sogliola fillets of sole
filetto (di manzo) fillet of beef
finocchio fennel
formaggi misti variety of cheeses
fragole strawberries
frappé whisked fruit or milk drink ice
frittata type of omelette
fritto misto mixed seafood in batter
frittura di pesce variety of fried fish
frutta fruit
frutti di mare seafood
funghi mushrooms
gamberetti shrimp
gamberi prawn
gamberoni king prawns
gazzosa clear lemonade
gelatina jelly
gelato ice cream
gnocchi flour and potato dumplings
granchio crab
granita drink with crushed ice
grigliata di pesce grilled fish
grigliata mista mixed grill (meat or fish)
grissini thin, crisp breadsticks
indivia endive
insalata salad
insalata di mare seafood salad
insalata di pomodori tomato salad
insalata mista mixed salad
insalata verde green salad
lamponi raspberries
latte milk
lattuga lettuce
legumi legumes
lenticchie lentils
limone lemon
lingua tongue
macedonia di frutta fruit salad
maiale pork

maionese mayonnaise
mandorla almond
manzo beef
marroni chestnuts
medaglioni di vitello veal medallions
mela apple
melanzane aubergine
melone melon
menta mint
menu turistico tourist menu
meringata meringue pie
merluzzo cod
millefoglie layered pastry slice with
    confectioner's custard
minestra in brodo noodle soup
mirtilli bilberries
more mulberries or blackberries
nasello hake
nocciole hazelnuts
noci walnuts
nodino veal chop
olio oil
origano oregano
ossobuco stewed shin of veal
ostriche oysters
pane bread
panino filled roll
panna cream
parmigiano parmesan cheese
pasta e piselli pasta with peas
pasticcio di maccheroni baked macaroni
pastina in brodo noodle soup
patate potatoes
patate fritte chips
pecorino strong, hard sheep's milk cheese
pepe pepper (spice)
peperoni peppers
pera pear
pesca peach
pesce fish
pesce in carpione marinaded fish

piselli peas
pollo chicken
pollo al forno/arrosto roast chicken
polpette meatballs
polpettone meatloaf
pomodori tomatoes
pomodori ripieni stuffed tomatoes
pompelmo grapefruit
porri leeks
primi piatti first courses
prosciutto cotto cooked ham
prosciutto e fichi cured ham with figs
prugne plums
purè di patate mashed potatoes
quaglie quails
radicchio chicory
rapanelli radishes
razza skate
risi e bisi risotto with peas and ham
riso rice
risotto ai funghi mushroom risotto
risotto alla castellana risotto with mushroom, ham, cream and cheese
risotto alla milanese risotto flavoured with saffron
salame salami
sale salt
salmone affumicato smoked salmon
salsa di pomodoro tomato sauce
salsa tartara tartar sauce
salsiccia sausage
saltimbocca alla romana slices of veal stuffed with ham and sage and fried
salvia sage
sarde ai ferri grilled sardines
scaloppine veal escalopes
scamorza alla griglia grilled soft cheese
scampi alla griglia grilled scampi
secondi piatti second courses, main courses
sedano celery

senape mustard
sogliola sole
sorbetto sorbet, soft ice cream
spaghetti aglio, olio e peperoncino spaghetti with garlic, oil and crushed chilli pepper
spaghetti al pesto spaghetti in crushed basil, garlic, oil and parmesan dressing
spaghetti al pomodoro spaghetti in tomato sauce
spaghetti al ragù spaghetti with meat sauce
spaghetti alla carbonara spaghetti with egg, chopped bacon and cheese sauce
spaghetti alla puttanesca spaghetti with anchovies, capers and black olives in tomato sauce
spaghetti alle vongole spaghetti with clams
spaghetti all'amatriciana spaghetti with chopped bacon and tomato sauce, typical of Rome
spezzatino di vitello veal stew
spinaci spinach
stracciatella soup of beaten eggs cooked in boiling, clear broth
strudel di mele apple strudel
succo juice
tacchino ripieno stuffed turkey
tagliata finely cut beef fillet cooked in the oven
tagliolini thin soup noodles
tartine small sandwiches
tartufo round ice cream covered in cocoa or chocolate
tè tea
tè con latte tea with milk
tè con limone lemon tea
tiramisù dessert made with coffee-soaked sponge fingers, eggs, Marsala, mascarpone and cocoa powder

tonno tuna
torta tart, flan
torta salata savoury flan
torta ai carciofi artichoke flan
torta al cioccolato chocolate tart
torta al formaggio cheese flan
torta di mele apple tart
torta di noci walnut tart
torta di ricotta type of cheesecake
torta di zucchine courgette flan
torta gelato ice-cream tart
tortellini small pasta shapes filled with minced pork, ham, parmesan and nutmeg
tortellini alla panna tortellini with cream
tortellini al pomodoro tortellini with tomato sauce
tortellini al ragù tortellini with mince and tomato sauce
tortellini in brodo tortellini in clear broth
tortelloni di magro/di ricotta pasta shapes filled with cheese, parsley and chopped vegetables
trancio di pesce spada swordfish steak
trenette col pesto type of flat spaghetti with crushed basil, garlic, oil and cheese sauce
triglie mullet (fish)
trippa tripe
trota trout
trota affumicata smoked trout
trota al burro trout cooked in butter
trota alle mandorle trout with almonds
trota bollita boiled trout
uova eggs
uova al tegamino con pancetta fried eggs and bacon
uova alla coque boiled eggs
uova farcite eggs with tuna and capers

uova sode hard-boiled eggs
uva grapes
uva bianca white grapes
uva nera black grapes
vellutata di asparagi creamed asparagus with egg yolks
vellutata di piselli creamed peas with egg yolks
verdura vegetables
vermicelli very fine, thin pasta, often used in soups
vino wine
vino bianco white wine
vino da dessert dessert wine
vino da pasto table wine
vino da tavola table wine
vino rosso red wine
vitello veal
vitello tonnato cold sliced veal in tuna, anchovy, oil and lemon sauce
vongole clams
würstel hot dog
zabaione creamy dessert made from beaten eggs, sugar and Marsala wine
zafferano saffron
zucca pumpkin
zucchine courgette
zucchine al pomodoro chopped courgette in tomato, garlic and parsley sauce
zucchine ripiene stuffed courgette
zuccotto ice-cream cake with sponge fingers, cream and chocolate
zuppa soup
zuppa di cipolle onion soup
zuppa di cozze mussel soup
zuppa di lenticchie lentil soup
zuppa di pesce fish soup
zuppa di verdura vegetable soup
zuppa inglese trifle

NORWEGIAN

CONTENTS

INTRODUCTION

Pronunciation

When reading the imitated pronunciation, stress that part which is underlined. Pronounce each syllable as if it formed part of an English word and you will be understood sufficiently well. Remember the points below, and your pronunciation will be closer to the correct Norwegian.

EW	try to say 'ee' with your lips rounded (or the French 'u')
Hy	the 'hu' sound as in 'huge'
I	the 'i' sound as in 'high'
ow	as in 'cow'
ur	the 'u' sound as in 'fur'

Norwegian Alphabetical Order

In the lists called *Things You'll See* and in the Menu Guide we have followed Norwegian alphabetical order. The following letters are listed after z: **æ, ø, å.**

'You'

There are two words for 'you': **du** (addressing one person) and **dere** (addressing two or more people). The polite form **De** is seldom used.

Genders and the Definite/Indefinite Article

Norwegian has three genders for nouns – masculine, feminine and neuter. Since most feminine words can also have a masculine form, in this phrase book we have mainly used masculine and neuter forms, giving only essential feminine ones.

The definite article (English 'the') is used as an ending in Norwegian and shows the gender of the noun: **-en** (masculine), **-et** (neuter).Where used, **-a** is the feminine word ending.

When you see translations given in the form **gutt(en)** or
hus(et), the form **gutten** will mean 'the boy' and **huset** 'the
house'. Note that the final -**t** of the definite article ending is
always silent: **huset** <u>hoo</u>sseh. The indefinite article ending
(English 'a', 'an') is the same as the definite article but is placed
before the noun as a separate word: **en** or **et**. For example,
'a boy' is **en gutt** and 'a house' is **et hus**.

VERBS

Verbs are given in the infinitive form: '(to) speak' (**å**) **snakke**.
To form the present tense for all persons add 'r' to the infinitive:
jeg snakker 'I speak', **du snakker** 'you speak' and so on.

USEFUL PHRASES

Yes/no
Ja/nei
yah/nɪ

Thank you
Takk
takk

No, thank you
Nei takk
nɪ takk

Please *(offering)*
Vær så god
varshawgo

I don't understand
Jeg forstår ikke
yɪ forshtawr ikkeh

Do you speak English/French/German?
Snakker du engelsk/fransk/tysk?
snakker doo eng-elsk/fransk/tɛwsk

I can't speak Norwegian
Jeg snakker ikke norsk
yɪ snakker ikkeh norshk

I don't know
Jeg vet ikke
yɪ vayt ikkeh

Please speak more slowly
Kan du snakke langsommere
*kan doo sn**a**kkeh l**a**ng-sawmereh*

Please write it down for me
Kan du skrive det opp for meg?
*kan doo skr**ee**veh deh op for mɪ*

My name is …
Jeg heter …
*yɪ h**ay**ter*

How do you do, pleased to meet you
God dag, hyggelig å hilse på deg
*go dahg h**ew**geli aw h**i**lseh paw dɪ*

Good morning/good afternoon/good evening
God mor'n/god dag/god kveld
*go-m**aw**rn/go-d**a**hg/go-kv**e**ll*

Good night *(when leaving late at night/at bedtime)*
God natt
*go-n**a**tt*

Goodbye
Morn'a; *(informal)* ha det
*m**o**rna; h**a**h-deh*

Excuse me, please
Unnskyld
*<u>oo</u>nsh**ew**l*

Sorry!
Om forlatelse!
*om forl**a**hdelseh*

I'm really sorry!
Jeg er virkelig lei meg!
yı ar vırkeli lı mı

Can you help me?
Kan du hjelpe meg?
kan doo yelpeh mı

Can you tell me …?
Kan du si meg …?
kan doo see mı

Can I have …?
Kan jeg få …?
kan yı faw

I would like a …
Jeg vil gjerne ha en/et …
yı vil yarneh hah ayn/et

I would like to …
Jeg vil gjerne …
yı vil yarneh

Would you like a …?
Vil du ha en/et …?
vil doo hah ayn/et

Is there … here?
Er det … her?
ar deh … har

Where can I get …?
Hvor kan jeg få …?
vohr kan yı faw

How much is it?
Hvor mye koster det?
vohr mEW-eh koster deh

What time is it?
Hvor mange er klokken?
vohr mang-eh ar klokken

I must go now
Jeg må gå nå
yı maw gaw naw

I've lost my way *(on foot)*
Jeg har gått meg bort
yı hahr gawt mı bohrt

Cheers!
Skål!
skawl

Do you take credit cards?
Tar du kredittkort?
tahr doo kredittkort

Where is the British/US embassy?
Hvor er den britiske/amerikanske ambassade?
vohr ar den britteeskeh/amayreekahnskeh ambassadeh

Where is the toilet?
Hvor er toalettet?
vohr ar toh-a-letteh

Excellent!
Fint!
feent

**I've lost my passport/money/room key/traveller's cheques/
credit cards**

Jeg har mistet /mitt pass/mine penger/nøkkelen til rommet
mitt/mine reisesjekker/mine kredittkort

*yı hahr meestet /mıtt pass/meeneh peng-er/nurkel-en til rohm-eh
mıtt/meeneh ray-seh-shekker/meeneh kredittkort*

THINGS YOU'LL HEAR

bare hyggelig!	you're welcome!
bra	good
det er riktig	that's right
fint	fine
god tur	have a good trip
hils …!	regards to …!
hva?	pardon?; sorry?
hva sa du?	sorry, what did you say?
hvordan går det?	how are things?
hvordan har du det?	how are you?
ja	yes
jaså?	is that so?
jeg forstår ikke	I don't understand
jeg vet ikke	I don't know
kom inn	come in
morn'a	cheerio
nei	no
om forlatelse!	I'm so sorry!
pass deg!	look out!
takk	thanks
tusen takk	thank you very much
unnskyld	excuse me
velkommen	welcome
vi ses	see you later
vær så god	here you are; please help yourself

DAYS, MONTHS, SEASONS

Sunday	søndag	_surn_dag
Monday	mandag	m_a_ndag
Tuesday	tirsdag	t_ee_rssdag
Wednesday	onsdag	_ohn_ssdag
Thursday	torsdag	t_a_wrssdag
Friday	fredag	fr_ay_dag
Saturday	lørdag	_lurr_dag
January	januar	yanoo-_ahr_
February	februar	febroo-_ahr_
March	mars	marsh
April	april	apr_ee_l
May	mai	mɪ
June	juni	_yoo_ni
July	juli	_yoo_li
August	august	ow_goo_st
September	september	sept_e_mber
October	oktober	okt_a_wber
November	november	nov_e_mber
December	desember	des_e_mber
Spring	vår	vawr
Summer	sommer	_so_mmer
Autumn	høst	hurst
Winter	vinter	v_i_nter
Christmas	Jul	yool
Christmas Eve	Julaften	_yoo_laften
New Year	Nyttår	n_EW_tawr
New Year's Eve	Nyttårsaften	n_EW_tawrsaften
Easter	Påske	_paw_skeh
Good Friday	Langfredag	langfr_ay_dag
Whitsun	Pinse	_pi_nseh
Midsummer Day	Sankthans	_sa_ngt-hanss

NUMBERS

Compound numbers are found in two forms in Norwegian. The newer form puts the tens before the units, eg: **tjueen** is 'twenty one'. The older form puts the units first, eg: **enogtyve** literally means 'one and twenty'. The old system is still used by many Norwegians and some people use a mixture of both systems.

0	null	*nooll*	10	ti	*tee*
1	en (ett*)	*ayn (ett)*	11	elleve	*elveh*
2	to	*toh*	12	tolv	*tawll*
3	tre	*tray*	13	tretten	*tretten*
4	fire	*feereh*	14	fjorten	*fyohrten*
5	fem	*fem*	15	femten	*femten*
6	seks	*seks*	16	seksten	*sisten*
7	sju/syv	*shoo/sEWv*	17	sytten	*surtten*
8	åtte	*awtteh*	18	atten	*atten*
9	ni	*nee*	19	nitten	*neetten*

20 tjue/tyve *Hyoo-eh/tEWveh*
21 tjueen/enogtyve *Hyoo-eh-ayn/ayn-aw-tEWveh*
22 tjueto/toogtyve *Hyoo-eh-toh/toh-aw-tEWveh*
30 tretti/tredve *tretti/tredveh*
40 førti/førr *furrti/furr*
50 femti *femti*
60 seksti *seksti*
70 sytti *surtti*
80 åtti *awtti*
90 nitti *neetti*
100 (ett) hundre *hoondreh*
110 hundre og ti *hoondreh aw tee*
200 to hundre *toh hoondreh*
300 tre hundre *tray hoondreh*
400 fire hundre *feereh hoondreh*
1,000 (ett) tusen *toossen*
10,000 ti tusen *tee toossen*
100,000 hundre tusen *hoondreh toossen*   *ett is the neuter
1,000,000 (en) million *milliyohn*   form of **en**

TIME

today	i dag	*ee-dahg*
yesterday	i går	*ee-gawr*
tomorrow	i morgen	*ee-mawern*
this week	denne uken	*den-eh ooken*
last week	i forrige uke	*ee forri-eh ookeh*
next week	neste uke	*nest-eh ookeh*
this morning	i morges	*ee-morges*
this afternoon	i ettermiddag	*ee-ettermiddag*
this evening/ tonight	i kveld	*ee-kvell*
in three days	om tre dager	*om tray dahger*
three days ago	for tre dager siden	*for tray dahger seeden*
late	sent	*saynt*
early	tidlig	*teeli*
soon	snart	*snahrt*
later on	senere	*saynereh*
at the moment	for øyeblikket	*for oyeblikkeh*
second	sekund(et)	*sekoon*
minute	minutt(et)	*minoott*
one minute	et minutt	*et minoott*
two minutes	to minutter	*toh minootter*
quarter of an hour	et kvarter	*et kvartayr*
half an hour	en halv time	*ayn hal teemeh*
three quarters of an hour	tre kvarter	*tray kvartayr*
hour	time(n)	*teemeh*
that day	den dagen	*den dahgen*
every day	hver dag	*var dahg*
all day	hele dagen	*hayleh dahgen*
the next day	neste dag	*nesteh dahg*
week	uke(n)	*ookeh*
month	måned(en)	*mawned*
year	år(et)	*awr*

TELLING THE TIME

Norway conforms to Central European Time, which is one hour in advance of GMT. The Norwegians put their clocks forward by an hour from the end of March until the end of September. When telling the time, it is important to note that, instead of saying 'half past' an hour, the Norwegians refer to the next hour coming, for example: 'half past one' in Norwegian is 'half two'.

Also, the minutes after 'quarter past' and before 'quarter to' the hour are linked to the half hour, for example: for 'twenty past three' the Norwegians would say 'ten to half four' and for 'twenty-five to one' they would say 'five past half one'. The 24-hour clock is used quite commonly in timetables, on radio and television and often when making appointments.

am	om formiddagen	*om formiddagen*
pm	om ettermiddagen	*om ettermiddagen*
one o'clock	klokken ett	*klokken ett*
ten past one	ti over ett	*tee awver ett*
quarter past one	kvart over ett	*kvart awver ett*
twenty past one	ti på halv to	*tee paw hal toh*
twenty-five past one	fem på halv to	*fem paw hal toh*
half past one	halv to	*hal toh*
twenty-five to two	fem over halv to	*fem awver hal toh*
twenty to two	ti over halv to	*tee awver hal toh*
quarter to two	kvart på to	*kvart paw toh*
ten to two	ti på to	*tee paw toh*
two o'clock	klokken to	*klokken toh*
13.00 (1 pm)	klokken tretten	*klokken tretten*
16.30 (4.30 pm)	seksten tretti	*sisten tretti*
at half past five	klokken halv seks	*klokken hal seks*
at seven o'clock	klokken sju	*klokken shoo*
noon	klokken tolv	*klokken tawll*
midnight	midnatt	*midnatt*

COMMUNICATIONS

Useful Words and Phrases

call	telefonsamtale(n)	*telefohnsamtahleh*
dialling tone	summetone(n)	*soommetohneh*
directory enquiries	opplysningen	*opplEWssning-en*
engaged	opptatt	*opptat*
enquiries	opplysninger	*opplEWssning-er*
extension	linje(n)	*leen-yeh*
internet	internett(et)	*internett(eh)*
mobile phone	mobiltelefon(en)	*mohbeel-telefohn(ayn)*
number	nummer(et)	*noommer*
payphone	telefon-automat(en)	*telefohn-owtohmaht*
phonecard	telefonkort(et)	*telefohn-kort(eh)*
reverse charge call	noteringsover-føring(en)	*nohtayringssawver-furring*
telephone	telefon(en)	*telefohn*
telephone directory	telefonkatalog(en)	*telefohnkatalawg*
Web site	web side(n)	*vebb seedeh(n)*
wrong number	feil nummer	*fil noommer*

Where is the nearest phone box?
Hvor er nærmeste telefonkiosk?
vohr ar narmesteh telefohnHyawsk

I would like a number in …
Jeg skal ha et nummer i …
yı skal hah et noommer ee

I would like to speak to …
Kan jeg få snakke med …?
kan yı faw snakkeh may

My number is …
Mitt nummer er …
mit noommer ar

I would like a number in …
Må jeg bede om et nummer i …
maw yi bay om it nawmor ee

Hello, this is … speaking
Hallo, det er …
hahloh, day air

Speaking
Det er (+ *name*)
day air

I would like to speak to …
Jeg vil gerne tale med …
yi vil gairner tahler meth

My number is …
Mit nummer er …
mit nawmor air

Could you leave him/her a message?
Kan du gi ham/henne en beskjed?
kan doo yee ham/henneh ayn beshay

I'll ring back later
Jeg ringer igjen senere
yi ring-er ee-yen saynereh

What's your fax number/email address?
Hva er ditt fax nummer/epost adresse?
vah ar ditt faks noommer/ay-pawst adresseh

Can I send an email/fax from here?
Kan jeg sende epost/en fax herfra?
kan yi senneh ay-pawst/ayn faks hayr-frah

THINGS YOU'LL HEAR

Hvem skal du snakke med?
Who would you like to speak to?

Hvem er det som snakker?
Who's speaking?

Hva er ditt nummer?
What is your number?

Han/hun er dessverre ikke inne
Sorry, he/she is not in

Han/hun kommer tilbake klokken ett
He/she will be back at one o'clock

Kan du ringe igjen i morgen?
Can you call back tomorrow?

Jeg skal si fra at du har ringt
I'll tell him/her you called

THINGS YOU'LL SEE

feilmelding	faults service
fjerntakst	operator; long-distance calls
fjernvalg	direct dialling
gebyr	fee
innenlands	national
i ustand	out of order
lokalsamtale	local call
retningsnummer	dialling code
takst	charges
utlandet	international

HOTELS

Useful Words and Phrases

balcony	balkong(en)	*balkong*
bathroom	bad(et)	*bahd*
bed	seng(en)	*seng*
bedroom	soverom(met)	*saw-verohm*
bill	regning(en)	*rining*
breakfast	frokost(en)	*frohkost*
dining room	spisesal(en)	*spee-seh-sahl*
dinner	middag(en)	*middag*
double bed	dobbeltseng(en)	*dobbeltseng*
double room	dobbeltrom(met)	*dobbeltrohm*
foyer	foyer(en)	*foh-a-yay*
full board	full pensjon	*full pangshohn*
half board	halv pensjon	*hal pangshohn*
head waiter	hovmester(en)	*hawvmester*
hotel	hotell(et)	*hotel*
hotel manager	hotellsjef(en)	*hotelshayf*
key	nøkkel(en)	*nurkel*
lift	heis(en)	*hiss*
lounge	salong(en)	*salong*
lunch	lunsj(en)	*'lunch'*
reception	resepsjon(en)	*resepshohn*
receptionist	resepsjonist(en)	*resepshohnist*
restaurant	restaurant(en)	*restoorang*
room	rom(met)	*rohm*
room service	romservice(n)	*rohm-'service'*
shower	dusj(en)	*doosh*
single room	enkeltrom(met)	*engkeltrohm*
toilet	toalett(et)	*toh-a-lett*
twin room	tomannsrom	*tohmanssrohm*

Have you any vacancies?
Har dere ledige rom?
hahr dereh laydi-eh rohm

I have a reservation
Jeg har reservert rom
yı hahr ressarvayrt rohm

I'd like a single/twin room
Kan jeg få et enkeltrom/tomannsrom?
kan yı faw et engkeltrohm/tohmansrohm

I'd like a room with a bathroom/balcony
Kan jeg få et rom med bad/balkong?
kan yı faw et rohm may bahd/balkong

Is there satellite/cable TV in the rooms?
Finnes det satelitt/kabel-TV på rommene?
finnes deh sahtaylitt/kahbel tayh-vayh paw rohmmehneh

I'd like a room for one night/three nights/one week
Kan jeg få et rom for en natt/tre netter/en uke?
kan yı faw et rohm for ayn natt/tray netter/ayn ookeh

What is the charge per night?
Hva koster det pr. natt?
vah koster deh par natt

Are there facilities for the disabled?
Er det tilrettelagt for funksjonshemmede?
ayr deh tilretteh-lahgt for foonkshohns-hemmedeh

When is breakfast/lunch/dinner?
Når er frokost/lunsj/middag?
nawr ar frohkost/lunch/middag

Please wake me at 7 o'clock
Kan du vekke meg klokken sju
kan doo vekkeh mı klokken shoo

Can I have breakfast in my room?
Kan jeg få frokost på rommet?
kan yı faw frohkost paw rohmeh

I'll be back at 10 o'clock
Jeg vil være tilbake klokken ti
yı vil var-eh tilbahkeh klokken tee

My room number is 205
Jeg har rom nummer to hundre og fem
yı hahr rohm noommer toh hoondreh aw fem

I'm leaving tomorrow
Jeg reiser i morgen
yı risser ee-mawern

Can I have the bill, please?
Kan jeg få regningen, takk?
kan yı faw rining-en takk

I'll pay by credit card
Jeg betaler med kredittkort
yı betahler may kredittkor

I'll pay cash
Jeg betaler kontant
yı betahler kontant

Can you get me a taxi?
Kan du få tak i en taxi?
kan doo faw tahk ee ayn taxi

Things You'll See

bad	bath
dusj	shower
frokost	breakfast
fullt	no vacancies
heis	lift
inngang	entrance
ledig	vacancies
nødutgang	emergency exit
regning	bill
rom	room
røyking forbudt	no smoking
skyv	push
trekk	pull
utgang	exit

Things You'll Hear

Det er dessverre fullt
I'm sorry, we're full

Vi har ingen enkeltrom igjen
We have no single rooms left

Hvor mange netter er det for?
For how many nights?

Kan du skrive navnet ditt her?
Please sign your name here

Hvordan vil du betale?
How will you be paying?

Kan du være så snill å betale på forhånd?
Please pay in advance

SHOPPING

I'd like …
Jeg skal ha …
yı skal hah

Do you have …?
Har du …?
hahr doo

How much is this?
Hvor mye koster denne (dette)?
vohr m<u>EW</u>-eh k<u>o</u>ster d<u>e</u>nneh (deh<u>tteh</u>)

Do you have any more of these?
Har du flere av disse?
hahr doo fl<u>ay</u>reh av d<u>e</u>esseh

Where do I pay?
Hvor skal jeg betale?
vohr skal yı bet<u>ah</u>leh

Have you anything cheaper?
Har du noe som er billigere?
hahr doo n<u>o</u>-eh som ar billi-ereh

Can I have a receipt?
Kan jeg få en kvittering?
kan yı faw ayn kvitt<u>ay</u>ring

Can I have a refund?
Kan jeg få pengene igjen?
kan yı faw p<u>e</u>ng-eneh ee-y<u>e</u>n

I'm just looking
Jeg bare ser
yı b<u>ah</u>reh sayr

EATING OUT

The Norwegian working day is from about 7 am to 3 or 4 pm and mealtimes are therefore quite early, with lunch mid-morning and dinner at about 4 pm. In hotels and restaurants, however, lunch is normally available between 12 and 2.30 and dinner is available all evening. Eating in hotels and restaurants can be quite expensive. However, you can get good-quality inexpensive meals at cafés which have a set menu **dagens rett** (_dahgenss ret_). Meatballs **kjøttkaker** (_Hyurt-kahker_), thick meat stew **brun lapskaus** (_broon lapskowss_) and pork chops with sweet and sour cabbage **svinekoteletter med surkål** (_sveeneh-koteletter may soorkawl_) are popular dishes. A service charge is usually included in the bill and additional tipping is up to you.

Norwegians eat a substantial breakfast **frokost** (_frohkost_) usually consisting of bread, cold meats, cured fish, a variety of jams and brown Norwegian goats' cheese.

Traditional dishes in Norway are plain and prepared from food which can be easily stored, ie salted, cured, smoked and dried. In the past, the staple diet consisted of various kinds of porridge, and soured cream porridge **rømmegrøt** (_rurmegrurt_), served sprinkled with cinnamon and sugar, was eaten on special occasions like Midsummer's Day. Nowadays, you are likely to come across **spekemat** (_spaykehmaht_), which is a selection of cold cured meats. These, together with sweet and sour salted herring **sursild** (_soorsill_), cured herring **spekesild** (_spaykehsill_), fermented trout **rakørret** (_rahkurret_) and cured salmon **gravlaks** (_grahvlaks_), are traditionally found in the Norwegian buffet **koldtbord** (_kawltbohr_).

Open sandwiches are available in most eating places. Waffles **vafler** (_vafler_), with soured cream and jam, are another favourite.

Licensing laws are strict, alcohol prices are high and the state has a monopoly on the sale of alcohol. Bring your duty-free allowance with you, otherwise you may have to buy spirits at the state-owned **Vinmonopolet** at treble the price. Beer is sold at supermarkets but not wine and spirits.

USEFUL WORDS AND PHRASES

beer	øl(et)	*url*
bill	regning(en)	*rining*
bottle	flaske(n)	*flaskeh*
buffet	koldtbord(et)	*kawltbohr*
cake	kake(n)	*kahkeh*
chef	kokk(en)	*kokk*
children's portion	barneporsjon(en)	*barneporshohn*
coffee	kaffe(n)	*kaffeh*
cup	kopp(en)	*kopp*
fork	gaffel(en)	*gaffel*
glass	glass(et)	*glass*
knife	kniv(en)	*k-neev*
menu	meny(en)	*menEW*
milk	melk(en)	*melk*
open sandwich	smørbrød(et)	*smurrbrur*
plate	tallerken(en)	*tal-arken*
receipt	kvittering(en)	*kvittayring*
schnapps	akevitt(en)	*akevitt*
serviette	serviett(en)	*sarvi-ett*
snack	smårett(en)	*smawrett*
soup	suppe(n)	*sooppeh*
spoon	skje(en)	*shay*
sugar	sukker(et)	*sookker*
table	bord(et)	*bohr*
tea	te(en)	*tay*
teaspoon	teskje(en)	*tayshay*
tip	tips(et)	*tips*
waiter	kelner(en)	*kelner*
waitress	serveringsdame(n)	*sarvayringssdahmeh*
water	vann(et)	*vann*
wine	vin(en)	*veen*
wine list	vinkart(et)	*veenkart*

A table for one/two, please
Kan jeg få et bord til en/to, takk?
kan yı faw et bohr til ayn/too takk

Can I see the menu?
Kan jeg få se menyen?
kan yı faw say men<u>Ew</u>en

Can I see the wine list?
Kan jeg få se vinkartet?
kan yı faw say v<u>ee</u>nkarteh

What would you recommend?
Hva vil du anbefale?
vah vil doo <u>ahn</u>befahleh

I'm allergic to nuts/shellfish
Jeg er allergisk mot nøtter/skalldyr
yı ar all<u>a</u>rgisk moht n<u>u</u>rttehr/sk<u>a</u>ll-dEwr

I'm vegetarian
Jeg er vegetarianer
yı ar vegget<u>ah</u>reeahnehr

Do you have any vegetarian dishes?
Har dere vegetarretter?
hahr d<u>ay</u>reh vegget<u>ah</u>r-retter

I'd like …
Kan jeg få …
kan yı faw

Just a cup of coffee, please
Bare en kopp kaffe, takk
b<u>ah</u>reh ayn kopp k<u>a</u>ffeh takk

Waiter/waitress!
Hallo!
hallo

Can we have the bill, please?
Kan vi få regningen, takk?
kan vee faw rining-en takk

I only want a snack
Jeg vil bare ha en smårett
yı vil bahreh hah ayn smawrett

Is there a set menu?
Er det en dagens rett?
ar deh ayn dahgenss rett

I didn't order this
Jeg har ikke bestilt dette
yı hahr ikkeh behstilt detteh

Can I have another knife/fork?
Kan jeg få en kniv/gaffel til?
kan yı faw ayn k-neev/gaffel til

May we have some more …?
Kan vi få litt mer …?
kan vee faw litt mayr

The meal was very good, thank you
Maten smakte deilig, takk!
mahten smahkteh dıli takk

Can we pay separately?
Kan vi betale hver for oss?
kan vee betahleh var for oss

MENU GUIDE

agurk(er) cucumber; pickled gherkins

and duck

ansjos anchovies

appelsin orange

aprikos apricot

bakt baked

betasuppe yellow pea, ham and vegetable soup

biff med løk fried steak with onions

bjørnebær blackberries, brambles

blandet kjøttrett a variety of meats diced and fried

blomkål cauliflower

bløtkokt egg soft-boiled egg

blåbær blueberries

blåskjell mussels

boller buns; dumplings; fish/meatballs

bringebær raspberries

brokkoli broccoli

brus fizzy drinks

bryst breast

brød bread

buljong clear soup, consommé

butterdeig flaky pastry

bønner beans

chips potato crisps

dampet steamed

drikkevarer drinks

druer grapes

dyrestek roast reindeer

eggekrem thick custard

eggeplomme egg yolk

eggerøre cold scrambled eggs

eple apple

erter peas

erter, kjøtt og flesk yellow pea soup and ham (with the ham served as the second course with boiled potatoes)

fasan pheasant

fenalår cured leg of mutton

fersken peach

filet fillet

fisk(e) fish

flaske bottle

flatbrød thin crispbread

flesk pork belly

flyndre sole

fløte cream

forloren meat loaf served as a roast

franskbrød white bread with poppy seeds

frisk(e) fresh

frityrstekt deep-fried

frokost breakfast

frokostblanding breakfast cereal

fromasj cold soufflé, mousse

frukt fruit

fylt stuffed

får mutton

gaffelbiter small fillets of herring soaked in strong marinade

grapefrukt grapefruit

grateng savoury hot soufflé

gravlaks cured salmon (gravad lax)

gressløk chives

griljert fried in breadcrumbs

grillben barbecued spare ribs

grovbrød wholemeal bread

gryte casserole

grønnsaker vegetables

grøt porridge made from flour, oats or rice; 'jelly' made from boiled fruit and fruit juice, and thickened with cornflour

gulrot carrot

gås goose

havre oatmeal

hellefisk halibut

helstekt fried or roasted whole

hjemmelaget home-made

honning honey

hovedrett main course

hummer lobster

hvalbiff whale steak

hveteboller buns

hvitløk garlic

hvit saus white sauce

hvitting whiting

hvitvin white wine

høns(e) chicken, poultry

hårdkokt egg hard-boiled egg

is ice cream, ice

jordbær strawberries

juice fruit juice

kaffe coffee

kake(r) cake(s); fish or meat cakes

kald cold

kaldrøkt cold smoked salmon

kalkun turkey

kalv(e) veal

kanel cinnamon

kapers capers

karbonade minced beef steak

karve caraway seeds

kavring rusk

kinakål Chinese leaves

kirsebær cherries

kjeks biscuits

kjøtt meat

kjøttkaker minced beef balls

knakkpølse small, thick smoked
  sausage

kneipbrød crusty wheaten bread

knekkebrød crispbread

kokt boiled, poached

koldtbord cold buffet

kotelett chop, cutlet

krabbe crab

kreps crayfish

kringle pretzel-shaped cake filled with
  almond paste, apples or raisins

kryddersild cured, spiced raw herring

kulturmelk, kulturmjølk soured milk

kveite halibut

kylling chicken

kål cabbage

kålrabi, kålrot swede

laks salmon

lam(me) lamb

lammerygg saddle of lamb

leskedrikk squash

lever liver

loff white bread

lumpe thin potato scone

lunsj lunch

løk onion

lår leg

mais sweetcorn

majones mayonnaise

makaroni macaroni

makron macaroon

mandel almond

marengs meringues

marinert marinated

medisterkaker fried meatballs made
  from minced pork

medisterpølse fried or poached pork
  sausage

mel flour

melk milk

meny menu

middag dinner

mjølk milk

moreller cherries

multer cloudberries (wild orange berries)

mørbrad sirloin

nygrodde poteter new potatoes boiled
  in their skins

nype rosehip

nypesuppe rosehip soup (usually served with whipped cream as a dessert)

nyrer kidneys

nøtter nuts

okse beef

oksehale oxtail

oksestek roast beef

ost cheese

ovnsbakt oven-baked

panert coated with breadcrumbs

pannekaker large thin pancakes

pepperrot horseradish

persille parsley

persillerot parsnip

pinnekjøtt salted, dried side of lamb, boiled and served with mashed turnip

pisket krem whipped cream

platte platter of cold meat or fish

plukkfisk poached cod in white sauce

pochert poached

postei pâté, vol-au-vent

poteter potatoes

potet gull crisps

purre leeks

pytt i panne fried, diced meat and potatoes, served with a fried egg

pære pear

pølser frankfurter sausages

pålegg sandwich spread or cold meat for sandwiches

rabarbra rhubarb

ragu stew

rakørret fermented trout

raspeball dumpling made from grated potato

reddiker radishes

reinsdyr reindeer

reke(r) prawns

remulade mayonnaise with chopped gherkins and spices

rett(er) dish(es), course(es)

reven, revet, revne grated

ribbe side of either pork or lamb

rips redcurrants

ris rice

rislapper small rice porridge pancakes eaten hot with jam

ristet toasted, fried, roast

rogn roe

rosenkål brussels sprouts

rosiner raisins

rugbrød rye bread

rullekake swiss roll

rundstykke crusty roll

rødbeter beetroot

rødgrøt med fløte soft red berry 'jelly' with cream

rødkål sweet and sour boiled red cabbage with caraway seeds

rødspette plaice

røkelaks smoked salmon

røket, røkt smoked

røkt svinekam smoked loin of pork

rømme soured cream

rørt(e) uncooked fruit mixed with sugar

rå raw

råkostsalat raw vegetable salad

råkrem whipped cream with yolks of egg

saft juice, squash

saftsuppe red fruit juice soup

salat lettuce; salad

saltpølse salami

sardiner sardines

saus sauce

sei coley

seibiff coley steaks with fried onions

selleri(rot) celeriac

semulegrøt semolina pudding served with red fruit sauce

sennep mustard

sild herring
sitron lemon
sitronbrus lemonade
sjokolade chocolate
skalldyr shellfish
skinke ham
skjell shells; puff pastry 'shells'
slangeagurk cucumber
smultringer doughnuts
smør butter
smørbrød open sandwich
smørgrøt sweet porridge made from white flour, served with cinnamon
snitter small open sandwiches
solbær blackcurrants
sopp mushroom
speilegg fried egg ('sunny side up')
spekemat tray of various kinds of cured and smoked cold meat and fish
spekepølse salami
spekesild cured, raw herring
spekeskinke cured leg of ham
spinat spinach
spisekart menu
stangselleri celery
stappe mashed
stek roast
stekt fried, roasted
stikkelsbær gooseberries
stuing in white or cream sauce
sukker sugar
sukkererter mangetout
sukrede rips redcurrants with sugar
suppe soup
surkål sweet and sour boiled cabbage with caraway seeds (sauerkraut)
sur og søt sweet and sour
sursild cured pickled herring
svin(e) pork
svinekam loin of pork
svor pork crackling

syltet preserved, pickled
syltetøy jam
søt sweet
tartarsaus mayonnaise with chopped egg, onion, capers and gherkins
te tea
terninger diced
terte tart, pastry
tilslørte bondepiker stewed apples with toasted breadcrumbs and cream
tiur capercaillie
tomat tomato
torsk cod
trollkrem whipped cream with egg whites and a sweet sauce
trøfler truffles
tunge tongue
tyttebær cowberries (like cranberries)
tørr dry
urter herbs
urtete herb tea
vafler waffles
valnøtter walnuts
vanilje vanilla
vaniljesaus custard sauce
vann water
vannbakkels choux pastry cakes filled with whipped cream
varm warm, hot
varm(e) retter hot dishes
varme pølser hot dogs
vegetarretter vegetarian dishes
vestkystsalat shellfish salad
vilt game
vindruer grapes
waleskringle choux pastry ring
wienerpølser frankfurter sausages
øl beer
ørret trout
østers oysters
ål eel

POLISH

CONTENTS

INTRODUCTION

Pronunciation

When reading the imitated pronunciation, stress the part that is underlined (usually the last but one syllable). Pronounce each syllable as if it formed part of an English word, and you will be understood sufficiently well. Note especially these points:

a	as in 'assist'
AWN	a nasal sound as in 'sawn' but with the 'n' barely sounded
ay	as in 'pay'
e, eh	'e' as in 'bed'
EN	as the 'en' in 'end' but a nasal sound and barely sounded
g	always hard as in 'get'
H	as the 'ch' in the Scottish word 'loch'
I	as the 'i' sound in 'wine'
J	as the 's' sound in 'leisure'
o	as in 'lot'
u	as in 'luck'
wuh	as the 'w' in 'well' but barely sounded
y	as in 'yes' (apart from *ay* above)
yuh	as the 'y' in 'yes' but barely sounded

Summary of Special Characteristics in Polish

ą	a nasal 'awn' sound as in 'sawn' or the French 'an'
c	'ts' as in 'cats'
ć, cz	'ch' as in 'challenge'
ch	'ch' as in Scottish 'loch'
dz	'j' as in 'jeans' when followed by **i** or **e** but otherwise 'dz' as in 'adze'
dź	'j' as in 'jeans'
dż	'd' as in 'dog' followed by 's' as in 'leisure'
ę	similar to 'en' in 'end' only nasal and barely sounded but, if at the end of the word, pronounced 'e' as in 'bed'

h	'ch' as in Scottish 'loch'
i	'ee' as in 'teeth'
j	'y' as in 'yes'
ł	'w' as in 'window'
ń	similar to the 'ni' in 'companion'
ó	'oo' as in 'soot'
rz	similar to the 's' in 'leisure' or, when it follows p, t or k, 'sh' as in 'shut'
ś, sz	'sh' as in 'shut'
y	similar to the 'i' in 'bit'
ź, ż	similar to the 's' in 'leisure'

Note also the following:
i in the middle of a word following c, dz, n, s or z softens these sounds and remains silent:

ci	'ch' as in 'cheap'
dzi	'j' as in 'jeans'
ni	'n-yuh' sound as the 'ni' in 'companion'
si	'sh' as in 'show'
zi	's' as in 'leisure'

i at the end of a word following c, dz, n, s or z softens the preceding sound but is also pronounced:

ci	'chee' as in 'cheese'
dzi	'jee' as in 'jeep'
ni	'n-yee' as the 'ni' in 'companion' plus 'ee', the 'y' sound being barely perceptible
si	'shee' as in 'sheet'
zi	's' as in 'leisure' plus 'ee'

POLITE FORMS OF ADDRESS

Polite forms of address are commonly used in Polish. In the phrases, the alternatives shown by (*to a man*) and (*to a woman*) indicate the forms to be used. A man is addressed as **pan**, 'Mr' or 'sir', a woman as **pani**, 'madam' or 'Ms'. The familiar forms for 'you', **ty** (*singular*) and **wy** (*plural*), can be used among friends and when speaking to young people.

USEFUL PHRASES

Yes/No
Tak/nie
tak/n-yeh

Thank you
Dziękuję
jENkoo-yeh

No, thank you
Nie, dziękuję
n-yeh jENkoo-yeh

Please
Proszę
prosheh

I don't understand
Nie rozumiem
n-yeh rozoom-yem

Do you speak English/French/German?
Czy mówi pan (*to a man*)/pani (*to a woman*) po angielsku/
  francusku/niemiecku?
chi moovee pan/panee po ang-yelskoo/frantsooskoo/n-yem-yetskoo

I can't speak Polish
Nie mówię po polsku
n-yeh moov-yeh po polskoo

I don't know
Nie wiem
n-yeh v-yem

Please speak more slowly
Proszę mówić wolniej
prosheh mooveech voln-yay

Please write it down for me
Proszę mi to napisać
prosheh mee to napeesach

My name is …
Nazywam się …
nazivam sheh

Pleased to meet you
Bardzo mi miło pana (*to a man*)/panią (*to a woman*) poznać
bardzo mee meewo pana/pan-yAWN poznach

Good morning/afternoon
Dzień dobry
jen-yuh dobri

Good evening
Dobry wieczór
dobri v-yechoor

Good night
Dobranoc
dobranots

Goodbye
Do widzenia
do veedzen-ya

How are you?
Jak się pan (*to a man*)/pani (*to a woman*) miewa?
yak sheh pan/panee m-yeva

Very well, thank you
Dziękuję, dobrze
jɛnkoo-yeh dobjeh

Excuse me, please
Przepraszam
psheprasham

Sorry!
Przepraszam!
psheprasham

I'm really sorry
Bardzo mi przykro
bardzo mee pshikro

Can you help me?
Czy mógłby pan (_to a man_)/mogłaby pani (_to a woman_) mi pomóc?
chi moogwuhbi pan/mogwabi panee mee pomoots

Can you tell me …?
Czy mógłby pan (_to a man_)/mogłaby pani (_to a woman_) mi
   powiedzieć …?
chi moogwuhbi pan/mogwabi panee mee pov-yejech

Can I have …?
Poproszę …?
poprosheh

I would like …
Chciałbym (_man_)/Chciałabym (_woman_) …
Hchawuhbim/Hchawabim

Is there … here?
Czy jest tu …?
chi yest too

Where can I get …?
Gdzie mogę dostać …?
gjeh mogeh dostach

How much is it?
Ile kosztuje?
eeleh koshtoo-yeh

What time is it?
Która jest godzina?
ktoora yest gojeena

I must go now
Muszę już iść
moosheh yooj eesh-ch

I've lost my way
Zgubiłem (*man*)/zgubiłam (*woman*) się
zgoobeewem/zgoobeewam sheh

Cheers!
Na zdrowie!
na zdrov-yeh

Do you take credit cards?
Czy przyjmuje pan (*to a man*)/pani (*to a woman*) karty kredytowe?
chi pshi-yuhmoo-yeh pan/panee karti kreditoveh

Where is the toilet?
Gdzie jest toaleta?
gjeh yest to-aleta

Go away!
Proszę odejść!
prosheh odaysh-ch

I've lost my passport/money/traveller's cheques/credit cards
Zgubiłem (*man*)/zgubiłam (*woman*) paszport/pieniądze/czeki
  podróżne/karty kredytowe
*zgoobeewuhem/zgoobeewuham pashport/p-yenyAWNje/tshekee
  podroojne/karti kreditowe*

Where is the British/US embassy?
Gdzie jest brytyjska/amerykańska ambasada?
gjeh yest britiyska/amerikan-yska ambasada

Is there wheelchair access?
Czy jest tam dostęp dla wózków inwalidzkich?
chi yest tam dostehp dla voozkoov eenva-leejkeeH

Are guide dogs allowed?
Czy psy przewodnicy są dozwolone?
chi psi pshewodneeci sAWN dozwolone

THINGS YOU'LL HEAR

Chwileczkę	One moment
Co słychać?	How are you?
Wszystko w porządku, dziękuję	Very well, thank you
– a co u pana/pani?	– and you?
Do zobaczenia	See you later
Naprawdę?	Is that so?
Nie ma	We haven't got any
Nie rozumiem	I don't understand
Proszę	Here you are, Please
Proszę bardzo	You're welcome
Słucham?	Pardon?
Tak jest	That's right
Uwaga!	Look out!
Wspaniale!	Excellent!

DAYS, MONTHS, SEASONS

Sunday	niedziela	*n-yejela*
Monday	poniedziałek	*pon-yejawek*
Tuesday	wtorek	*vtorek*
Wednesday	środa	*shroda*
Thursday	czwartek	*chvartek*
Friday	piątek	*p-yAWNtek*
Saturday	sobota	*sobota*
January	styczeń	*stichen-yuh*
February	luty	*looti*
March	marzec	*majets*
April	kwiecień	*kv-yechen-yuh*
May	maj	*mI*
June	czerwiec	*cherv-yets*
July	lipiec	*leep-yets*
August	sierpień	*sherp-yen-yuh*
September	wrzesień	*vjeshen-yuh*
October	październik	*paj-jerneek*
November	listopad	*leestopad*
December	grudzień	*groojen-yuh*
Spring	wiosna	*v-yosna*
Summer	lato	*lato*
Autumn	jesień	*yeshen-yuh*
Winter	zima	*jeema*
Christmas	Boże Narodzenie	*boje narodzen-yeh*
Christmas Eve	Wigilia	*veegeel-ya*
New Year	Nowy Rok	*novi rok*
New Year's Eve	Sylwester	*silvester*
Easter	Wielkanoc	*v-yelkanots*

NUMBERS

0 zero *zero*	10 dziesięć *jeshENCh*
1 jeden *yeden*	11 jedenaście *yedenash-cheh*
2 dwa *dva*	12 dwanaście *dvanash-cheh*
3 trzy *tshi*	13 trzynaście *tshinash-cheh*
4 cztery *chteri*	14 czternaście *chternash-cheh*
5 pięć *p-yENch*	15 piętnaście *p-yENtnash-cheh*
6 sześć *shesh-ch*	16 szesnaście *shesnash-cheh*
7 siedem *sh-yedem*	17 siedemnaście *shedemnash-cheh*
8 osiem *oshem*	18 osiemnaście *oshemnash-cheh*
9 dziewięć *jev-yENch*	19 dziewiętnaście *jev-yENtnash-cheh*

20 dwadzieścia *dvajesh-cha*
21 dwadzieścia jeden *dvajesh-cha yeden*
22 dwadzieścia dwa *dvajesh-cha dva*
30 trzydzieści *tshijesh-chee*
40 czterdzieści *chterjesh-chee*
50 pięćdziesiąt *p-yENchjeshAWNt*
60 sześćdziesiąt *shesh-chjeshAWNt*
70 siedemdziesiąt *shedemjeshAWNt*
80 osiemdziesiąt *oshemjeshAWNt*
90 dziewięćdziesiąt *jev-yENchjeshAWNt*
100 sto *sto*
110 sto dziesięć *sto jeshENCh*
200 dwieście *dv-yesh-cheh*
300 trzysta *tshista*
400 czterysta *chterista*
500 pięćset *p-yENchset*
600 sześćset *shesh-chset*
700 siedemset *shedemset*
800 osiemset *oshemset*
900 dziewięćset *jev-yENchset*
1000 tysiąc *tishAWNts*
100,000 sto tysięcy *sto tishENtsi*
1,000,000 milion *meel-yon*

TIME

today	dzisiaj	*jeesh*ı
yesterday	wczoraj	*vch*o*r*ı
tomorrow	jutro	*y*oo*tro*
this week	w tym tygodniu	*vtim tig*o*dn-yoo*
last week	w zeszłym tygodniu	*vzeshwim tig*o*dn-yoo*
next week	w przyszłym tygodniu	*vpshishwim tig*o*dn-yoo*
this morning	dzisiaj rano	*jeesh*ı *r*a*no*
this afternoon	dzisiaj popołudniu	*jeesh*ı *popow*oo*dn-yoo*
this evening	dzisiaj wieczorem	*jeesh*ı *v-yech*o*rem*
tonight	dzisiejszej nocy	*jesh*ay*shay n*o*tsi*
late	późno	*p*oo*jno*
early	wcześnie	*vch*e*shn-yeh*
soon	nie długo	*n-yeh dw*oo*go*
minute	minuta	*meen*oo*ta*
quarter of an hour	kwadrans	*kv*a*drans*
half an hour	pół godziny	*p*oo*wuh goj*ee*ni*
three quarters of an hour	trzy kwadranse	*tji kvadr*a*nseh*
hour	godzina	*goj*ee*na*
every day	codziennie	*tsoj*e*n-yeh*

TELLING THE TIME

There are several ways of telling the time in Polish. For time on the hour, use first, second, third for one, two, three, etc. So 'one o'clock' is **pierwsza** (*p-*y*ervsha*), 'two o'clock' is **druga** (*dr*oo*ga*) and so on. Poles leave out the words 'hour' and 'minutes'.

For time past and to the hour, say the hour followed by the minutes: 'ten past ten' is therefore **dziesiąta dziesięć** (*jesh*AWN*ta jesh*ENCH). 'Ten forty' is **dziesiąta czterdzieści** (*jesh*AWN*ta chterj*e*sh-chee*). Time past the hour can also be expressed using **po** meaning 'after', for example 'ten past ten' is **dziesięć po dziesiątej** (*jesh*ENCH *po jesh*AWN*tay*).

Another way of expressing time to the hour is to use **za** 'before', followed by the minutes and the hour which is approaching: so 'twenty to eleven' is **za dwadzieścia jedenasta** (*za dvaj<u>e</u>sh-cha yeden<u>a</u>sta*).

For half past, use either the past hour followed by thirty, so 'half past ten' is **dziesiąta trzydzieści** (*jesh<u>AWN</u>ta tshij<u>e</u>sh-chee*); or alternatively you can say 'half to' the hour approaching – **w pół do jedenastej** (*v p<u>oo</u>wuh do yeden<u>a</u>stay*).

Kwadrans ('quarter') is sometimes used, so 'quarter past ten' is **kwadrans po dziesiątej** (*kv<u>a</u>drans po jesh<u>AWN</u>tay*).

1 o'clock	pierwsza	p-y<u>e</u>rvsha
2 o'clock	druga	dr<u>oo</u>ga
3 o'clock	trzecia	tsh<u>e</u>cha
4 o'clock	czwarta	chv<u>a</u>rta
5 o'clock	piąta	p-y<u>AWN</u>ta
6 o'clock	szósta	sh<u>oo</u>sta
7 o'clock	siódma	sh<u>oo</u>dma
8 o'clock	ósma	<u>oo</u>sma
9 o'clock	dziewiąta	jev-y<u>AWN</u>ta
10 o'clock	dziesiąta	jesh<u>AWN</u>ta
11 o'clock	jedenasta	yeden<u>a</u>sta
12 o'clock	dwunasta	dvoon<u>a</u>sta
ten past one	dziesięć po pierwszej	jesh<u>E</u>NCH po p-y<u>e</u>rvshay
quarter past one	kwadrans po pierwszej	kv<u>a</u>drans po p-y<u>e</u>rvshay
half past one	w pół do drugiej	vp<u>oo</u>wuh do dr<u>oo</u>g-yay
twenty to two	za dwadzieścia druga	za dvaj<u>e</u>sh-cha dr<u>oo</u>ga
quarter to two	za kwadrans druga, za piętnaście druga	za kv<u>a</u>drans dr<u>oo</u>ga, za p-y<u>E</u>Nt<u>n</u>ash-cheh dr<u>oo</u>ga
at seven o'clock	o siódmej	o sh<u>oo</u>dmay
noon	południe	pow<u>oo</u>dn-yeh
midnight	północ	p<u>oo</u>wuhnots

COMMUNICATIONS

USEFUL WORDS AND PHRASES

code	kod	*kod*
dialling tone	sygnał	*sygnawuh*
email address	adres email	*adres eemeyl*
enquiries	informacja	*eenformats-ya*
extension	wewnętrzny	*vevnENtshni*
mobile phone	telefon komórkowy	*telefon komoorkovi*
number	numer	*noomer*
operator	centrala	*tsentrala*
payphone	automat telefoniczny	*awtomat telefoneechni*
reverse charge call	rozmowa R	*rozmova err*
telephone	telefon	*telefon*
telephone box	budka telefoniczna	*boodka telefoneechna*
telephone card	karta telefoniczna	*karta telefoneechna*
telephone token	żeton	*jeton*
Web site	strona internetowa	*strona eenternetova*
wrong number	pomyłka	*pomiwuhka*

Where is the nearest phone box?
Gdzie jest najbliższa budka telefoniczna?
gjeh yest nIbleejsha boodka telefoneechna

I would like a number in …
Poproszę number w …
poprosheh noomer v

I would like to speak to …
Chciałbym (*man*)/chciałabym (*woman*) rozmawiać z …
Hchawuhbim/Hchawabim rozmav-yach z

My number is …
Mój numer jest …
moo-yuh noomer yest

I would like to reverse the charges
Poproszę rozmowę R
vpoprosheh rozmoveh err

Could you leave him a message?
Czy można zostawić wiadomość?
chi mojna zostaveech v-yadomosh-ch

I'll ring back later
Zadzwonię poźniej
zadzvon-yeh poojn-yay

Sorry, wrong number
Przepraszam, pomyłka
psheprasham pomiwuhka

Please tell him … called (*man/woman*)
Proszę powiedzieć mu, że … dzwonił/dzwoniła
prosheh pov-yejech moo je … dzvon-yeewuh/dzvon-yeewa

Ask him to call me back, please
Proszę, poprosić go żeby oddzwonił
prosheh poprosheech go jebi odzvon-yeewuh

→

298

Jaki jest pana/pani numer?
What is your number?

Przepraszam, ale nie ma go
Sorry, he's not in

Wróci o …
He'll be back at … o'clock

Proszę zadwonić jutro
Please call again tomorrow

Przekażę mu, że pan dzwonił/pani dzwoniła
I'll tell him you called

THINGS YOU'LL SEE

adres email	email address
automatyczne połączenie	direct dialling
budka telefoniczna	telephone box
centrala	operator
fotokopiarka	photocopier
informacja	enquiries
karta telefoniczna	phonecard
kod	code
międzynarodowa	international
nieczynny	out of order
opłata	charges
pogotowie	ambulance
rozmowa miejscowa	local call
rozmowa międzymiastowa	long-distance call
rozmowa zagraniczna	international call
strona internetowa	Web site
żeton	telephone token

HOTELS

Useful Words and Phrases

balcony	balkon	b<u>a</u>lkon
bathroom	łazienka	wa<u>je</u>nka
bed	łóżko	w<u>oo</u>jko
bedroom	sypialnia	sip-<u>ya</u>ln-ya
bill	rachunek	ra<u>hoo</u>nek
breakfast	śniadanie	shn-yad<u>a</u>n-yeh
dining room	jadalnia	yad<u>a</u>ln-ya
dinner	kolacja	kol<u>a</u>ts-ya
double room	pokój dwuosobowy	p<u>o</u>koo-yuh dvoo-osob<u>o</u>vi
foyer	foyer	f<u>o</u>-yeh
full board	pełne utrzymanie	p<u>e</u>wuhneh ootjim<u>a</u>n-yeh
guest house	zajazd	z<u>a</u>-yazd
hotel	hotel	H<u>o</u>tel
inn	gospoda	gosp<u>o</u>da
key	klucz	kl<u>oo</u>ch
lift	winda	v<u>ee</u>nda
lounge	hall	H<u>a</u>l
lunch	obiad	<u>o</u>b-yad
manager	kierownik	k-yer<u>o</u>vneek
reception	recepcja	rets<u>e</u>pts-ya
receptionist (*male*)	recepcjonista	retsepts-yon<u>ee</u>sta
(*female*)	recepcjonistka	retsepts-yon<u>ee</u>stka
restaurant	restauracja	restawr<u>a</u>ts-ya
room	pokój	p<u>o</u>koo-yuh
shower	prysznic	pr<u>i</u>shneets
single room	pokój	p<u>o</u>koo-yuh
	jednoosobowy	yedno-osob<u>o</u>vi
toilet	toaleta	to-al<u>e</u>ta
twin room	pokój z dwoma	p<u>o</u>koo-yuh z dv<u>o</u>ma
	lóżkami	wooj<u>ka</u>mee
youth hostel	schronisko	sHron<u>ee</u>sko
	młodzieżowe	muhwoje<u>jo</u>veh

Have you any vacancies?
Czy ma pan (*to a man*)/pani (*to a woman*) wolne pokoje?
chi ma pan/panee volneh poko-yeh

I have a reservation
Mam rezerwację
mam rezervats-yeh

I'd like a single/double room
Poproszę pokój jednoosobowy/dwuosobowy
poprosheh pokoo-yuh yedno-osobovi/dvoo-osobovi

I'd like a twin room
Poproszę pokój z dwoma lóżkami
poprosheh pokoo-yuh z dvoma woojkamee

Is there satellite/cable TV in the rooms?
Czy jest w pokojach telewizja satelitarna/kablowa?
chi yest w pokoyaн tele-vizya satelee-tarna/kablova

I'd like a room with a bathroom/balcony
Poproszę pokój z łazienką/balkonem
poprosheh pokoo-yuh z wajenkAWN/balkonem

I'd like a room for one night/two/three nights
Poproszę pokój na jedną dobę/dwie/trzy doby
poprosheh pokoo-yuh na yednAWN dobeh/dv-yeh/tshi dobi

What is the charge per night?
Ile kosztuje za dobę?
eeleh koshtoo-yeh za dobeh

There's no hot water/toilet paper/soap
Nie ma ciepłej wody/papieru toaletowego/mydła
n-yeh ma chepway vodi/pap-yeroo to-aletovego/midwa

What time is breakfast/dinner?
O której jest śniadanie/kolacja?
o ktooray yest shn-yadan-yeh/kolats-ya

Please call me at … o'clock
Proszę mnie obudzić o … godzinie
prosheh mn-yeh oboojeech o … gojeen-yeh

Can I have breakfast in my room?
Czy można zjeść śniadanie w pokoju?
chi mojna z-yesh-ch shn-yadan-yeh vpoko-yoo

I'm leaving tomorrow
Wyjeżdżam jutro
vi-yejd-jam yootro

At what time do I have to be out of my room?
O której trzeba opuścić pokój?
o ktooray tsheba opoosh-cheech pokoo-yuh

Can I have the bill, please?
Proszę o rachunek
prosheh o raноonek

I'll pay by credit card
Zapłacę kartą kredytową
zapwatseh kartAWN kreditovAWN

I'll pay cash
Zapłacę gotówką
zapwatseh gotoovkAWN

Can you get me a taxi?
Czy może pan (*to a man*)/pani (*to a woman*) sprowadzić mi taksówkę?
chi mojeh pan/panee sprovajeech mee taksoovkeh

THINGS YOU'LL SEE

ciągnąć	pull
łazienka	bathroom
obiad	lunch
pchnąć	push
prysznic	shower
rachunek	bill
recepcja	reception
restauracja	restaurant
rezerwacja	reservation
śniadanie	breakfast
toaleta, W.C.	toilet
winda	lift
wyjście	exit

THINGS YOU'LL HEAR

Przepraszam, nie mamy wolnych pokoi
I'm sorry, we're full

Nie ma żadnych jednoosobowych pokoi
There are no single rooms left

Nie ma żadnych dwuosobowych pokoi
There are no double rooms left

Ile dób?
How many nights?

Proszę zapłacić z góry
Please pay in advance

Proszę wypełnić formularz
Please fill in this form

SHOPPING

Where is the … department?
Gdzie jest dział z …?
gjeh yest jawuh z

Do you have …?
Czy ma pan (*to a man*)/pani (*to a woman*) …?
chi ma pan/panee

How much is this?
Ile to kosztuje?
eeleh to koshtoo-yeh

Where do I pay?
Gdzie się płaci?
gjeh sheh pwachee

Have you anything cheaper?
Czy jest coś tańszego?
chi yest tsosh tan-yushego

Can I have a receipt?
Czy mogę otrzymać paragon?
chi mogeh otshimach paragon

Can I have a refund?
Proszę o zwrot
prosheh o zvrot

I'm just looking
Chcę tylko popatrzyć
Htseh tilko popatshich

EATING OUT

Poles usually have their main meal of the day relatively early, between 3 and 5 pm. Restaurants, **restauracja** (*restawrats-ya*), fall into four categories: **kat.S** (very high standard), **kat.I**, **kat.II** and **kat.III**. In the better restaurants, you will now pay more but get a wider range of food. Most larger hotels have **kat.S** or **kat.I** restaurants. While small restaurants in the lower categories frequently offer high quality food, **kat.S** restaurants are known for their slow service. There are various other places where you can get food and drink:

Bar – offers both soft and alcoholic drinks, and snacks.

Mleczny bar (*mlechni bar*) – literally a 'milk bar' which is open during the day and where you can eat dishes based on dairy products, cereals, vegetables but no meat or fish. No alcoholic drinks are served. In the **mleczny bar** you go straight to the cashier, tell them what you want to eat, pay and take your receipt to the kitchen window. Then you are called to collect it. The **mleczny bar** is excellent value for money. The **Naleśniki z serem** (*naleshneekee zeh serem*) – pancakes with soft white cheese and sour cream – are well worth trying as are the different types of dumplings.

Cocktail bar – surprisingly these sell no alcoholic drinks, only milk shakes, cream cakes and ice cream.

Kawiarnia (*kav-yarn-ya*) – basically a café offering coffee, tea, soft and alcoholic drinks as well as pastries, cakes and often breakfasts and light snacks.

Winiarnia (*veen-yarn-ya*) – a wine bar. Food is not sold here.

Piwiarnia (*peev-yarn-ya*) – a bar that mainly sells beer. Again food is not usually served. Be careful of the company!

In addition to the traditional places, foreign fast-food chains can now be found in the larger towns.

Restaurants and most cafés have cloakroom facilities and you are expected to tip the cloakroom attendant as well as the toilet attendant. (Don't be surprised if you are asked to pay extra for toilet paper and the use of soap.)

Useful Words and Phrases

beer	piwo	*peevo*
bill	rachunek	*raHoonek*
bottle	butelka	*bootelka*
bowl	miska	*meeska*
cake	ciasto	*chasto*
chef	szef kuchni	*shef kooHnee*
coffee	kawa	*kava*
cup	filiżanka	*feeleejanka*
fixed menu	obiad firmowy	*ob-yad feermovi*
fork	widelec	*veedelets*
glass	szklanka	*shklanka*
knife	nóż	*nooj*
menu	menu,	*men-yoo,*
	jadłospis	*yadwospees*
milk	mleko	*mleko*
plate	talerz	*talej*
receipt	przepis	*pshepees*
sandwich	kanapka	*kanapka*
serviette	serwetka	*servetka*
snack	przekąska	*pshekAWNska*
soup	zupa	*zoopa*
spoon	łyżka	*wijka*
sugar	cukier	*tsook-yer*
table	stolik	*stoleek*
tea	herbata	*Herbata*
teaspoon	łyżeczka	*wijechka*
tip	napiwek	*napeevek*
vodka	wódka	*voodka*
waiter	kelner	*kelner*
waitress	kelnerka	*kelnerka*
water	woda	*voda*
wine	wino	*veeno*
wine list	karta win	*karta veen*

A table for one/two, please
Stolik dla jednej osoby/dwóch osób, proszę
stoleek dla yednay osobi/dvooH osoob prosheh

Can I see the menu?
Czy mogé poprosić o jadłospis?
chi mogeh poprosheech o yadwospees

Can I see the wine list?
Czy mogę poprosić o kartę win?
chi mogeh poprosheech o karteh veen

What would you recommend?
Co pan (*to a man*)/pani (*to a woman*) poleca?
tso pan/panee poletsa

Is this suitable for vegetarians?
Czy to się nadaje dla wegetarianinów?
chi to sheh nadaye dla vegetaryaneenoov

I'm allergic to nuts/shellfish
Jestem uczulony (*man*)/uczulona (*woman*) na orzechy/małże
yestem oochooloni/oochoolona na ojeHi/mawuhje

Do you do children's portions?
Czy ma Pan (*to a man*)/Pani (*to a woman*) porcje dla dzieci?
chi ma pan/panee portsye dla jyechee

Just a cup of coffee, please
Tylko kawę proszę
tilko kaveh prosheh

Waiter/waitress!
Proszę pana/panią!
prosheh pana/pan-yAWN

I only want a snack
Tylko przekąskę proszę
tilko pshek<u>AWN</u>skeh pr<u>o</u>sheh

Is there a set menu?
Czy jest obiad firmowy?
chi yest <u>o</u>b-yad feerm<u>o</u>vi

I didn't order this
Tego nie zamawiałem (*man*)/zamawiałam (*woman*)
t<u>e</u>go n-yeh zamav-y<u>a</u>wem/zamav-y<u>a</u>wam

May we/I have some more ...?
Możemy/mogę poprosić o więcej ...?
moj<u>e</u>mi/m<u>o</u>geh popr<u>o</u>shech o v-y<u>EN</u>tsay

Can we have the bill, please?
Poproszę o rachunek
popr<u>o</u>sheh o raH<u>oo</u>nek

The meal was very good, thank you
Bardzo było smaczne, dziękuję
b<u>a</u>rdzo b<u>i</u>wo sm<u>a</u>chneh jENk<u>oo</u>-yeh

THINGS YOU'LL SEE

restauracja	restaurant
samoobsługa	self-service
smacznego	enjoy your meal
szatnia	cloakroom
szatnia obowiązkowa	cloakroom obligatory
toaleta płatna 200 zł.	charge for toilet 200 złotys
toalety	toilets

MENU GUIDE

agrest gooseberries
babka cake made with eggs and butter
bakalie fruit and nuts
baranina mutton, lamb
barszcz czerwony beetroot soup
bawarka milky tea
bażant pheasant
befsztyk beef steak
bezy meringues
biała kiełbasa white sausage – pork sausage with garlic
biały ser white cheese
bita śmietana whipped cream
bitki wołowe beef cutlets
bliny blinis – small thick, rich pancakes
boczek bacon
bób broad beans
brukiew turnips
brukselki brussel sprouts
brzoskwinia peach
budyń custard-like pudding
bułka white bread
bułeczka roll
buraki beetroot
bryzol grilled beef steak
cebula onion
chleb bread
chleb żytni rye bread
chrzan horseradish
ciasto cake, pastry
cielecina veal
comber saddle
cukier sugar
cynaderki kidneys
cytryna lemon
czarna porzeczka blackcurrants
czekolada chocolate
czereśnia cherry

czosnek garlic
daktyle dates
dania miesne meat dishes
dania rybne fish dishes
dania z drobiu poultry dishes
dania z jaj egg dishes
deser dessert
dorsz cod
drób poultry
dynia pumpkin
dziczyzna game
drożdżówka brioche, Danish pastry
dżem jam
faszerowany stuffed
fasola beans, kidney beans
fasola szparagowa French beans
filet cielecy veal escalope
flądra flounder
frytki chips
galaretka jelly
geś goose
gofry waffles
gołąbki stuffed cabbage leaves
golonka boiled leg of pork
gotowany boiled
grochówka pea soup
groch włoski chickpeas
groszek peas
gruszka pear
grzanki toast, croûtons, garlic bread
gulasz goulash
herbata tea
herbatniki biscuits
homar lobster
indyk turkey
jabłko apple
jagody bilberries
jagnie lamb

jajecznica scrambled eggs
jajka przepiórcze quails' eggs
jajka sadzone fried eggs
jajko egg
jajko na miękko soft-boiled egg
jajko na twardo hard-boiled egg
jarski vegetarian
jarzyny vegetables
jeżyny blackberries
jogurt yoghurt
kabanos dried, smoked pork sausage
kaczka duck
kakao cocoa
kalafior cauliflower
kalarepa kohlrabi
kanapka sandwich
kapuśniak cabbage soup
kapusta cabbage
kapusta czerwona red cabbage
kapusta kiszona sauerkraut
karczochy artichokes
karmazyn haddock
karp carp
kartofelki sauté sauté potatoes
kartoflanka potato soup
kartofle potatoes
kartofle w mundurkach baked potatoes
kasza any type of boiled grain or cereal
kasza gryczana buckwheat
kasza jęczmienna barley porridge
kasza manna semolina
kasza perłowa pearl barley
kaszanka black pudding
kasztany chestnuts
kawa coffee
kawa po staropolsku traditional Polish-style coffee containing spices
kawior caviar
kefir drinking yoghurt
kiełbasa sausage
kisiel a thickened kind of jelly

klopsiki minced meatballs
klopsy minced meatballs
kluski dumplings, noodles
kminek caraway seed
knedle plum dumplings
kołacz rich cake made with eggs and butter
kołduny meatballs made of minced lamb or mutton and boiled
konfitury jam, preserves
koper dill
kopytka potato dumplings
kotlet chop, cutlet
kotlet mielony minced meat burger
kotlet siekany hamburger steak
kotlet wieprzowy pork chop
kotlet wołowy beef cutlet
krem z czekoladą cream sprinkled with chocolate
kremówka a type of millefeuille cake, custard slice
krewetki shrimps
krokiety croquettes
kromka chleba slice of bread
królik rabbit
krupnik barley soup, spiced hot mead
kukurydza corn on the cob
kulebiak pie with meat, fish or cabbage
kura chicken
kurcze po polsku roast chicken stuffed with liver and bread
kurczak pieczony roast chicken
kuropatwa partridge
kwaśne mleko sour milk
leniwe pierogi dumplings with white cheese
leszcz bream
lody ice cream
łazanki dish similar to lasagne
łosoś salmon
łosoś wędzony smoked salmon

majeranek marjoram
majonez mayonnaise
makaron macaroni, pasta
makowiec poppy seed cake
makrela mackerel
maliny raspberries
mandarynki tangerines
marchew carrot
margaryna margarine
marynowany marinated
masło butter
masło roślinne hard margarine made
  from vegetable oil
maślaki large-cap wild mushrooms
maślanka buttermilk
mazurek a kind of thin cake
mielonka a type of luncheon meat
mielony minced
mieso meat
migdały almonds
miód honey
mizeria cucumber in sour cream
mleko milk
mocno wysmażony well-done
morele apricots
mostek cielecy veal brisket
murzynek chocolate cake
mus jabłeczny apple mousse
mus owocowy fruit mousse
musztarda mustard
nadzienie stuffing
naleśniki pancakes
napoleonka a type of millefeuille cake,
  custard slice
nerki kidneys
ocet vinegar
ogórek cucumber
ogórek kiszony cucumber pickled in
  brine
ogórek konserwowy pickled gherkins
  in vinegars

olej oil
oliwa olive oil
oliwki olives
omlet omelette
oszczypek smoked ewes' milk cheese
orzechy włoskie walnuts
orzeszki peanuts
orzeszki laskowe hazelnuts
owoce fruit
ozorki cielece veal tongue
ozór tongue
panierowany in breadcrumbs
papryka paprika
papryka zielona green peppers
parówki frankfurters
pasztecik savoury pastries
pasztet terrine, pâté
pasztetówka liver sausage
pączki doughnuts
pieczarki button mushrooms
pieczeń roast
pieprz pepper
piernik spiced honeycake
pierogi ravioli-like dumplings
pietruszka parsley
pikantny spicy
piwo beer
placek tart
płatki owsiane porridge oats
po angielsku rare
polędwica sirloin
polędwica sopocka smoked fish fillet
pomarańcza orange
pomidor tomato
pory leeks
porter stout
porzeczka czarna blackcurrants
porzeczka czerwona redcurrants
przecier purée
przekładaniec layer cake
przepiórki quail

przystawki entrées
pstrąg trout
ptyś cream puff
pyzy large dumplings
rabarbar rhubarb
racuszki kind of pancake with apple
rak crayfish
ratafia fruit liqueur
renklody greengages
rodzynki raisins
rolmopsy rollmop herrings
rosół broth
rozbef roast beef
rozmaryn rosemary
rumsztyk rumpsteak
ryba fish
ryż rice
rzodkiewki radishes
salceson brawn
sałatka salad
sałatka owocowa fruit salad
sandacz perch
sardynki sardines
sarnina deer
schab joint of pork
ser cheese
sernik cheesecake
sezamki sesame seeds
sękacz fancy layer cake
seler celery
serdelki kind of sausage eaten hot
słodki sweet
smażony fried
sok juice
sola sole
solony salted
sos sauce, gravy
sól salt
stek steak
surówka crudités, raw vegetables
surowy raw

suszone śliwki prunes
szaszłyk mutton kebab
szczupak pike
sznycel escalope
szparagi asparagus
szpinak spinach
sztuka mięsa boiled beef
szynka ham
śledź herring
śliwki plums
śmietana sour cream
śmietanka cream
truskawki strawberries
tuńczyk tuna fish
twarożek soft white cream cheese
tymianek thyme
uszka small parcels of pasta filled with cabbage and mushrooms
wafle wafers
wątroba liver
wędzony smoked
węgorz eel
wieprzowina pork
winogrona grapes
wiśnie cherries
woda water
woda mineralna mineral water
wołowina beef
zając hare
zakąski snacks
zalewajka potato and rye soup
ziemniaki potatoes
zioła herbs
zrazy naturalne fillets of beef
zsiadłe mleko sour milk
zupa soup
z rusztu grilled
z wody poached
żeberka spareribs
żurawina cranberries
żurek sour rye-flour soup

PORTUGUESE

CONTENTS

PRONUNCIATION

When reading the imitated pronunciation, stress the part that is underlined. Pronounce each syllable as if it formed part of an English word, and you will be understood sufficiently well. Avoid pauses between the syllables. The Portuguese tend to link the sound of a terminal vowel with the beginning of the next word. They have a 'soft' pronunciation and will often swallow word endings. Given this complex sound structure it is not always easy to transcribe Portuguese in terms of English spelling. Remember the points below, and your pronunciation will be even closer to the correct Portuguese.

j   As in *ajood<u>a</u>hr* (for **ajudar**): this should be sounded as you would in the s in 'pleasure', soft not hard.

ng As in *nowng* (for **não**): it represents the nasal sound made when the vowels a, e, i, o or u precede m or n, and the nasal diphthongs ão, ãe, ãi, and õe. If you are familiar with the French pronunciation of words like 'monter' and 'environ', then the Portuguese nasal sound should be no problem to you. Don't give the g of *ng* its full (hard) value as in 'sing' – treat the letter combination as a symbol of the nasal sound.

r   As in *rak<u>e</u>ttuh* (for **raqueta**): the initial r of a word should be rolled and aspirated, to create a 'hrr' sound from the back of the throat.

u   As in *k<u>a</u>h-zuh duh b<u>a</u>hn-yoo* (for **casa de banho**): this is a dull u sound, as in the o in 'mother'.

BRAZILIAN PORTUGUESE

For Brazilian Portuguese, word endings are not swallowed as
in Portuguese, and vowel sounds are clearly pronounced. The
ão sound is heavily nasalised as in Portugal. The letter r at the
beginning of a word is pronounced as an h so Rio (as in Rio de
Janeiro) actually sounds like hee-oo. A double r, in the middle
of a word, also sounds like the English h. The s as in **cortes** is
more like a z, whereas in Portuguese it is like the English sh.

   Where the Portuguese word differs from the Brazilian, the
Brazilian equivalent has been given next to it, as in the
following example (**levantar** is the Portuguese and **tirar** the
Brazilian equivalent);

Posso levantar/tirar (*Braz*) **dinheiro com este cartão de crédito?**

Where the whole sentence (or most of the sentence) is different,
the Brazilian equivalent will be repeated on a separate line and
have (*Braz*) preceding it:

Desculpe, enganei-me no número
dushk__oolp__, engan__a__y-muh noo n__oo__meroo

(*Braz*) Desculpe, foi engano
dushk__oolp__, foy en-gah-noh

In Things You'll See or Hear, the whole Brazilian phrase has
been given afterward:

casa de banho/banheiro (*Braz*)	bathroom
não fumadores/não fumantes (*Braz*)	non-smokers

USEFUL PHRASES

Yes/No
Sim/Não
seeng/nowng

Thank you
Obrigado *(said by a man)*
obreegah-doo

Obrigada *(said by a woman)*
obreegah-duh

No, thank you
Não obrigado *(said by a man)*
nowng obreegah-doo

Não obrigada *(said by a woman)*
nowng obreegah-duh

Please
Por favor
poor fuh-vor

I don't understand
Não compreendo/entendo *(Braz)*
nowng kompree-endoo/ain-taing-doh

Do you speak English/French/Spanish?
Fala inglês/francês/espanhol?
fah-luh eenglesh/fransesh/shpan-yoll

I can't speak Portuguese
Eu não falo português
eh-oo nowng fah-loo poortoo-gesh

Please speak more slowly
Por favor, fale mais devagar
poor fuh-vor, fahl mysh duvagahr

Please write it down for me
Não se importa de me escrever isso?
nowng see eemportuh duh mushkrevair eessoo

Good morning
Bom dia
bong dee-uh

Good afternoon
Boa tarde
boh-uh tard

Good night
Boa noite
boh-uh noyt

Goodbye
Adeus/Até logo *(Braz)*
adeh-oosh/ahteh loh-guh

How are you?
Como está?/Como vai? *(Braz)*
koh-moo shta/koh-moo vaee

Excuse me, please
Se faz favor/Com licença *(Braz)*
suh fash fuh-vor/kong lee-saing-sah

Sorry!
Desculpe!
Dushkoolp

317

I'm really sorry
Tenho muita pena/Sinto muito (Braz)
tenyo mweentuh peh-nuh/seento mweentoo

Can you help me?
Pode-me ajudar?
pod-muh ajoodar

Can you tell me …?
Pode-me dizer …?
pod-muh deezair

Can I have …?
Dá-me …?/Me dá …? (Braz)
da-muh/meh dah

I would like …
Queria …/Gostaria … (Braz)
kree-uh/gos-tah-ree-uh

Is there … here?
Há … aqui?
ah … akee

Where is the toilet?
Onde é a casa de banho?
ondeh uh kah-zuh duh bahn-yoo

(Braz) Onde é o banheiro
ong-deh er oh bang-eh-roh

Is there a highchair/cot/baby changing room?
Há uma cadeira alta/um berço/um vestiário para bébés?
ah oomah kah-day-ruh al-tuh/oom behr-su/oom vesh-tee-aree-oo
  pahr-uh beh-besh

Where can I get …?
Onde posso arranjar …?
onduh possoo arranjahr

How much is it?
Quanto custa?
kwantoo kooshtuh

Do you take credit cards?
Aceitam cartões de crédito?
assay-towng kartoyngsh duh kredditoo

Can I pay by cheque?
Posso pagar com cheque?
possoo pagahr kong shek

What time is it?
Que horas são?
kee orush sowng

I must go now
Tenho que me ir embora
tenyo kuh muh eer emboruh

(Braz) Tenho que ir embora
teng-ho keh eer eng-boh-rah

Cheers! *(toast)*
Saúde!
sa-ood

Go away!
Vá-se/Vai *(Braz)* embora!
vassuh/vaee emboruh

Is there wheelchair access?
Têm acesso para cadeiras de rodas?
tay-ayng asseh-soo pahr-uh kah-day-rash deh ro-dash

Are guide dogs allowed?
Permitem cães de guia?
per-mee-tang kaingsh deh guahr-duh

THINGS YOU'LL SEE OR HEAR

aberto	open
casa de banho/ **banheiros** (*Braz*)	toilet
com licença	excuse me
de nada	don't mention it
empurre	push
encerrado	closed
entrada	entrance
fechado	closed
homens	men
horário de abertura	opening times
lavabos	toilet
muito prazer!	pleased to meet you!
não falo inglês	I don't speak English
não faz mal	never mind
não fumar	no smoking
obrigado	thank you
perdão	sorry
perigo de morte	danger
proibida a entrada	no admittance
puxe	pull
saída	exit
sanitários/WC	toilet
senhoras	women
um momento, por favor	one moment, please

DAYS, MONTHS, SEASONS

Sunday	Domingo	*doomeengo*
Monday	Segunda-feira	*segoonduh fay-ruh*
Tuesday	Terça-feira	*tairsuh fay-ruh*
Wednesday	Quarta-feira	*kwartuh fay-ruh*
Thursday	Quinta-feira	*keentuh fay-ruh*
Friday	Sexta-feira	*sayshtuh fay-ruh*
Saturday	Sábado	*sabadoo*
January	Janeiro	*janay-roo*
February	Fevereiro	*fuvray-roo*
March	Março	*marsoo*
April	Abril	*abreel*
May	Maio	*my-oo*
June	Junho	*joon-yoo*
July	Julho	*jool-yoo*
August	Agosto	*agoshtoo*
September	Setembro	*setembroo*
October	Outubro	*oh-toobroo*
November	Novembro	*noovembroo*
December	Dezembro	*dezembroo*
Spring	Primavera	*preema-vairuh*
Summer	Verão	*verowng*
Autumn	Outono	*otoh-noo*
Winter	Inverno	*eemvairnoo*
Christmas	Natal	*natahl*
Christmas Eve	Véspera de Natal	*veshpurruh duh natahl*
Good Friday	Sexta-feira Santa	*seshtuh fay-ruh santuh*
Easter	Páscoa,	*pahsh-kwuh-wuh,*
	Semana Santa	*seman-uh santuh*
New Year	Ano Novo	*ah-noo noh-voo*
New Year's Eve	Véspera de Ano	*veshpuh-ruh dah-noo*
	Novo	*noh-voo*

NUMBERS

0 zero _zairoo_
1 um _oom_
2 dois _doysh_
3 três _tresh_
4 quatro _kwatroo_

5 cinco _seeng-koo_
6 seis _saysh_
7 sete _set_
8 oito _oytoo_
9 nove _nov_

10 dez _desh_
11 onze _onz_
12 doze _doze_
13 treze _trez_
14 catorze/quatorze (Braz) _katorz/katorzeh_
15 quinze _keenz_
16 dezasseis/dezesseis (Braz) _dezassaysh/dez-eh-seh-is_
17 dezassete/dezessete (Braz) _dezaset/dez-eh-setee_
18 dezoito _dezoytoo_
19 dezanove/dezenove (Braz) _dezanov/dez-eh-noh-vee_
20 vinte _veent_
21 vinte e um _veent ee oom_
22 vinte e dois _veent ee doysh_
30 trinta _treentuh_
31 trinta e um _treentuh ee oom_
32 trinta e dois _treentuh ee doysh_
40 quarenta _kwarentuh_
50 cinquenta _seeng-kwentuh_
60 sessenta _sessentuh_
70 setenta _setentuh_
80 oitenta _oytentuh_
90 noventa _nooventuh_
100 cem _sayng_
110 cento e dez _sentoo ee desh_
200 duzentos _doozentoosh_
1000 mil _meel_
1,000,000 um milhão _oom meel-yowng_

TIME

today	hoje	_oje_
yesterday	ontem	_ontayng_
tomorrow	amanhã	_amanyang_
this week	esta semana	_eshtuh semah-nuh_
last week	a semana passada	_uh semah-nuh passah-duh_
next week	a semana que vem	_uh semah-nuh kuh vayng_
this morning	esta manhã/	_eshtuh manyang/_
	hoje de manhã (Braz)	_hoe-gee deh manyang_
this afternoon	esta tarde/	_eshtuh tard_
	hoje à tarde (Braz)	_hoe-gee ah tard_
this evening	esta noite/	_eshtuh noyt_
	hoje de noite (Braz)	_hoe-gee deh noyt_
tonight	esta noite	_eshtuh noyt_
in three days	dentro de três dias/	_dentroo duh tresh dee-ush_
	em três dias (Braz)	_ehm tresh dee-ush_
three days ago	há três dias	_ah tresh dee-ush_
late	tarde	_tard_
early	cedo	_seh-doo_
soon	em breve	_ayng brev_
second	segundo	_segoondoo_
minute	minuto	_meenootoo_
ten minutes	dez minutos	_desh meenootoosh_
quarter of	um quarto de hora/	_oom kwartoo doruh/_
an hour	quinze minutos (Braz)	_king-zeh mee-noo-toes_
half an hour	meia hora	_may-yuh oruh_
hour	a hora	_oruh_
day	o dia	_dee-uh_
week	a semana	_semah-nuh_
fortnight	a quinzena	_keenzaynuh_
month	o mês	_mesh_
year	o ano	_ah-noo_

TELLING THE TIME

In Portuguese you always put the hour first when talking about minutes past the hour. Use the word **e** for 'past' (eg 3.20 = **três e vinte** or 'three and twenty'). For minutes to the hour the minutes come first. Use the word **para** for 'to' (eg 6.40 = **vinte para as sete** or 'twenty to seven'). The 24-hour clock is used officially in timetables and enquiry offices.

In Brazilian Portuguese you never use the word 'quarter' when telling the time, instead you say fifteen to the hour or fifteen past the hour (eg 2.15 = **duas e quinze** and 2.45 = **quinze para as três**).

one o'clock	uma hora	<u>oo</u>muh <u>o</u>ruh
ten past one	uma e dez	<u>oo</u>muh ee desh
quarter past one	uma e um quarto/ uma e quinze (Braz)	<u>oo</u>muh ee oom kw<u>a</u>rtoo/<u>oo</u>mah eh <u>king</u>-zeh
twenty past one	uma e vinte	<u>oo</u>muh ee veent
half past one	uma e meia	<u>oo</u>muh ee m<u>ay</u>-yuh
twenty to two	vinte para as duas	veent prash d<u>oo</u>-ush
quarter to two	um quarto para as duas/quinze para as duas (Braz)	oom kw<u>a</u>rtoo prash d<u>oo</u>-ush/<u>king</u>-seh pah-rah as d<u>oo</u>-as
ten to two	dez para as duas	desh prash d<u>oo</u>-ush
two o'clock	duas horas	d<u>oo</u>-uz <u>o</u>rush
13.00 (1 pm)	treze horas	tr<u>e</u>zee <u>o</u>rush
16.30 (4.30 pm)	dezasseis e trinta/ dezesseis e trinta (Braz)	dezass<u>ay</u>z ee tr<u>e</u>entuh dez-eh-<u>seh</u>-is ee tr<u>e</u>entuh
20.10 (8.10 pm)	vinte e dez	veent ee desh
at half past five	às cinco e meia	ash s<u>ee</u>ng-koo ee m<u>ay</u>-yuh
at seven o'clock	às sete horas	ash set <u>o</u>rush
noon	meio-dia	m<u>ay</u>-yoo-d<u>ee</u>-uh
midnight	meia-noite	m<u>ay</u>-yuh-n<u>oy</u>t

COMMUNICATIONS

Useful Words and Phrases

code	o indicativo/	eendeekuh-*teevoo*/
	o código (Braz)	*coh*-de-go
dialling tone	o sinal de chamada	seen*al* deh shum*ah*-duh
email address	o endereço de email	endeh-re-soo deh ee-mayl
emergency	a emergência	eemer-j*enss*-yuh
extension	a extensão	eeshten*sowng*
number	o número	n*oo*meroo
operator	a telefonista	tulluh-foon*eesh*tuh
payphone	o telefone público/	tulluh-fonn p*oo*blikoo/
	o orelhão (Braz)	oh-reh-lee-aw
reverse charge	a chamada paga	sham*ah*-duh p*ah*-guh
call	no destinatário/	noo dushteenat*ar*-yoo/
	a chamada a cobrar (Braz)	sha-*mah*-da ah *ko*-bra
telephone	o telefone	tulluh-f*onn*
telephone box	a cabina telefónica/	kab*ee*nuh tulluh-fonnikuh/
	o orelhaõ (Braz)	oh-reh-lee-aw
telephone	a lista telefónica/	l*ee*shtuh tulluh-fonnikuh/lees-tah
directory	a lista telefônica (Braz)	teh-leh-*foh*-nee-ka

Where is the nearest phone box?
Onde fica a cabina telefónica/o orelhão(Braz) mais próxima?
onduh feekuh uh kabeenuh tulluh-fonnikuh/oo oh-reh-lee-aw mysh prossimuh

I would like a number in …
Queria um número em …
kree-uh oom noomeroo ayng

I would like to speak to …
Queria falar com …
kree-uh falahr kong

My number is …
O meu número de telefone é o …
oo meh-oo noomeroo duh tulluh-fonn eh oo

Hello, this is … speaking
Está, é o/a …
shtah, eh oo/uh

(*Braz*) Alô, aqui é o/a …
ah-low, a-key eh oh/ah

Is that …?
É o/a …?
eh oo/uh

Could you leave him a message?
Pode-lhe deixar um recado?
podl-yuh dayshahr oom rekah-doo

Sorry, I've got the wrong number
Desculpe, enganei-me no número
dushkoolp, enganay-muh noo noomeroo

(*Braz*) Desculpe, foi engano
dushkoolp, foy en-gah-noh

I'll ring back later
Volto a telefonar mais tarde
voltoo uh tulluh-foonar mysh tard

What's your fax number/email address?
Qual é o seu número de fax/endereço de email?
kwal eh oo she-oo noo-meyro deh fax/endeh-re-soo deh ee-mayl

Can I send an email/fax from here?
Posso enviar um email/um fax daqui?
possoo envee-ahr oom ee-mayl/man-dahr oom fax duh-kee

THINGS YOU'LL HEAR

Com quem quer falar?
Whom would you like to speak to?

Quem fala?
Who's speaking?

De que número fala?
What is your number?

Desculpe, mas ele não está
(Braz) Sinto muito, mas ele não está
Sorry, he's not in

Volte a telefonar amanhã, por favor
Please call again tomorrow

Eu digo-lhe que telefonou
I'll tell him you called

THINGS YOU'LL SEE

avariado/não funciona (*Braz*)	out of order
cabina telefónica	telephone box
cartão telefónico	phonecard
chamada internacional	international call
chamada local	local call
correio electrónico	email
endereço de email	email address
fax	fax machine
informações	enquiries
página na internet/web site (*Braz*)	Web site
serviço internacional	international calls
tarifas	charges
telefone	telephone
telemóvel/cellular (*Braz*)	mobile phone

HOTELS

balcony	a varanda	*varanduh*
bathroom	a casa de banho/	*kah-zuh duh bahn-yoo/*
	o banheiro (*Braz*)	*bang-eh-roh*
bed	a cama	*kah-muh*
bedroom	o quarto	*kwartoo*
bill	a conta	*kontuh*
breakfast	o pequeno almoço/	*pekeh-noo almoh-soo/*
	o café da manhã (*Braz*)	*café dah mang-nya*
dining room	a sala de jantar	*sah-lah duh jantahr*
dinner	o jantar	*jantahr*
double room	o quarto de casal	*kwartoo duh kazal*
foyer	o foyer/o salão (*Braz*)	*fwy-ay/sahlang*
full board	pensão completa	*payng-sowng komplettuh*
half board	meia-pensão	*may-yuh payng-sowng*
hotel	o hotel	*oh-tell*
key	a chave	*shahv*
lift	o ascensor/	*ash-sayng-sor/*
	o elevador (*Braz*)	*eh-lev-ah-door*
lounge	a sala	*sah-luh*
lunch	o almoço	*almoh-soo*
manager	o gerente	*jerrent*
reception	a recepção	*russepsowng*
receptionist	o recepcionista	*russepss-yooneeshtuh*
restaurant	o restaurante	*rushtoh-rant*
room	o quarto	*kwartoo*
room service	o serviço de quartos	*sur-veeso duh kwartoosh*
shower	o duche/o chuveiro (*Braz*)	*doo-sh sho-veh-roh*
single room	o quarto individual/	*kwartoo eendeeveedwal/*
	de solteiro (*Braz*)	*duh sol-teh-roh*
toilet	a casa de banho/	*kah-zuh duh bahn-yoo/*
	banheiro (*Braz*)	*bah-nhei-roh*
twin room	o quarto com duas	*kwartoo kong doo-ush*
	camas	*kah-mush*

Have you any vacancies?
Têm vagas?
t<u>a</u>y-ayng v<u>a</u>h-gush

I have a reservation
Eu fiz uma reserva
<u>e</u>h-oo feez <u>oo</u>ma rez<u>ai</u>rvuh

I'd like a single/double room
Queria um quarto individual/de casal
kr<u>ee</u>-uh oom kw<u>a</u>rtoo eendeeveedw<u>a</u>l/duh kaz<u>a</u>l

(Braz) Queria um quarto de solteiro/de casal
kr<u>ee</u>-uh oom kw<u>a</u>rtoo dee sol-<u>teh</u>-roh/duh kaz<u>a</u>l

I'd like a twin room
Queria um quarto com duas camas
kr<u>ee</u>-uh oom kw<u>a</u>rtoo kong d<u>oo</u>-ush k<u>a</u>h-mush

I'd like a room with a bathroom/balcony
Queria um quarto com casa de banho/com varanda
kr<u>ee</u>-uh oom kw<u>a</u>rtoo kong k<u>a</u>h-zuh duh b<u>a</u>nyoo/kong var<u>a</u>nduh

(Braz) Queria um quarto com o banheiro/com varanda
kr<u>ee</u>-uh oom kw<u>a</u>rtoo kong oh bang-<u>eh</u>-roh/kong var<u>a</u>nduh

I'd like a room for one night/three nights
Queria um quarto só por uma noite/três noites
kr<u>ee</u>-uh oom kw<u>a</u>rtoo soh poor <u>oo</u>muh noyt/poor tresh noytsh

Is there satellite/cable TV in the rooms?
Os quartos têm tv via satélite/tv por cabo?
osh kwartoosh tay-ayng teh-vea vee-uh sateh-lee-tuh/teh-vee poor ka-bu

What is the charge per night?
Qual é o preço por noite?
kwal eh oo pr<u>e</u>h-soo poor noyt

When is breakfast/dinner?
A que horas é o pequeno almoço/o jantar?
uh kee oruz eh oo pekeh-noo almoh-soo/oo jantahr

(*Braz*) A que horas é o café da manhã/o jantar?
uh kee oruz eh oo café deh mang-nya/oo jantahr

Would you have my luggage brought up, please?
Pode-me/Poderia (*Braz*) levar a bagagem, por favor?
pod-muh/poh-deh-ree-ah luhvahr uh bagah-jayng, poor fuh-vor

Please call me at … o'clock
Chame-me às … horas, por favor
shamu-muh ash … orush, poor fuh-vor

Can I have breakfast in my room?
Posso tomar o pequeno almoço no quarto?
possoo toomahr oo pekeh-noo almoh-soo/noo kwartoo

(*Braz*) Posso tomar o café da manhã no quarto?
possoo toomahr oo café deh mang-nya noo kwartoo

My room number is …
O número do meu quarto é o …
oo noomeh-roo doo meh-oo kwartoo eh oo

I'm leaving tomorrow
Vou-me embora amanhã
voh-muh emboruh amanyang

Can I have the bill, please?
A conta, por favor
uh kontuh, poor fuh-vor

Can you get me a taxi?
Pode-me chamar um taxi?
pod-muh shamahr oom taksee

THINGS YOU'LL SEE

água fria	cold water
água quente	hot water
almoço	lunch
banheira	bathtub
casa de banho/	bathroom, toilet
banheiro (*Braz*)	
chuveiro	shower
conta	bill
elevador	lift
jantar	dinner
pequeno almoço/	breakfast
café da manhã (*Braz*)	
recepção	reception
reserva	reservation
restaurante	restaurant
saída de emergência	emergency exit
telefonista	switchboard operator

THINGS YOU'LL HEAR

Tenho muita pena, mas estamos cheios
(*Braz*) Sinto muito, mas estamos cheios
I'm very sorry, but we're full

Não temos quartos individuais
(*Braz*) Não temos quarto de solteiros
There are no single rooms left

Não há vagas
No vacancies

É/Por (*Braz*) favor pagar adiantado
Please pay in advance

SHOPPING

Where is the … department?
Onde é a secção de …?
ondeh uh seksowng duh

Do you have …?
Tem …?
tayng

How much is this?
Quanto é que isto custa?
kwantoo eh kee eeshtoo kooshtuh

Where do I pay?
Onde é que se paga?
ondeh kuh suh pah-guh

Do you take credit cards?
Aceita cartões de crédito?
asay-tuh car-tow-eensh de credee-too

Can I have a receipt?
Pode-me/Poderia (*Braz*) dar uma factura/um recibo (*Braz*),
  por favor?
pod-muh/poh-deh-ree-ah dar oomuh faktooruh/oom heh-see-bow,
  poor fuh-vor

Can I have a refund?
Pode-me/Pode (*Braz*) devolver o dinheiro?
pod-muh/poh-deh duvvolvair oo deen-yay-roo

That's fine
Está bem
shtah bayng

EATING OUT

Portugal and Brazil offer a variety of places to eat:

Café: A general café that sells all kinds of food and drinks and is well worth trying for a quick snack. Full meals are also often available.

Churrascaria: A restaurant specializing in barbecued dishes.

Confeitaria *(Braz)*: A bakery/café that sells bread and cakes, and also serves snacks, juices, milkshakes and coffee.

Esplanada: Pavement café

Lanchonete *(Braz)*: A café-bar selling sandwiches and light meals as well as cakes, sweets and drinks.

Pastelaria: A cake shop that also serves tea, coffee, beer, sandwiches and light snacks. In Brazil, this is a place specializing in **pasteis** (savoury pastries with fillings), and other snacks, but not cakes or sweet pastries.

Restaurante: Restaurant.

Snack-bar: A combined café, bar and restaurant not to be confused with the English idea of a snack-bar. Service is provided at the counter or, for a little extra, at a table. There is usually a good variety of set menus at reasonable prices (look for **pratos combinados** or, in Brazil, **pratos do dia** – dish of the day).

Useful Words and Phrases

beer	a cerveja	ser_vay_-juh
bill	a conta	k_o_ntuh
bottle	a garrafa	garr_ah_-fuh
bowl	a tigela	teej_e_lluh
cake	o bolo	b_oh_-loo
chef	o cozinheiro	koozeen-y_ay_-roo
coffee	o café	kuff_eh_
cup	a chávena/a xícara (Braz)	sh_a_venuh/she-_ka-rah_
fork	o garfo	g_a_rfoo
glass	o copo	k_o_poo
knife	a faca	f_ah_-kuh
menu	a ementa/o cardápio (Braz)	eem_e_ntuh/car-_dap_-eo
milk	o leite	layt
plate	o prato	pr_ah_-too
receipt	o recibo	russ_ee_boo
restaurant	o restaurante	rushtoh-r_a_nt
sandwich	a sandes/	sandj/
	o sanduíche (Braz)	sand-_weech_-eh
serviette	o guardanapo	gwarduh-n_a_poo
snack	a refeição ligeira/	refay-s_ow_ng leej_a_yruh/
	o lanche (Braz)	lang-sheh
soup	a sopa	s_oh_ppuh
spoon	a colher	kool-y_ai_r
sugar	o açúcar	ass_oo_kar
table	a mesa	m_e_zuh
tea	o chá	sha
teaspoon	a colher de chá	kool-y_ai_r duh sha
tip	a gorjeta	goorj_e_tuh
waiter	o empregado de mesa/	empreg_ah_-doo duh m_e_zuh/
	a garçom (Braz)	gah-_song_
waitress	a empregada de mesa/	empreg_ah_-duh duh m_e_zuh/
	a garçonete (Braz)	gah-song-_etche_
water	a água	_ah_g-wuh
wine	o vinho	v_ee_nyoo
wine list	a lista dos vinhos	l_ee_shtuh doosh v_ee_nyoosh

A table for one, please
Uma mesa para uma pessoa, por favor
_oo_muh m_e_zuh p_a_r-uh _oo_muh pess_o_h-uh, poor fuh-v_o_r

A table for two/three, please
Uma mesa para duas/três pessoas, por favor
_oo_muh m_e_zuh p_a_r-uh d_oo_-ush/tresh pess_o_h-ush, poor fuh-v_o_r

Can we see the menu, please?
Pode trazer a ementa/o cardápio (Braz), por favor?
pod traz_ai_r uh eem_e_ntuh/oh car-_dap_-eo, poor fuh-v_o_r

Can we see the wine list, please?
Pode trazer a lista dos vinhos, por favor?
pod traz_ai_r uh l_ee_shtuh doosh v_e_enyoosh, poor fuh-v_o_r

Do you do children's portions?
Servem porções para crianças?
servaing poo-soyngsh pahr-uh kree-ang-sash

What would you recommend?
O que é que nos aconselha?
oo kee eh kuh nooz akons_e_ll-yuh

(Braz) O que pode sugerir?
oo kee p_oh_deh s_oo_jeh-reer

Is this suitable for vegetarians?
Isto é apropriado para vegetarianos?
eeshtoo eh aproo-pree-ahdoo pahr-uh veh-jeh-tah-ree-ahnoos

I'd like …
Queria …
kr_ee_-uh

Just a cup of coffee, please
Só um café, por favor
soh oom kuffeh, poor fuh-vor

Waiter!/Waitress!
Se faz favor!
suh fash fuh-vor

(*Braz*) Garçom! Garçonete!
gah-song gah-song-etche

Can we have the bill, please?
Pode trazer a conta, por favor?
pod trazair uh kontuh, poor fuh-vor

I only want a snack
Só quero uma refeição ligeira
soh kairoo oomuh ruffay-sowng leejay-ruh

(*Braz*) Só quero lanchar
soh kairoo lang-shah

Is there a set menu?
Qual é o prato do dia?
kwal eh prato doh dea

I didn't order this
Eu não pedi isto
eh-oo nowng pedee eeshtoo

May we have some more …?
Pode trazer mais …?
pod trazair mysh

The meal was very good, thank you
A comida estava óptima/ótima, obrigado
uh koomeeduh shtah-vuh ottimmuh/oh-ti-moh, obgrigah-doo

MENU GUIDE

açorda thick bread soup
açúcar sugar
aipo celery
alcachofras artichokes
alface lettuce
alho garlic
alho francês leek
almôndegas meatballs
alperces apricots
amêijoas clams
ameixas plums
amêndoas almonds
ao natural plain
arroz rice
arroz doce sweet rice dessert
atum tuna
avelãs hazelnuts
azeitonas olives
bacalhau cod
bacalhau à Zé do Pipo cod in egg sauce
batata assada baked potato
batata palha thinly cut chips
batatas potatoes
batatas cozidas boiled potatoes
batatas fritas french fries
batidos/batida (Braz) milkshakes
bem passado well done
berbigão clam-like shellfish
beringelas aubergines
besugos sea bream (fish)
beterraba beetroot
bica small black coffee
bifanas pork slice in a roll
bife steak
bife à cortador thick, tender steak
bife de alcatra rump steak
bife de atum tuna steak
bife grelhado grilled steak

bifes de peru turkey steaks
bifinhos de porco small slices of pork
bola de carne meatball cooked in dough
bolo cake
borrego à moda do Minho marinated lamb in the Minho style
branco white
cachorros/cachorro quente (Braz) hot dogs
café coffee
café pingado espresso coffee with a touch of milk
caldeirada fish stew
caldo soup
camarões prawns
canela cinnamon
canja de galinha chicken soup
caracóis snails
caranguejos crabs
carapaus mackerel
caril curry
carioca small weak black coffee
carne à jardineira meat and vegetable stew
carne de vaca assada roast beef
carne de vaca guisada stewed beef
carne estufada stewed meat
carneiro mutton
carnes meats
carnes frias selection of cold meats
castanhas chestnuts
cerejas cherries
cerveja beer
chá de limão lemon tea
chá de mentol mint tea
chanfana de porco pork casserole
chocolate quente hot chocolate
chocos cuttlefish

chouriço spiced sausage
churros long, tube-shaped fritters
cimbalino espresso coffee
codorniz quail
coelho rabbit
cogumelos mushrooms
compota stewed fruit
conquilhas baby clams
coração heart
corvina large sea fish
costeletas chops
couve branca white cabbage
couve-flor cauliflower
couve roxa red cabbage
couves de bruxelas Brussels sprouts
couves guisadas com salsichas stewed cabbage and sausage
cozido à portuguesa Portuguese stew (with chicken, sausage etc)
creme de marisco cream of shellfish soup
doce dessert, jam, sweet made from eggs and sugar
doce de ovos custard-like sweet made from eggs and sugar
dourada dory (sea fish)
ementa menu
empadão de carne large meat pie
empadão de peixe large fish pie
encharcada sweet made of almonds and eggs
enguias eels
ensopado de borrego lamb stew
ensopado de enguias eel stew
entrecosto entrecôte
ervilhas peas
escalope panado breaded escalope
espargos asparagus
esparguete à bolonhesa spaghetti bolognese
esparregado puréed spinach

espetada kebab
faisão pheasant
farófias whipped egg white with cinnamon
farturas long, tube-shaped fritters
fatias recheadas slices of bread with fried mince
febras de porco thin pork slices
feijão verde French bean
feijoada bean stew
figos figs
filete fillet
filhozes sugared buns
folhado de carne meat roll with puff pastry
folhado de salsicha sausage roll
frango chicken
frango assado roast chicken
frango na púcara chicken casserole with port and almonds
fruta fruit
funcho fennel
galão large milky coffee
galinha de África guinea fowl
galinha de fricassé chicken fricassee
gambas prawns
garoto small milky coffee
gelado ice cream
gelado de baunilha vanilla ice cream
geleia preserve
groselha currant similar to blackcurrant
iogurte yoghurt
iscas à portuguesa fried liver and boiled potatoes
lagosta lobster
lagostins crayfish
lampreia à moda do Minho marinated lamprey served in the Minho style
lampreia de ovos egg dessert shaped as a lamprey
laranjas oranges

lasanha lasagne
leitão à Bairrada suckling pig from Bairrada
leite milk
leite creme light custard with cinnamon
língua tongue
linguado à meunière sole meunière
linguado grelhado/frito/no forno grilled/fried/baked sole
lista menu
lombo de porco loin of pork
lombo de vaca sirloin
lulas squid
maçã assada baked apple
maçãs apples
macedónia de frutas fruit cocktail
mal passado rare
manteiga butter
marinada marinade
marisco shellfish
marmelos quince
mazagrin iced coffee with lemon
meia de leite large white coffee
meia desfeita cod and chickpeas with olive oil and vinegar
melancia watermelon
melão melon
mexilhões mussels
migas à alentejana thick bread soup
mil folhas sweet, flaky pastry
molho sauce
molho branco white sauce
molho holandês hollandaise sauce
molho inglês brown sauce
molho velouté white sauce made from egg yolks and cream
morangos strawberries
morena beer
mousse de fiambre ham mousse
napolitanas long, flat biscuits
nêsperas loquats (fruit)

nozes walnuts
omolete/omelete (Braz) omelette
ovo estrelado fried egg
ovo quente soft-boiled egg
ovos escalfados poached eggs
ovos mexidos scrambled eggs
ovos verdes stuffed eggs
pão de centeio rye bread
pão de milho corn bread
pão integral wholemeal bread
pão torrado toasted bread
pargo sea bream
parrilhada fish grill
pastéis de nata puff pastry with egg custard filling
pastéis de Tentugal custard pie with almonds and nuts
pastelinhos de bacalhau cod fishcakes
pataniscas salted cod fritter
pato assado roast duck
pato com laranja duck à l'orange
peixe fish
peixe espada swordfish
pequeno almoço continental breakfast
pêras pears
perdizes na púcara partridge casserole
perna de carneiro leg of lamb
peru turkey
pescada cozida boiled hake
pêssego careca nectarine
pêssegos peaches
pimenta pepper
pimentos peppers (red or green)
piperate pepper stew
pratos combinados mixed dishes
pregos thin slice of steak in a roll
pudim de laranja orange flan
pudim de ovos egg pudding
pudim flan type of crème caramel
puré de batata mashed potatoes
puré de castanhas chestnut purée

queijo cheese
rabanadas French toast
raia skate
remoulade dressing with mustard and herbs
requeijão curd cheese
rillete potted pork and goose meat
rins kidneys
rissol rissole
robalo rock bass
rolo de carne meat loaf
sabayon dessert with egg yolks and white wine
sal salt
salada salad
salada mista mixed salad
salmão salmon
salmão fumado smoked salmon
salmonetes grelhados grilled mullet
salsicha sausage
sandes sandwich
santola spider crab
santola gratinada spider crab au gratin
sapateira spider crab
sardinhas assadas grilled sardines
sobremesas desserts
solha flounder
sonhos dried dough with cinnamon
sopa soup
sumo juice
toranja grapefruit
torresmos small rashers of bacon
tortilha Spanish omelette (with potato)
tosta toasted sandwich
toucinho do céu egg dessert
truta trout
uvas brancas/pretas white/black grapes
veado assado roast venison
vieiras recheadas stuffed scallops
vinagre de estragão tarragon vinegar
xarope syrup

BRAZILIAN MENU GUIDE

abacaxi pineapple
acarajé fried bean dumpling
angu polenta
bacalhoada baked salt cod with potato
bife steak
bobó de camarão cassava and prawns
caldo de cana sugarcane juice
carne de boi/vaca beef
carne de sol dried salt beef
churrasco barbecued meat
cocada dessert made of coconut
couve a mineira chopped spring greens
coxinha de galinha chicken dumplings
damasco apricot
dendê palm oil
empadinha pie
farofa side dish of cassava flour and eggs
feijão preto black beans
feijoada black bean and meat stew
galinha/frango chicken
goiaba guava
linguiça sausage
mamão papaya
mandioca/aipim cassava
maracujá passion fruit
moqueca fish or prawn stew
palmito palm heart
pão de queijo cheese bread
pastel thin fried pasty
pirão savoury cream
porco pork
pudim creme caramel
quibe deep fried minced meat
quindim coconut dessert
salgadinho savoury filled pastries
siri crab
tutu mashed beans with eggs and bacon
vatapá spicy thick cream
xinxim de galinha chicken with prawns

SPANISH

CONTENTS

INTRODUCTION

PRONUNCIATION

When reading the imitated pronunciation, stress the part that is underlined. Pronounce each syllable as if it formed part of an English word and you will be understood sufficiently well. Remember the points below and your pronunciation will be even closer to the correct Spanish.

g	always hard as in 'get'
H	represents the guttural sound of 'ch'
I	pronounced as 'eye'
ow	as in 'cow'
s	always sound the Spanish 's' as a double 'ss' as in 'missing', *never* like the 's' in 'easy'
th	as in 'thin', *not* as in 'they'
y	always as in 'yet', *not* as in 'eye' (eg **bien** *byen*, **siento** *sy<u>en</u>toh*)

Don't be worried by the varying pronunciations you are certain to hear in some parts of Spain. An example is the sounding of 'z' (and of 'c' before e or i) like an English 's' – in this instance we recommend that you don't copy it, but lisp the sound as we have imitated it. Similarly, in certain circumstances, the Spanish 'v' can be pronounced as either a 'v' or a 'b', so that **vaca** sounds like 'baca'.

GENDERS AND ARTICLES

Spanish has two genders for nouns – masculine and feminine. We generally give the definite article ('the') – **el** for masculine nouns, **la** for feminine nouns, **los** for masculine plural nouns and **las** for feminine plural nouns. Where the indefinite article ('a, an') is more appropriate, we have given **un** for masculine nouns and **una** for feminine nouns, or the words for 'some' – **unos** (masculine) and **unas** (feminine).

USEFUL PHRASES

Yes, No, OK etc

Yes/No
Sí/No
see/noh

OK
Vale
baleh

That's fine
Está bien
esta byen

That's right
Eso es
essoh ess

Greetings, Introductions

How do you do? Pleased to meet you
¿Qué tal?, mucho gusto
keh tal, mootchoh goostoh

Good morning/good evening/good night
Buenos días/buenas tardes/buenas noches
bweh-noss dee-ass/bweh-nass tardess/bweh-nass notchess

Goodbye/Bye
Adiós
ad-yoss

How are you?   *(familiar)*
¿Cómo está usted?   ¿Cómo estás?
koh-moh esta oosteh   *koh-moh estass*

My name is …
Me llamo …
meh yah-moh

343

What's your name? *(familiar)*
¿Cómo se llama usted?   ¿Cómo te llamas?
k<u>oh</u>-moh seh y<u>ah</u>-ma oost<u>eh</u>   k<u>oh</u>-moh teh y<u>ah</u>-mass

This is … *(introducing a man/woman)*
Éste/ésta es …
<u>e</u>steh/<u>e</u>sta ess

Hello/Hi!
¡Hola!
<u>oh</u>-la

PLEASE, THANK YOU, APOLOGIES

Thank you/No, thank you
Gracias/No, gracias
gr<u>a</u>th-yass/noh gr<u>a</u>th-yass

Please
Por favor
por fa-v<u>or</u>

Excuse me! *(when sneezing, etc.)*
¡Perdón!
pair-d<u>on</u>

Sorry!
¡Perdón!/Lo siento
pair-d<u>on</u>/loh sy<u>e</u>ntoh

WHERE, HOW, ASKING

Excuse me, please *(to get past)*
¿Me hace el favor?
meh <u>ah</u>-theh el fa-v<u>or</u>

Can you tell me …?
¿Puede decirme …?
pw<u>eh</u>-deh deth<u>ee</u>r-meh

Would you like a …?
¿Quiere un/una …?
kyeh-reh oon/oona

(familiar)
¿Quieres un/una …?
kyeh-rehs oon/oona

Would you like to …?
¿Le gustaría …?
leh goostaree-a

(familiar)
¿Te gustaría …?
teh goostaree-a

Is there … here?
¿Hay … aquí?
i … akee

What's that?
¿Qué es eso?
keh ess esso

How much is it?
¿Cuánto es?
kwantoh ess

Where is the …?
¿Dónde está el/la …?
dondeh esta el/la

Is there wheelchair access?
¿Hay acceso para sillas de ruedas?
i akthesoh a parra seeyahs de rooedas

Are there facilities for the disabled?
¿Hay acceso a minusválidos?
i akthesoh a meenoosvaleedos

ABOUT ONESELF

I'm from …
Soy de …
soy deh

I'm … years old
Tengo … años
teng-goh … ahn-yoss

I'm a …
Soy …
soy

I'm married/divorced
Estoy casado/divorciado
estoy kasadoh/deevorss-yah-doh

I'm single
Soy soltero
soy soltairoh

I have … sisters/brothers/children
Tengo … hermanas/hermanos/hijos
teng-goh … airmah-nass/airmah-noss/ee-Hoss

HELP, PROBLEMS

Can you help me?
¿Puede ayudarme?
pweh-deh ayoodarmeh

I don't understand
No comprendo
noh komprendoh

Does anyone here speak English?
¿Hay alguien aquí que hable inglés?
i algyen akee keh ahbleh eengless

I can't speak Spanish
No hablo español
noh ah-bloh esspan-yoll

I don't know
No sé
noh seh

Please speak more slowly
Por favor, hable más despacio
por fa-vor ah-bleh mass desspath-yoh

Please write it down for me
Por favor, escríbamelo
por fa-vor eskreeba-meh-loh

I've lost my way
Me he perdido
meh eh pairdeedoh

Go away!
¡Váyase!
vah-ya-seh

LIKES, DISLIKES, SOCIALIZING

I like/love …
Me gusta/encanta el/la …
meh goosta/enkanta el/la

I don't like …
No me gusta el/la …
noh meh goosta el/la

I hate …
Detesto …
detestoh

Do you like …?
¿Le gusta …?
leh goosta

It's delicious/awful!
¡Es delicioso/horrible!
ess deleeth-yohsoh/orreebleh

I don't drink/smoke
No bebo/fumo
noh beboh/foomoh

Do you mind if I smoke?
¿Le importa que fume?
leh eemporta keh foomeh

What would you like (to drink)?
¿Qué quiere (beber/tomar)?
keh kyeh-reh bebair/tomar

I would like a …
Quería …
keh-ree-a

Nothing for me, thanks
No quiero nada, gracias
noh kyeh-roh nada grath-yass

Cheers! *(toast)*
¡Salud!
saloo

THINGS YOU'LL HEAR

¡adelante!	come in!
aquí tiene	here you are
¡bien!	good!
¡buen viaje!	have a good trip!
¿cómo?	excuse me?
¡cuánto lo siento!	I'm so sorry!
¡cuidado!	look out!
de acuerdo	OK
de nada	you're welcome, don't mention it
eso es	that's right
¡hasta luego!	goodbye! see you later!
¡hola!	hello! hi!
muchas gracias	thank you very much
por favor	please
¿qué ha dicho?	what did you say?
sírvase usted mismo	help yourself

DAYS, MONTHS, SEASONS

Sunday	domingo	*dom<u>ee</u>ngoh*
Monday	lunes	*l<u>oo</u>ness*
Tuesday	martes	*m<u>a</u>rtess*
Wednesday	miércoles	*my<u>a</u>irkoh-less*
Thursday	jueves	*Hw<u>eh</u>-vess*
Friday	viernes	*vy<u>a</u>irness*
Saturday	sábado	*s<u>a</u>bbadoh*
January	enero	*enn<u>eh</u>-roh*
February	febrero	*febr<u>eh</u>-roh*
March	marzo	*m<u>a</u>rthoh*
April	abril	*abr<u>ee</u>l*
May	mayo	*m<u>a</u>yyoh*
June	junio	*H<u>oo</u>n-yoh*
July	julio	*H<u>oo</u>l-yoh*
August	agosto	*ag<u>o</u>stoh*
September	septiembre	*set-y<u>e</u>mbreh*
October	octubre	*okt<u>oo</u>breh*
November	noviembre	*nov-y<u>e</u>mbreh*
December	diciembre	*deeth-y<u>e</u>mbreh*
Spring	primavera	*preema-v<u>eh</u>-ra*
Summer	verano	*ver<u>ah</u>-noh*
Autumn	otoño	*ot<u>o</u>n-yoh*
Winter	invierno	*eemb-y<u>a</u>irnoh*
Christmas	Navidad	*navee-d<u>a</u>*
Christmas Eve	Nochebuena	*notcheh-bw<u>eh</u>-na*
Easter	Pascua,	*p<u>a</u>skwa,*
	Semana Santa	*sem<u>ah</u>-na s<u>a</u>nta*
Good Friday	Viernes Santo	*vy<u>a</u>irness s<u>a</u>ntoh*
New Year	Año Nuevo	*<u>ah</u>n-yoh nw<u>eh</u>-voh*
New Year's Eve	Nochevieja	*notcheh-vy<u>eh</u>-Ha*

NUMBERS

0 cero *theh-roh*
1 uno, una* *oonoh, oona*
2 dos *doss*
3 tres *tress*
4 cuatro *kwatroh*
5 cinco *theenkoh*
6 seis *sayss*
7 siete *see-eh-teh*
8 ocho *otchoh*
9 nueve *nweh-veh*

10 diez *dyeth*
11 once *ontheh*
12 doce *doh-theh*
13 trece *treh-theh*
14 catorce *katortheh*
15 quince *keentheh*
16 dieciséis *dyeth-ee-sayss*
17 diecisiete *dyeth-ee-see-eh-teh*
18 dieciocho *dyeth-ee-otchoh*
19 diecinueve *dyeth-ee-nweh-veh*

20 veinte *vaynteh*
21 veintiuno *vayntee-oonoh*
22 veintidós *vayntee-doss*
30 treinta *traynta*
31 treinta y uno *traynti oonoh*
32 treinta y dos *traynti doss*
40 cuarenta *kwarenta*
50 cincuenta *theen-kwenta*
60 sesenta *sessenta*
70 setenta *setenta*
80 ochenta *otchenta*
90 noventa *noh-venta*
100 cien *thyen*
110 ciento diez *thyentoh dyeth*
200 doscientos, doscientas *doss-thyentoss, doss-thyentass*
500 quinientos, quinientas *keen-yentoss, keen-yentass*
1,000 mil *meel*
1,000,000 un millón *mee-yon*

* When **uno** precedes a masculine noun, it loses the final **o**,
e.g. '1 point' is **un punto**. Feminine nouns take **una**, e.g.
'1 bag', **una bolsa**. Numbers in the hundreds, 200, 300, etc.,
use the form ending in **-as** with feminine nouns, e.g. '300
notes', **trescientos billetes**; '300 weeks', **trescientas semanas**.

TIME

today	hoy	*oy*
yesterday	ayer	*ayy<u>ai</u>r*
tomorrow	mañana	*man-y<u>ah</u>-na*
this week	esta semana	*<u>e</u>sta sem<u>ah</u>-na*
next week	la semana que viene	*la sem<u>ah</u>-na keh vy<u>e</u>h-neh*
this morning	esta mañana	*<u>e</u>sta man-y<u>ah</u>-na*
this afternoon	esta tarde	*<u>e</u>sta t<u>a</u>rdeh*
this evening	esta tarde/noche	*<u>e</u>sta t<u>a</u>rdeh/n<u>o</u>tcheh*
tonight	esta noche	*<u>e</u>sta n<u>o</u>tcheh*
last night	anoche	*ann<u>o</u>tcheh*
tomorrow morning	mañana por la mañana	*man-y<u>ah</u>-na por la man-y<u>ah</u>-na*
in three days	dentro de tres días	*d<u>e</u>ntro deh tress d<u>ee</u>-ass*
three days ago	hace tres días	*<u>a</u>h-theh tress d<u>ee</u>-ass*
late	tarde	*t<u>a</u>rdeh*
early	temprano	*tempr<u>ah</u>-noh*
soon	pronto	*pr<u>o</u>ntoh*
later on	más tarde	*mass t<u>a</u>rdeh*
at the moment	en este momento	*en <u>e</u>steh mom<u>e</u>ntoh*
second	un segundo	*seg<u>oo</u>ndoh*
minute	un minuto	*meen<u>oo</u>toh*
quarter of an hour	un cuarto de hora	*kw<u>a</u>rtoh deh <u>o</u>ra*
half an hour	media hora	*m<u>e</u>h-dya <u>o</u>ra*
three quarters of an hour	tres cuartos de hora	*tress kw<u>a</u>rtoss deh <u>o</u>ra*
hour	la hora	*<u>o</u>ra*
day	el día	*d<u>ee</u>-a*
every day	todos los días	*t<u>o</u>doss loss d<u>ee</u>-ass*
the next day	al día siguiente	*al d<u>ee</u>-a seegy<u>e</u>nteh*
week	la semana	*sem<u>ah</u>-na*
month	el mes	*mess*
year	el año	*<u>ah</u>n-yoh*

TELLING THE TIME

'O'clock' is not normally translated in Spanish unless it is for emphasis, when **en punto** would be used. For example: (**es**) **la una** (**en punto**) is '(it's) one o'clock'. The plural form of the verb is used for all other hours, eg (**son**) **las cinco** (**en punto**) is '(it's) five o'clock'.

The word 'past' is translated as **y** (= 'and'). In order to express minutes after the hour, state the hour followed by **y** plus the number of minutes: so **las seis y diez** is 'ten past six'. The word 'to' is translated as **menos** (= 'less'). So, for example, **las diez menos veinte** is 'twenty to ten'. The word for 'quarter' is **cuarto**; **las siete menos cuarto** is 'quarter to seven' and **las cinco y cuarto** is 'quarter past five'. The half hour is expressed using **y media**, so **las seis y media** is '6.30'.

The word 'at' is translated as **a** followed by **las**. For example, **a las tres y cuarto** is 'at quarter past three'. Remember to change **las** to **la** when using 'one', thus 'at 1.30' becomes **a la una y media**.

what time is it?	¿qué hora es?	*keh ora ess*
am	de la mañana	*deh la man-yah-na*
pm *(up to 8 pm)*	de la tarde	*deh la tardeh*
(from 8 pm)	de la noche	*deh la notcheh*
one o'clock	la una	*la oona*
ten past one	la una y diez	*la oona ee dyeth*
quarter past one	la una y cuarto	*la oona ee kwartoh*
1.30	la una y media	*la oona ee meh-dya*
twenty to two	las dos menos veinte	*lass doss meh-noss vaynteh*
quarter to two	las dos menos cuarto	*lass doss meh-noss kwartoh*
two o'clock	las dos (en punto)	*lass doss (en poontoh)*
at seven o'clock	a las siete	*a lass see-eh-teh*
noon	mediodía	*meh-dyoh dee-a*
midnight	medianoche	*meh-dya notcheh*

COMMUNICATIONS

Useful Words and Phrases

code	el prefijo	*preh-fee-Hoh*
dialling tone	la señal para marcar	*sen-yal parra markar*
email address	la dirección de email	*deerektheeon deh eemail*
emergency	una emergencia	*emmair-Henth-ya*
extension	extensión	*ekstenth-yon*
fax machine	el fax	*fax*
internet	el internet	*internet*
mobile phone	el teléfono móvil	*teh-leffonoh mohbeel*
number	el número	*noomeh-roh*
operator	la operadora	*opeh-radora*
phonecard	una tarjeta de teléfono	*tar-Heh-ta deh teh-leffonoh*
reverse charge call	una llamada a cobro revertido	*yamah-da a kobroh reh-vair-teedoh*
telephone	un teléfono	*teh-leffonoh*
Web site	la web site	*'web site'*
wrong number	el número equivocado	*noomeh-roh eh-keevoh-kah-doh*

Where is the nearest phone box?
¿Dónde está la cabina telefónica más cercana?
dondeh esta la kabeena tehleh-fonnika mass thair-kah-na

I would like a number in …
Quiero un número de …
kyeh-roh oon noomeh-roh deh

I would like to speak to …
Quería hablar con …
keh-ree-a ablar kon

Hello, this is … speaking
Hola, soy …
oh-la soy

Could you leave him/her a message?
¿Podría dejarle un recado?
podr__ee__-a deh-Harleh oon reh-k__ah__-doh

I'll call back later
Volveré a llamar luego
volveh-r__eh__ a yam__a__r lw__eh__-goh

What's your fax number/email address?
¿Cual es su número de fax/dirección de email?
kwal ess soo n__oo__meh-roh deh fax/deerekthee__o__n de eemail

Can I use the photocopier/fax machine?
¿Puedo usar la fotocopiadora/el fax
pw__eh__-doh oos__a__r la fotokopeead__o__ra/el fax

THINGS YOU'LL HEAR

¿Con quién quiere que le ponga?
Who would you like to speak to?

Se ha equivocado de número
You've got the wrong number

¿Quién es?
Who's speaking?

Al aparato/Al habla/Soy yo
Speaking

¿Cuál es su teléfono?
What is your number?

Lo siento, no está
Sorry, he/she's not in

Vuelva a llamar mañana, por favor
Please call again tomorrow

Le diré que le/la ha llamado usted
I'll tell him/her you called

EMERGENCIES

USEFUL WORDS AND PHRASES

accident	un accidente	*akthee-denteh*
ambulance	una ambulancia	*amboolanth-ya*
breakdown	una avería	*aveh-ree-a*
burglary	un robo	*roh-boh*
crash	un accidente	*akthee-denteh*
emergency	una emergencia	*emair-henth-ya*
fire	un fuego	*fwehgoh*
(*large*)	un incendio	*eenthend-yoh*
fire brigade	los bomberos	*bombeh-ross*
police	la policía	*poleethee-a*
police station	la comisaria	*kommeessaree-a*

Help!
¡Socorro!
sokorroh

Stop!
¡Pare!
pareh

Get an ambulance!
¡Llame a una ambulancia!
yah-meh a oona amboolanth-ya

Hurry up!
¡Dése prisa!
deh-seh preessa

My address is …
Mi dirección es …
mee deerekth-yon ess

My passport/car has been stolen
Me han robado el pasaporte/el coche
meh an robah-doh el passaporteh/el kotcheh

HOTELS

Useful Words and Phrases

balcony	el balcón	bal-kon
bathroom	el cuarto de baño	kwartoh deh bahn-yoh
bed	la cama	kah-ma
bed and breakfast	alojamiento y desayuno	aloh-Hamyentoh ee dessa-yoonoh
bedroom	la habitación	abbee-tath-yon
bill	la cuenta	kwenta
breakfast	el desayuno	dessa-yoonoh
car park	el aparcamiento	aparkamyentoh
dining room	el comedor	kommeh-dor
dinner	la cena	theh-na
double bed	la cama doble	kah-ma doh-bleh
double room	una habitación doble	abbee-tath-yon doh-bleh
full board	pensión completa	penss-yon kompleh-ta
guesthouse	la pensión	penss-yon
half board	media pensión	meh-dya penss-yon
hotel	el hotel	oh-tell
key	la llave	yah-veh
lift	el ascensor	ass-then-sor
lunch	la comida	komee-da
maid	la camarera	kamareh-ra
manager	el director	deerek-tor
reception	la recepción	reh-thepth-yon
room	la habitación	abbee-tath-yon
room service	el servicio de habitaciones	sairveeth-yoh deh abbeetath-yoh-ness
shower	la ducha	dootcha
single bed	la cama individual	kah-ma eendeeveed-wal
single room	una habitación individual	abbee-tath-yon eendeeveed-wal
toilets	los servicios	vattair, retreh-teh
twin room	una habitación con dos camas	abbee-tath-yon kon doss kah-mass

Do you have any vacancies?
¿Tienen alguna habitación libre?
tyeh-nen algoona abbee-tath-yon leebreh

I have a reservation
He hecho una reserva
eh etchoh oona reh-sairva

I'd like a single room
Quería una habitación individual
keh-ree-a oona abbee-tath-yon eendeeveed-wal

I'd like a room with a balcony/bathroom
Quería una habitación con balcón/cuarto de baño
keh-ree-a oona abbee-tath-yon kon bal-kon/kwartoh deh bahn-yoh

Is there satellite/cable TV in the rooms?
¿Hay televisión por satélite/por cable en las habitaciones?
i televeesseeon por sateleete/por kable en las abbee-tath-yoh-ness

I'd like a room for one night/three nights
Quería una habitación para una noche/para tres noches
keh-ree-a oona abbee-tath-yon parra oona notcheh/parra tress notchess

What is the charge per night?
¿Cuál es la tarifa por noche?
kwal ess la tarreefa por notcheh

When is breakfast/dinner?
¿A qué hora es el desayuno/la cena?
a keh ora ess el dessa-yoonoh/la theh-na

Please wake me at … o'clock
Haga el favor de llamarme a las …
ah-ga el fa-vor deh yamar-meh a lass

Can I have breakfast in my room?
¿Pueden servirme el desayuno en mi habitación?
pweh-den sair-veermeh el dessa-yoonoh en mee abbee-tath-yon

My room number is …
El número de mi habitación es …
el noomeh-roh deh mee abbee-tath-yon ess

There is no toilet paper in the bathroom
No hay papel higiénico en el cuarto de baño
noh I papel ee-Hyeneekoh en el kwartoh deh bahn-yoh

The window won't open
No se puede abrir la ventana
noh seh pweh-deh abreer la ventah-na

There isn't any hot water
No hay agua caliente
noh I ahg-wa kalyenteh

I'm leaving tomorrow
Me marcho mañana
meh martchoh man-yah-na

When do I have to vacate the room?
¿A qué hora tengo que desocupar la habitación?
a keh ora teng-goh keh dessokoopar la abbee-tath-yon

Can I have the bill, please?
¿Me da la cuenta, por favor?
meh da la kwenta por fa-vor

I'll pay by credit card
Pagaré con tarjeta (de crédito)
pagareh kon tar-Heh-ta deh kredeetoh

I'll pay cash
Pagaré al contado
pagareh al kontahdoh

Can you get me a taxi?
¿Puede llamar a un taxi?
pweh-deh yamar a oon taksee

THINGS YOU'LL SEE

almuerzo	lunch
ascensor	lift
completo	no vacancies
cuarto de baño	bathroom
cuenta	bill
desayuno	breakfast
empujar	push
entrada	entrance
prohibida la entrada	no admission
prohibido el paso	staff only
salida de emergencia	emergency exit
servicio	toilets
tirar	pull

THINGS YOU'LL HEAR

Lo siento, está lleno
I'm sorry, we're full

No nos quedan habitaciones individuales/dobles
There are no single/double rooms left

¿Para cuántas noches?
For how many nights?

¿Va a pagar al contado, o con tarjeta?
Will you be paying by cash or credit card?

Haga el favor de pagar por adelantado
Please pay in advance

Tiene que desocupar la habitación antes de las doce
You must vacate the room by noon

SHOPPING

Excuse me, where is/are …? *(in a supermarket)*
Por favor, ¿dónde está/están …?
por fa-vor dondeh esta/estan

Do you have …?
¿Tienen …?
tyeh-nen

How much is this?
¿Cuánto es esto?
kwantoh ess estoh

Where do I pay?
¿Dónde se paga?
dondeh seh pah-ga

Do you take credit cards?
¿Puedo pagar con tarjeta de crédito?
pweh-doh pagar kon tar-Heh-ta deh kredeetoh

Can I have a receipt?
¿Me da un recibo?
meh da oon retheeboh

Have you anything cheaper?
¿Tiene usted algo más barato?
tyeh-neh oosteh algoh mass barah-toh

Can I have a refund?
¿Pueden devolverme el dinero?
pweh-den deh-volvair-meh el deeneh-roh

That's fine. I'll take it
Está bien. Me lo llevo
esta byen. meh loh yeh-voh

It isn't what I wanted
No es lo que yo quería
noh ess loh keh yoh keh-ree-a

EATING OUT

You can eat in a variety of places:

Restaurante: These have an official rating (1–5 forks), but this depends more on the variety of dishes served than on the quality.

Cafetería: Not to be confused with the British term. It is a combined bar, café and restaurant. Service is provided at the counter or, for a little extra, at a table. There is usually a good variety of set menus at reasonable prices (look for **platos combinados**).

Fonda: Offers inexpensive, good food that is representative of regional dishes.

Hostería or **Hostal:** A restaurant that usually specializes in regional dishes.

Parador: Belonging to the previously state-run hotels, they offer a first-rate service in select surroundings.

Café or **Bar:** Both are general cafés selling all kinds of food and drink (again, they are not to be confused with British establishments of the same name). Well worth trying if you just want a quick snack. In some places, they serve free **tapas** (starters) with alcoholic drinks. Full meals are often available.

Merendero: Outdoor **café** on the coast or in the country. Usually inexpensive and a good buy.

Generally, breakfast in Spain is at 8 am, lunch is at 2 pm and dinner (the main evening meal) is at 10 pm.

Useful Words and Phrases

beer	una cerveza	*thairveh-tha*
bill	la cuenta	*kwenta*
bottle	la botella	*boh-tay-ya*
bread	el pan	*pan*

butter	la mantequilla	*manteh-kee-ya*
cake	un pastel	*pastell*
carafe	una jarra	*Harra*
chef	el cocinero	*kothee-neh-roh*
children's portion	una ración especial para niños	*rath-yon espethyal parra neen-yoss*
coffee	el café	*kaffeh*
cup	la taza	*tah-tha*
dessert	el postre	*postreh*
fork	el tenedor	*teneh-dor*
glass	el vaso	*vah-soh*
half litre	medio litro	*meh-dyoh leetroh*
knife	el cuchillo	*kootchee-yoh*
main course	el segundo plato	*segoondoh plah-toh*
menu	la carta	*karta*
milk	la leche	*letcheh*
napkin	la servilleta	*sairvee-yeh-ta*
pepper	la pimienta	*peemyenta*
plate	el plato	*plah-toh*
receipt	un recibo	*retheeboh*
salt	la sal	*sal*
sandwich (*Spanish*)	un sandwich un bocadillo	*sand-weetch boh-kadee-yoh*
soup	la sopa	*soh-pa*
spoon	la cuchara	*kootchah-ra*
starter	el primer plato	*primair plah-toh*
sugar	el azúcar	*athookar*
table	una mesa	*meh-sa*
tea	el té	*teh*
teaspoon	la cucharilla	*kootcha-ree-ya*
tip	una propina	*propeena*
waiter	el camarero	*kamma-reh-roh*
waitress	la camarera	*kamma-reh-ra*
water	el agua	*ahg-wa*
wine	el vino	*veenoh*
wine list	la carta de vinos	*karta deh veenoss*

A table for one, please
Una mesa para una persona, por favor
<u>oo</u>na m<u>eh</u>-sa p<u>a</u>rra <u>oo</u>na pairs<u>oh</u>-na por fa-v<u>o</u>r

A table for two/three, please
Una mesa para dos/tres personas, por favor
<u>oo</u>na m<u>eh</u>-sa p<u>a</u>rra doss/tress pairs<u>oh</u>-nass por fa-v<u>o</u>r

Is there a highchair?
¿Hay sillita de niño?
i see-y<u>ee</u>ta deh n<u>ee</u>n-yo

Can we see the menu/wine list?
¿Nos trae la carta/la carta de vinos?
noss tr<u>ah</u>-eh la k<u>a</u>rta/la k<u>a</u>rta deh v<u>ee</u>noss

What would you recommend?
¿Qué recomendaría usted?
keh rekomenda-r<u>ee</u>-a oost<u>eh</u>

I'd like …
Quería …
keh-r<u>ee</u>-a

Just a cup of coffee, please
Un café nada más, por favor
oon kaff<u>eh</u> n<u>ah</u>-da mass por fa-v<u>o</u>r

I only want a snack
Sólo quiero una comida ligera
s<u>oh</u>-loh kee-<u>eh</u>-roh <u>oo</u>na komm<u>ee</u>da lee-H<u>eh</u>-ra

Is there a set menu?
¿Hay menú del día?
i meh-n<u>oo</u> dell d<u>ee</u>-a

A litre carafe of house red, please
Una jarra de litro de tinto de la casa, por favor
<u>oo</u>na H<u>a</u>rra deh l<u>ee</u>troh deh t<u>ee</u>ntoh deh la k<u>ah</u>-sa por fa-v<u>o</u>r

Do you have any vegetarian dishes?
¿Tiene algún plato vegetariano?
tyeh-neh algoon plah-toh veh-Hetaryah-noh

Could we have some water?
¿Nos trae agua, por favor?
noss trah-eh ahg-wa por fa-vor

Can you warm this bottle/baby food for me?
¿Podría calentar este biberón/comida para niño?
po-dreea kalentar este beeberon/komeeda parra neen-yoh

Waiter/waitress!
¡Oiga, por favor!
oy-gah por fa-vor

I didn't order this
No he pedido esto
noh eh pedeedoh estoh

May we have some more …?
¿Nos trae más …?
noss trah-eh mass

Can I have another knife/fork?
¿Me trae otro cuchillo/tenedor?
meh trah-eh otroh kootchee-yoh/teneh-dor

Can we have the bill, please?
¿Nos trae la cuenta, por favor?
noss trah-eh la kwenta por fa-vor

Could I have a receipt, please?
¿Me puede dar un recibo, por favor?
meh pweh-deh dar oon retheeboh por fa-vor

The meal was very good, thank you
La comida ha sido muy buena, gracias
la kommeeda a seedoh mwee bweh-na grath-yass

MENU GUIDE

aceitunas olives
aguacate avocado
ahumados smoked fish
ajo garlic
albaricoques apricots
albóndigas meatballs
alcachofas artichokes
alcaparras capers
almejas clams
almendras almonds
alubias con ... beans with ...
anchoas anchovies
anguila eel
arenque herring
arroz rice
arroz con leche rice pudding
asados roast meat
atún tuna
avellanas hazelnuts
azúcar sugar
bacalao cod
batido milk shake
bebidas drinks
berenjenas aubergine
besugo al horno baked sea bream
bistec de ternera veal steak
bizcochos sponge fingers
bonito al horno baked tuna
bonito con tomate tuna with tomato
boquerones fritos fried anchovies
brazo gitano swiss roll
brevas figs
buñuelos light fried pastries
cachelada pork stew
calabacines courgette, vegetable marrow
calabaza pumpkin
calamares squid
caldeirada fish soup

caldereta gallega vegetable stew
caldo de ... ... soup
camarones baby prawns
canelones canneloni
cangrejos de río river crabs
caracoles snails
caramelos sweets
carnes meats
carro de queso cheese board
castañas chestnuts
cebolla onion
cebolletas spring onions
centollo spider crab
cerezas cherries
cerveza beer
cesta de frutas a selection of fresh fruit
champiñón mushrooms
chanquetes fish (similar to whitebait)
chipirones baby squid
chirimoyas custard apples
chocos squid
chuleta chop
chuletón large chop
churros deep-fried pastry strips
cigalas crayfish
ciruelas plums, greengages
ciruelas pasas prunes
cochinillo asado roast suckling pig
cocido stew made with meat, chickpeas
  and vegetables
cocktail de bogavante lobster cocktail
cocochas (de merluza) hake stew
codornices quail
col cabbage
coles de Bruselas Brussels sprouts
coliflor cauliflower
conejo asado roast rabbit
congrio conger eel

contra de ternera con guisantes veal stew with peas

contrafilete de ternera veal fillet

copa ... ... cup, glass of wine

cordero asado roast lamb

cordero chilindrón lamb stew with onion, tomato, peppers and eggs

costillas de cerdo pork ribs

crema catalana crème brûlée

crema de cangrejos cream of crab soup

crema de espárragos cream of asparagus soup

crema de legumbres cream of vegetable soup

crocante ice cream with chopped nuts

croquetas croquettes

cuajada curds

dátiles dates

embutidos sausages

empanada gallega fish pie

empanada santiaguesa fish pie

empanadillas de bonito small tuna pies

empanadillas de carne small meat pies

ensalada salad

entrecot a la parrilla grilled entrecôte

entrecot de ternera veal entrecôte

escalope a la milanesa breaded veal with cheese

escalope a la plancha grilled veal

escalope de lomo de cerdo escalope of pork fillet

escalope de ternera veal scallop

escalope empanado breaded scallops

espadín a la toledana kebab

espaguetis italiana spaghetti

espárragos asparagus

espinacas spinach

estofado de ... ... stew

fabada (asturiana) bean stew with sausage

faisán pheasant

fiambres cold meats

fideos thin pasta, noodles

flan crème caramel

fresas con nata strawberries and cream

fruta fruit

gallina en pepitoria chicken stewed with peppers

gambas shrimp

garbanzos chickpeas

gazpacho andaluz cold tomato soup from Andalusia

gelatina de ... ... jelly

gratén de ... ... au gratin (baked in a cream and cheese sauce)

grelo turnip

guisantes con jamón peas with ham

guisantes salteados sautéed peas

habas broad beans

habichuelas beans

helado ice cream

hígado liver

higos con miel y nueces figs with honey and nuts

higos secos dried figs

horchata (de chufas) cold almond-flavoured milk drink

huevos eggs

huevos escalfados poached eggs

huevos fritos fried eggs

huevos rellenos stuffed eggs

huevos revueltos scrambled eggs

jamón ham

jerez sherry

judías verdes green beans

jugo juice

langosta lobster

langostinos king prawns

laurel bay leaves

leche frita egg and milk pudding

leche merengada cold milk with meringues

lechuga lettuce
lengua tongue
lenguado sole
lentejas lentils
liebre estofada stewed hare
lombarda rellena stuffed red cabbage
lombarda salteada sautéed red cabbage
lomo curado pork loin sausage
lonchas de jamón sliced, cured ham
longaniza cooked Spanish sausage
lubina sea bass
macarrones macaroni
macedonia de fruta fruit salad
manises peanuts
manitas de cordero lamb shank
manos de cerdo pigs' feet
mantecadas small sponge cakes
mantequilla butter
manzanas apples
mariscada cold mixed shellfish
mariscos del día fresh shellfish
mariscos del tiempo seasonal shellfish
medallones de anguila eel steaks
medallones de merluza hake steaks
mejillones mussels
melocotón peach
melón melon
membrillo quince jelly
menestra de legumbres vegetable stew
menú de la casa set menu
menú del día menu of the day
merluza hake
mermelada jam
mero grouper (type of fish)
morcilla blood sausage
morros de cerdo pigs' cheeks
morros de vaca cows' cheeks
mortadela salami-type sausage
morteruelo kind of pâté
nabo turnip
naranjas oranges

natillas cold custard
níscalos wild mushrooms
nísperos medlars (similar to crab apple)
nueces walnuts
paella fried rice with various seafood
and chicken
paella castellana meat paella
paella de marisco shellfish paella
paella de pollo chicken paella
paella valenciana shellfish, rabbit and
chicken paella
paleta de cordero lechal shoulder of
lamb
pan bread
pan de higos dried fig cake with cinnamon
panache de verduras vegetable stew
panceta bacon
parrillada de caza mixed grilled game
parrillada de mariscos mixed grilled
shellfish
pasas raisins
pastel de … … cake
pastel de ternera veal pie
pasteles cakes
patatas potatoes
patatas fritas chips
patitos rellenos stuffed duckling
pato duck
pavo turkey
pecho de ternera breast of veal
pechuga de pollo breast of chicken
pepinillos gherkins
pepino cucumber
peras pears
perdices partridges
perejil parsley
pescaditos fritos fried fish
pestiños sugared pastries flavoured
with aniseed
pez espada ahumado smoked swordfish

picadillo de ternera minced veal
pimienta black pepper
pimientos peppers
pimientos morrones bell peppers
pimientos rellenos stuffed peppers
pimientos verdes green peppers
piña pineapple
pinchos morunos kebabs
piñones pine nuts
pisto fried mixed vegetables
pisto manchego vegetable marrow with onion and tomato
plátanos bananas
pollo chicken
pomelo grapefruit
potaje castellano thick broth
potaje de garbanzos chickpea stew
potaje de habichuelas white bean stew
potaje de lentejas lentil stew
puchero canario casserole of meat, chickpeas and corn
pulpitos con cebolla baby octopus with onions
pulpo octopus
puré de patatas mashed potatoes
purrusalda cod with leeks and potatoes
queso cheese
quisquillas shrimps
rábanos radish
rape monkfish
raya skate
remolacha beets
repollo cabbage
requesón cream cheese, cottage cheese
revuelto scrambled eggs
riñones kidneys
rodaballo turbot (fish)
romero rosemary
roscas sweet pastries
sal salt
salchichas sausages

salchichas de Frankfurt hot dogs
salchichón white sausage with pepper
salmón salmon
salmonetes red mullet
salsa sauce
salsa allioli/ali oli mayonnaise with garlic
sandía watermelon
sardinas sardines
setas a la plancha grilled mushrooms
setas rellenas stuffed mushrooms
sobreasada soft red sausage with cayenne pepper
solomillo fillet steak
solomillo frío cold roast beef
sopa soup
sopa castellana vegetable soup
sopa de gallina chicken soup
sopa mallorquina soup with tomato, meat and eggs
sopa sevillana fish soup
sorbete sorbet
tallarines noodles
tarta cake
tencas tench
ternera asada roast veal
tocinillos del cielo crème caramel
tomates rellenos stuffed tomatoes
tomillo thyme
tordo thrush
torrijas sweet pastries
tortilla Alaska baked Alaska
tortilla Spanish omelette
tournedó tournedos (fillet steak)
trucha trout
turrón nougat
uvas grapes
vieiras scallops
zanahorias carrots
zarzuela de mariscos seafood stew
zumo de … … juice

SWEDISH

CONTENTS

INTRODUCTION

Pronunciation

When reading the imitated pronunciation, stress the part which is underlined. Pronounce each syllable as if it formed part of an English word, and you will be understood sufficiently well. Remember the points below, and your pronunciation will be even closer to the correct Swedish.

ai	as in 'fair' or 'stair'
ew	like the sound in 'dew'
EW	try to say 'ee' with your lips rounded
oo	as in 'book' or 'soot'
OO	as in 'spoon' or 'groom'
r	should be strongly pronounced

Swedish Alphabetical Order

In the lists of Things You'll See and in the Menu Guide we have followed Swedish alphabetical order. The following letters are listed after z: å, ä, ö.

'You'

There are two words for **you**: **du** and **ni**. Ni is the polite form; **du** is the familiar form. But unlike in some other European countries it is not necessarily impolite to address a complete stranger with the familiar form. In fact many Swedes consider the polite form to be old-fashioned. In many cases in this book we have given you a choice.

The Definite/Indefinite Articles

The commonest form of the definite article ('the') in Swedish is as a suffix (eg **en, et**) added to the end of a word. When you see translations given in the form **hus(et)** or **bil(en)**, the form **huset** will mean 'the house' and **bilen** 'the car'. 'A house' is **ett hus** and 'a car' is **en bil**.

USEFUL PHRASES

Yes/no
Ja/nej
yah/nay

Thank you
Tack
tack

No, thank you
Nej tack
nay tack

Please *(offering)*   *(asking for something, accepting something)*
Varsågod   Tack
vahrshawgood   *tack*

I don't understand
Jag förstår inte
yah furshtawr inteh

Do you speak English/French/German?
Talar du engelska/franska/tyska?
tahlar dew engelska/franska/tewska

I can't speak Swedish
Jag talar inte svenska
yah tahlar inteh svenska

I don't know
Jag vet inte
yah veat inteh

Please speak more slowly
Kan du/ni tala långsammare, tack
kan dEW/nee tahla lawngssamareh tack

Please write it down for me
Var snäll och skriv upp det för mig
vahr snell ock skreev ewp deat fur may

My name is …
Jag heter …
yah heater

How do you do, pleased to meet you
Hej, trevligt att träffas
hay, treavligt att treffas

Good morning/good afternoon/good evening
God morgon/goddag/god afton
goo morron/goodahg/goo afton

Good night *(when going to bed)*
Godnatt
goonatt

Goodbye
Adjö; *(informal word)* hejdå
ahyur; haydaw

How are you?
Hur mår du?
hEwr mawr dEW

Excuse me, please
Ursäkta
Ewrshekta

Sorry!
Förlåt!
furrlawt

I'm really sorry
Jag är mycket ledsen
yah air mewkeh layssen

Can you help me?
Kan du hjälpa mig?
kan dew yelpa may

Can you tell me …?
Kan du säga mig …?
kan dew saya may

Can I have …?
Kan jag få …?
kan yah faw

I would like a …
Jag skulle vilja ha en/ett …
yah skewleh vilya hah ehn/ett

Would you like a …?
Vill du/ni ha en/ett …?
vill dew/nee hah ehn/ett

Is there … here?
Finns det en/ett … här?
finnss day ehn/ett … hair

Where can I get …?
Var kan jag få …?
vahr kan yah faw

How much is it?
Hur mycket kostar det?
hEWr mEWkeh kostar deat

What time is it?
Hur mycket är klockan?
hEWr mEWkeh air klockan

I must go now
Jag måste gå nu
yah mawsteh gaw nEW

I've lost my way
Jag har tappat bort mig
yah har tappat bort may

I've lost my passport/room key/traveller's cheques
Jag har förlorat mit pass/min rumsnyckel/mina resecheckar
yah har furlorat mitt pass/min rewmssnEWckel/mina reasecheckar

Cheers! *(toast)*
Skål!
skawl

Do you take credit cards?
Tar ni kreditkort?
tahr ni kredeetkoort

Where is the toilet?
Var är toaletten?
vahr air too-aletten

Excellent!
Utmärkt!
EWtmerkt

THINGS YOU'LL HEAR

adjö	goodbye
akta dig!	look out!
bra	good
förlåt	sorry
hej	hi; hello
hej, trevligt att träffas	how do you do, nice to meet you
hur står det till?	how are you?
hursa?	pardon?
ja	yes
jag förstår inte	I don't understand
jag vet inte	I don't know
just det	that's right
lycklig resa	bon voyage
nej	no
stig in	get in
tack	thanks
tack, bra	very well, thank you
tack så mycket	thank you very much
ursäkta	excuse me
varsågod	please; you're welcome; here you are
vi ses senare	see you later
välkommen	welcome

THINGS YOU'LL SEE

att hyra	to let
damer	women
drag	pull
ej …	no …, do not …
ej ingång/utgång	no entrance/exit
fritt inträde	admission free
fullsatt	no vacancies

→

förbjudet	forbidden
gata	street
herrar	men
hiss	lift
ingång	entrance
inte	not
kassa	cash register, sales counter
korvkiosk	hot dog stand
ledigt	vacant/free
livsfara	danger
luciadagen	St Lucia's Day (13th December)
lägenhet att hyra	flat for rent
nymålat	wet paint
nödutgång	emergency exit
polis	police
privat	private
rabatt	reduced prices
rea	sale
reserverad	reserved
semesterstängt	closed for holidays
skjut	push
stängt	closed
till salu	for sale
tillträde förbjudet	no admittance
toaletter	toilets
tystnad	silence, quiet
upplysningar	information
upptaget	engaged
utförsäljning	sale
utgång	exit
utsålt	sold out
väg	road
öppet	open

DAYS, MONTHS, SEASONS

Sunday	söndag	*surndahg*
Monday	måndag	*mawndahg*
Tuesday	tisdag	*teessdahg*
Wednesday	onsdag	*oonssdahg*
Thursday	torsdag	*toorshdahg*
Friday	fredag	*fraydahg*
Saturday	lördag	*lurrdahg*
January	januari	*yanewahree*
February	februari	*febrewahree*
March	mars	*mahrsh*
April	april	*ahpreel*
May	maj	*mah-ee*
June	juni	*yEwnee*
July	juli	*yEwlee*
August	augusti	*ahgewstee*
September	september	*septemberr*
October	oktober	*oktooberr*
November	november	*noovemberr*
December	december	*dessemberr*
Spring	vår	*vawr*
Summer	sommar	*sommahr*
Autumn	höst	*hurst*
Winter	vinter	*vinter*
Christmas	jul	*yEwl*
Christmas Eve	julafton	*yEwlafton*
Good Friday	långfredag	*lawngfraydahg*
Easter	påsk	*pawsk*
Whitsun	pingst	*pingst*
New Year	nyår	*nEW-awr*
New Year's Eve	nyårsafton	*nEW-awrsh-afton*
Midsummer	midsommarafton	*midsommahrafton*

NUMBERS

0	noll	*noll*		
1	ett	*ett*		
2	två	*tvaw*		
3	tre	*tray*		
4	fyra	*fEWra*		

5	fem	*fem*
6	sex	*sex*
7	sju	*shEW*
8	åtta	*otta*
9	nio	*nee-oo*

10 tio *tee-oo*
11 elva *elva*
12 tolv *tolv*
13 tretton *tretton*
14 fjorton *f-yoorton*
15 femton *femton*
16 sexton *sexton*
17 sjutton *shewton*
18 arton *ahrton*
19 nitton *nitton*
20 tjugo *chEWgoo*
21 tjugoett *chEWgo-ett*
22 tjugotvå *chEWgo-tvaw*
30 trettio *tretti*
31 trettioett *tretti-ett*
32 trettiotvå *tretti-tvaw*
40 fyrtio *furrti*
50 femtio *femti*
60 sextio *sexti*
70 sjuttio *shewti*
80 åttio *otti*
90 nittio *nitti*
100 (ett) hundra *(ett) hewndra*
110 (ett) hundratio *(ett) hewndra-teeoo*
200 tvåhundra *tvawhewndra*
1,000 (ett) tusen *(ett) tEWssen*
100,000 (ett) hundra tusen *(ett) hewndra tEWssen*
1,000,000 en miljon *ayn milyoon*

TIME

today	i dag	*ee dahg*
yesterday	i går	*ee gawr*
tomorrow	i morgon	*ee morron*
the day before yesterday	i förrgår	*ee furrgawr*
the day after tomorrow	i övermorgon	*ee urvermorron*
this week	den här veckan	*dayn hair veckan*
last week	förra veckan	*furra veckan*
next week	nästa vecka	*nesta vecka*
this morning	i morse	*ee morsheh*
this afternoon	i eftermiddag	*ee eftermiddahg*
this evening	i kväll	*ee kvell*
tonight	i natt	*ee natt*
yesterday afternoon	i går eftermiddag	*ee gawr eftermiddahg*
last night	i går kväll	*ee gawr kvell*
tomorrow morning	i morgon bitti	*ee morron bittee*
tomorrow night	i morgon kväll	*ee morron kvell*
in three days	om tre dagar	*om trea dahgar*
three days ago	för tre dagar sedan	*furr trea dahgar seadan*
late	sen	*sean*
early	tidig	*teedig*
soon	snart	*snahrt*
later on	senare	*seanareh*
at the moment	just nu	*yewst nEW*
second	en sekund	*sekewnd*
minute	en minut	*meenEWt*
two minutes	två minuter	*tvaw meenEWter*
quarter of an hour	en kvart	*ehn kvahrt*
half an hour	en halvtimme	*ehn halvtimmeh*
three quarters of an hour	tre kvart	*trea kvahrt*

hour	en timme	*timmeh*
every day	varje dag	*vahryeh dahg*
all day	hela dagen	*heala dahgen*
the next day	nästa dag	*nesta dahg*
week	vecka	*vecka*
month	månad	*mawnad*
year	år	*awr*

TELLING THE TIME

Sweden conforms to Central European time, which is one hour ahead of GMT. The Swedes put their clocks forward by an hour from the end of March until the end of October.

In telling the time it is important to note that, instead of saying 'half past' an hour, the Swedes refer to the next hour coming (for example, 'half past one' is said in Swedish as 'half two'). Also, the 24-hour clock is used much more commonly than in the UK, both in the written form, as in timetables, and verbally, as when using an information desk or when making appointments.

am	förmiddag(en)	*furmiddahg*
pm	eftermiddag(en)	*eftermiddahg*
one o'clock	klockan ett	*klockan ett*
ten past one	tio över ett	*teeoo urver ett*
quarter past one	kvart över ett	*kvahrt urver ett*
half past one	halv två	*halv tvaw*
twenty to two	tjugo i två	*chEwgoo ee tvaw*
quarter to two	kvart i två	*kvahrt ee tvaw*
two o'clock	klockan två	*klockan tvaw*
13.00	klockan tretton	*klockan tretton*
16.30	sexton och trettio	*sexton ock tretti*
at half past five	halv sex	*halv sex*
at seven o'clock	klockan sju	*klockan shEW*
noon	klockan tolv	*klockan tolv*
midnight	midnatt	*meednatt*

COMMUNICATIONS

USEFUL WORDS AND PHRASES

code	riktnummer	*riktnewmer*
dialling tone	kopplingston	*kopplingston*
email address	email-adress	*ee-mail adress*
emergency	nödfall	*nurdfall*
extension	anknytning(en)	*ank-newtning*
mobile phone	mobiltelefon(en)	*mobiltelefawn*
number	nummer (numret)	*newmer*
operator	växel(n)	*vexel*
(in hotel)	telefonist(en)	*telefawneest*
phonecard	telefonkort(et)	*telefawnkoort*
reverse charge call	b-a samtal (-numret)	*bea-ah samtahl*
telephone	en telefon	*telefawn*
telephone box	en telefonkiosk	*telefawn-cheeosk*
wrong number	fel nummer	*fayl newmer*

Where is the nearest phone box?
Var finns närmaste telefonkiosk?
vahr finnss nairmasteh telefawn-cheeosk

I would like a number in …
Jag skulle vilja ha ett nummer i …
yah skewleh vilya hah ett newmer ee

I would like to speak to …
Kan jag få tala med …?
kan yah faw tahla med

My number is …
Mitt nummer är …
mitt newmer air

Could you leave him a message?
Får jag lämna ett meddelande?
fawr yah lemna ett meadealandeh

I'll ring back later
Jag ringer senare
yah ringer seanareh

What's your fax number/email address?
Vad har du för faxnummer/email-adress?
vahd hahr dew fur faxnewmmer/ee-mail adress

Can I send an email/fax from here?
Kan jag skicka et email/fax härifrån?
kan yah skicka ett eemail/fax hair-eefrawn

THINGS YOU'LL SEE

direktval	direct dialling
email	email
email addres	email address
faxmaskin	fax machine
information	enquiries
internationell	international
internationellt samtal	international call
i olag	out of order
lokalsamtal	local call
lyft luren	lift receiver
nödsamtal	emergency call
rikssamtal	long-distance call
riktnummer	code
Tele	public telephone office
telefonsvarare	answering machine
telefonkiosk	telephone box
websida	Web site

THINGS YOU'LL HEAR

Vem vill du tala med?
Who would you like to speak to?

Du har fått fel nummer
You've got the wrong number

Vem är det som talar?
Who's speaking?

Jag kopplar vidare
I'll put you through

Vad har du for nummer?
What is your number?

Tyvärr, han är inte anträffbar
Sorry, he's not in

Han kommer tillbaka klockan …
He'll be back at … o'clock

Ring på nytt i morgon
Please call again tomorrow

Jag skall meddela honom att du har ringt
I'll tell him you called

Tyvärr är alla linjer upptagna
Sorry, all lines are busy

Försök på nytt senare
Please try later

HOTELS

Useful Words and Phrases

balcony	en balkong	*balkong*
bathroom	ett badrum	*bahdrewm*
bed	en säng	*seng*
bedroom	ett sovrum	*sawvrewm*
bill	räkning(en)	*raikning*
breakfast	frukost(en)	*frewkost*
dining room	matsal(en)	*mahtssahl*
dinner	middag	*middahg*
double room	ett dubbelrum	*doobelrewm*
foyer	lobby(n)	*lobbee*
full board	helpension	*haylpangshoon*
half board	halvpension	*halvpangshoon*
hotel	ett hotell	*hootell*
key	nyckel(n)	*newckel*
lift	en hiss	*hiss*
lounge	sällskapsrum(met)	*sellskahps-rewm*
lunch	lunch(en)	*lewnch*
manager	direktör(en)	*direkturr*
reception	reception(en)	*resseptshoon*
receptionist	receptionist(en)	*ressept-shooneest*
restaurant	en restaurang	*restawrang*
room	ett rum	*rewm*
room service	rumsbetjäning(en)	*rewmss-bechaining*
shower	en dusch	*dewsh*
single room	ett enkelrum	*enkelrewm*
toilet	en toalett	*too-alett*
twin room	ett rum med två sängar	*rewm med tvaw sengar*

Do you have any vacancies?
Har ni några lediga rum?
hahr nee noorgra laydiga rewm

I have a reservation
Jag har beställt rum
yah hahr bestellt rewm

I'd like a single/double room
Jag skulle vilja ha ett enkelrum/dubbelrum
yah skewleh vilya hah ett enkelrewm/doobelrewm

I'd like a room with a bathroom/balcony
Jag skulle vilja ha ett rum med bad/balkong
yah skewleh vilya hah ett rewm med bahd/balkong

I'd like a room for one night/three nights
Jag skulle vilja ha ett rum för en natt/tre nätter
yah skewleh vilya hah ett rewm furr ehn natt/tray netter

Is there satellite/cable TV in the rooms?
Finns det satellit/kabel TV på rummen?
finns deat sateleet/kahbel teavea paw rewmmen

What is the charge per night?
Vad kostar det per natt?
vah kostar deat pair natt

Is there wheelchair access?
Är det rullstolsvänligt?
air deat rewllstoolsvainligt

Are there facilities for the disabled?
Är det anpassat för rörelsehindrade?
air deat anpassat fur rurelsehindrade

When is breakfast/dinner?
När serveras frukosten/middagen?
nair sairvearass frewkosten/middahgen

Please call me at ... o'clock
Kan ni/du väcka mig klockan ... tack
kan nee/dEW vaikka may klockan ... tack

Can I have breakfast in my room?
Kan jag få frukost på rummet?
kan yah faw frewkost paw rewmmet

My room number is ...
Mitt rumsnummer är ...
mitt rewmss-newmmer ay

I'm leaving tomorrow
Jag reser i morgon
yah raysser ee morron

Can I have the bill, please?
Kan jag få räkningen?
kan yah faw raikningen

I'll pay by credit card
Jag betalar med kreditkort
yah betahlar med kredeetkoort

I'll pay cash
Jag betalar kontant
yah betahlar kontant

Can you get me a taxi?
Kan jag få en taxi?
kan yah faw ehn taxee

THINGS YOU'LL SEE

bottenvåning	ground floor
drag	pull
fullbelagt, fullbokat	no vacancies
nödutgång	emergency exit
rum med frukost	bed and breakfast
räkning	bill
skjut, tryck	push

THINGS YOU'LL HEAR

Tyvärr, vi är fullbokade
I'm sorry, we're full

Vi har inga lediga enkelrum/dubbelrum
There are no single rooms/double rooms left

För hur många nätter?
For how many nights?

För hur många personer?
For how many people?

Hur betalar ni?
How will you be paying?

Fyll i den här blanketten
Please fill in this form

Var snäll och skriv under här
Please sign your name here

Var vänlig och betala i förskott
Please pay in advance

SHOPPING

Where is the … department?
Var ligger … avdelningen?
vahr ligger … ahvdealningen

Do you have …?
Har du/ni …?
hahr dEW/nee

How much is this?
Hur mycket kostar den här?
hEWr mEWkeh kostar dehn hair

Do you have any more of these?
Har du/ni fler av den här sorten?
hahr dEW/nee flear ahv dehn hair sorten

Where do I pay?
Var kan jag betala?
vahr kan yah betahla

Have you anything cheaper?
Finns det någonting billigare?
finnss deat nawgonting billigareh

Can I have a receipt?
Kan jag få ett kvitto, tack?
kan yah faw ett kvitto, tack

Can I have a refund?
Kan jag få pengarna tillbaka?
kan yah faw pengarna tillbahka

I'm just looking
Jag ser mig bara omkring
yah sear may bahra omkring

EATING OUT

Swedish restaurants range from the expense-account variety to smallish cafeterias. Look out for the **dagens rätt** (*dahgens rett*), the special dish of the day, which usually includes a main course, salad, soft drink and coffee.

The service charge is always included in the bill, so any additional tipping is up to you.

You should try the traditional **smörgåsbord** (*smurrgawssboord*) but, to do it justice, choose a day when you have a hearty appetite. You start off with herring or some other salt fish, move on to cold meats and salads then to hot dishes. Athough there is no dessert as such, you can finish off with cheeses and fruit.

In most towns you'll find fast food outlets serving hamburgers and pizzas. A typical Swedish institution is the **korvkiosk**, a hot-dog stand, open very late, serving different varieties of hamburgers and hot dogs.

The Swedes eat early. Lunch starts around 11.30 and dinner from 5 pm (or 7–8 pm if you are eating out).

Beer is Sweden's favourite drink and it comes in three categories: **lättöl** (*letturl*) which is class I, the weakest; **mellanöl** (*mellanurl*) or **folköl** (*follkurl*) which is class II and the most popular; and **starköl** which is class III and the strongest. **Snaps** is an aquavit flavoured with various herbs and drunk ice-cold, and **punsch** is a sweet arrack liqueur served with coffee after dinner. If you are not in a restaurant, alcoholic beverages – apart from **lättöl** which can be bought from grocery shops – are sold only by state-controlled shops called **Systembolaget** (*sewsteamboolahget*). You have to be at least 20 years old in order to be able to shop in these.

USEFUL WORDS AND PHRASES

beer	en öl	*url*
bill	nota(n)	*noota*
bottle	en flaska	*flaska*
cake	tårta(n)	*tawrta*

coffee	kaffe(t)	*kaffeh*
cup	kopp(en)	*kopp*
dessert	efterätt	*efterett*
fork	gaffel(n)	*gaffel*
glass	ett glas	*glahss*
knife	kniv(en)	*k-neev*
main course	huvudrätt	*hEWvEWdrett*
menu	meny(n),	*menEW,*
	matsedel(n)	*mahtseadel*
milk	mjölk(en)	*m-yurlk*
napkin	en servett	*sairvett*
plate	tallrik(en)	*tallreek*
receipt	kvitto(t)	*kvitto*
sandwich	en smörgås	*smurrgawss*
snack	matbit(en)	*mahtbeet*
soup	soppa(n)	*soppa*
spoon	sked(en)	*shead*
starter	förätt	*furrett*
sugar	socker(et)	*socker*
table	ett bord	*boord*
tea	te(et)	*tea*
teaspoon	tesked(en)	*teashead*
tip	dricks(en)	*dricks*
waiter	hovmästare(en)	*hawvmestareh*
waitress	servitris	*sairvitreess*
water	vatten(et)	*vatten*
wine	vin(et)	*veen*
wine list	vinlista(n)	*veenlista*

A table for one, please
Kan jag få ett bord för en person, tack?
kan yah faw ett boord fur ehn pairshoon, tack

A table for two, please
Kan jag få ett bord för två, tack?
kan yah faw ett boord fur tvaw, tack

Can I see the menu/wine list?
Kan jag få se menyn/vinlistan, tack?
kan yah faw sea menEWn/veenlistan, tack

What would you recommend?
Vad rekommenderar ni/du?
vah rekommendayrar nee/dEW

Do you do children's portions?
Går det att få barnportion?
gawr deat att faw barnportshOOn

Is this suitable for vegetarians?
Är det här lämpligt för vegetarianer?
air deat hair laimplit fur vehgetaree-ahner

I'd like …
Jag skulle vilja ha …
yah skewleh vilya hah

Just a cup of coffee, please
Bara en kopp kaffe, tack
bahra ehn kopp kaffeh, tack

Waiter/waitress! *(to get attention)*
Ursäkta!
EWrshekta

I only want a snack
Jag vill bara något litet att äta
yah vill bahra nawgot leeteht att aita

Is there a set menu?
Har ni en dagens rätt?
hahr nee ehn dahgens rett

I didn't order this
Jag beställde inte det här
yah bestelldeh inteh deat hair

May we have some more …?
Kan vi få litet mer av …?
kan vee faw leeteh mear ahv

Could I have another knife, please? *(a different one)*
Kan jag få en annan kniv, tack?
kan jah faw ehn annan k-neev tack

(an extra one)
Kan jag få en kniv till, tack?
kan jah faw en k-neev till tack

Can we have the bill, please?
Kan vi få notan?
kan vee faw nootan

Can we pay together/separately?
Kan vi betala tillsammans/var för sig?
kan vee betahla tillsammans/vahr fur say

The meal was very good, thank you
Det var mycket gott, tack
deat vahr mewkeh gott, tack

THINGS YOU'LL HEAR

Vad får det vara att dricka?
What would you like to drink?

Smaklig måltid
Enjoy your meal

MENU GUIDE

abborre perch
anka duck
apelsin orange
bakelse cake, pastry, tart
biff beef
biffgryta beef casserole
biffpaj beef pie
bigarrå white-heart cherries
björnbär blackberries, brambles
blekselleri celery
blodpudding black pudding
blomkål cauliflower
blåbär blueberries
braxen bream
bruna bönor brown beans
brylépudding caramel custard
brynt vitkålsoppa white cabbage soup
brysselkål Brussels sprouts
bräckt fried
bröd bread
buljong consommé
bullar sweet buns
bär berries
böckling smoked Baltic herring
bönor beans
chips crisps
dadlar dates
druvor grapes
duva pigeon
falukorv fried pork sausage
fasan pheasant
fisk fish
fiskbullar fish balls
fiskfärs minced fish
fiskgryta fish casserole
fiskpinnar fishfingers
flundra flounder
fläsk pork

fläskkorv spicy boiled pork sausage
forell trout
frukostflingor cereal
frukt fruit
fullkornsbröd wholemeal bread
fyllda stekta äpplen stuffed roast apples
förlorat ägg poached egg
getost goat's cheese
glaserad skinka glazed ham
glasmästarsill salt herring marinated
   with horseradish and carrots
glass ice cream
grahamsbröd brown bread
gravad lax/gravlax raw spiced salmon
griljerad skinka glazed ham
gräslök chives
gröna ärter green peas
grönkål kale
grönsaker vegetables
grönsallad lettuce
grön ärtpuré green pea purée
gul lök yellow onion
gurka cucumber
gås goose
gädda pike
gös pike-perch
hallon raspberries
hare hare
hasselnötter hazelnuts
helstekt whole roast
hjortron cloudberries
hummer lobster
hälleflundra halibut
höns chicken
inkokt cold boiled
inlagda rödbetor pickled beetroot
inlagd gurka pickled gherkins
inlagd sill marinated salt herring

isterband lightly smoked sausage, made from barley, pork and lard
jordgubbar strawberries
jordärtskockspuré artichoke purée
jos/juice juice
järpe hazel-grouse
kaffe coffee
kalkon turkey
kallskuret cold meats
kalops beef stew
kalvbräss calves' sweetbreads
kalvfilé fillet of veal
kalvfricassé veal fricasse
kalvgryta veal stew
kalvlever calf's liver
kalvrulader veal roulades
kalvschnitzel veal cutlet
kalvstek joint of veal
kalvsylta calves' brawn
kanin rabbit
karp carp
kassler smoked tenderloin of pork
katrinplommon prunes
kavring pumpernickel-type bread
knäckebröd crispbread
kokosnöt coconut
kokt boiled, poached
kokta majskolvar corn on the cob
kolja haddock
korv sausage
korvgryta sausage casserole
korvkaka oven-baked sausage and oatmeal dish
korvlåda sliced baked sausages
kotlett cutlet, chop
krabba crab
kronärtskockor artichokes
kroppkakor potato dumplings stuffed with chopped pork
krusbär gooseberries
kryddost cheese with caraway seeds

kräftor crayfish
kummel hake
kyckling chicken
kycklinglever chicken liver
kål cabbage
kåldolmar cabbage rolls stuffed with mince and rice
kålpudding cabbage and mince pudding
kålrötter swedes
kålsoppa cabbage soup
körsbär cherries
köttbullar meatballs
köttfärs minced beef
köttfärslimpa minced beef loaf
köttfärsrulader roulades of minced beef
köttgryta beef casserole
köttsoppa clear beef soup with meat and vegetables
lake burbot
lammfricassé lamb fricasse
lammsadel saddle of lamb
lammstek joint of lamb
lapskojs lobscouse, beef stew with mashed potatoes
lax salmon
laxpudding layers of salmon and potatoes baked in the oven
laxöring sea trout
legymsallad green vegetable salad
lever liver
leverbiff sliced fried liver
levergryta liver casserole
leverpastej liver paté
lutfisk dried fish, soaked in lye and cooked
löjrom roe from small whitefish
lök onion
lövbiff sliced beef fried with onions
majs maize, sweet corn
makaroner macaroni
makrill mackerel

mald leverbiff hamburger made of
minced liver
margarin margarine
marängsviss (hovdessert) meringue
layered with whipped cream and melted plain chocolate
matjessill a type of salt herring
mesost sweet brown cheese
mjukost soft white cheese
mjöl flour
mjölk milk
morkulla woodcock
morötter carrots
musslor mussels
nejonögon lampreys
njure kidney
njursauté sautéed kidneys
nyponsoppa rose-hip soup
nässelsoppa nettle soup
nötter nuts
olja oil
orre blackcock
ost cheese
ostron oysters
oststänger cheese sticks
oxfilé fillet of beef
oxjärpe type of cylindrical meatball
oxragu beef ragout
oxrulader rolled beef with stuffing
oxstek joint of beef
oxsvanssoppa oxtail soup
palsternacka parsnip
paltbröd black pudding
pannbiff beefburger
pannkakor pancakes
paprika green or red pepper
peppar pepper
pepparkakor ginger biscuits
pepparrotskött boiled beef with horseradish sauce
persika peach

piggvar burbot
plommon plum
pocherad forell poached trout
potatis potatoes
potatismos mashed potatoes
pressad potatis puréed potatoes
prinskorv mini-sausages
purjolök leek
pyttipanna hash of meat, potato and
onion
päron pears
pölsa barley and meat hash
rabarber rhubarb
raggmunkar potato pancakes
rapphöns partridge
renkött reindeer
renstek joint of reindeer
revbensspjäll spareribs
rimmad skinka salted ham
ripa ptarmigan (grouse)
ris rice
risgrynspudding rice pudding
rostat bröd toast
rotmos mashed turnips
russin raisins
råbiff steak tartare
rådjursstek joint of roedeer
rågbröd rye bread
rårivna morötter grated carrots
räkor shrimps
röda vinbär redcurrants
rödbetor beetroot
röding char
rödkål red cabbage
rödlök red onion
rödspätta plaice
rökt smoked
salt salt
saltgurka salt gherkin
salt sill salt herring
sardiner sardines

schalottenlök shallot
selleri celery
sellerikål celeriac
senap mustard
sik whitefish
sikrom whitefish roe
sill herring
sillbullar herring fish cakes
sillpudding herring soufflé
sjömansbiff beef, onions and potatoes
  casseroled in beer
skorpor rusks
slätvar brill
smultron wild strawberries
småbröd sweet biscuits
smör butter
smörgås sandwich
smörgåsbord the famous Scandinavian
  buffet table
sniglar snails
socker sugar
soppa soup
sotare tench
sparris asparagus
spenat spinach
sprängd anka salt duck
sprängd gås salt goose
squash pumpkin
stekt fried, roast
strömming Baltic herring
stuvad(e) in a white sauce
surkål sauerkraut
surstek marinated roast beef
surströmming fermented Baltic herring
svampgratinerad oxfilé fillet of beef
  and mushrooms au gratin
svarta vinbär blackcurrants
svartsoppa black soup made of goose
  blood
syltomelett sweet omelette with jam
te tea

tjäder capercailzie (grouse)
tomat tomato
torsk cod
tranbär cranberries
tunga tongue
tårta gateau
ugnsbakad skinka oven-baked ham
ugnskokt fiskfilé oven-baked fillet of
  fish
ugnsstekt revbensspjäll roast spare-ribs
valnöt walnuts
vetebröd tea loaf
vingelé currant jelly
vinkokt cooked in wine
vispgrädde whipped cream
vitkål white cabbage
vitling whiting
vitlök garlic
vitt formbröd white (British-style) bread
vitt matbröd white bread
våfflor waffles
wienerbröd Danish pastry
wienerkorv frankfurter-style sausage
ål eel
åkerbär arctic brambles
ångkokt salt sill steamed salt herring
ägg egg
äggröra scrambled eggs
älg elk
älgstek joint of elk
äppelkaka med vaniljsås apple crumble
  with vanilla sauce
äppelkräm apple compote
äppelmos apple purée
äpple apple
ärter peas
ärtsoppa (yellow) pea soup
ättika vinegar
ättikssill soused herring
ättiksströmming soused Baltic herring
öl beer

TRAVEL GUIDES PHRASE BOOKS

ARABIC • CZECH • DUTCH • EUROPEAN • FRENCH

GERMAN • GREEK • HEBREW • INDONESIAN

ITALIAN • JAPANESE • LATIN AMERICAN SPANISH

POLISH • PORTUGUESE • ROMANIAN • RUSSIAN

SPANISH • THAI • TURKISH

TRAVEL PACKS

DUTCH • FRENCH • GERMAN • GREEK • HEBREW

LATIN AMERICAN SPANISH • ITALIAN • PORTUGUESE

RUSSIAN • SPANISH

DK/HUGO IN THREE MONTHS
LANGUAGE COURSES

ARABIC • CHINESE • CZECH • DUTCH • FRENCH • GERMAN

GREEK • HEBREW • HINDI • ITALIAN • JAPANESE

LATIN AMERICAN SPANISH • NORWEGIAN • POLISH

PORTUGUESE • RUSSIAN • SCOTTISH GAELIC

SPANISH • SWEDISH • TURKISH • WELSH

COUNTRY GUIDES

AUSTRALIA • CANADA • CROATIA • CUBA • EGYPT • FRANCE
GERMANY • GREAT BRITAIN • GREECE: ATHENS & THE MAINLAND
HOLLAND • INDIA • IRELAND • ITALY • JAPAN • MEXICO • MOROCCO
NEW ZEALAND • NORWAY • POLAND • PORTUGAL • SCOTLAND
SINGAPORE • SOUTH AFRICA • SPAIN • THAILAND • TURKEY

REGIONAL GUIDES

BALI & LOMBOK • BARCELONA & CATALONIA • BRITTANY
CALIFORNIA • CANARY ISLANDS • CORSICA • CRUISE GUIDE TO
EUROPE & THE MEDITERRANEAN • EUROPE • FLORENCE AND TUSCANY
FLORIDA • HAWAII • JERUSALEM & THE HOLY LAND
GREAT PLACES TO STAY IN EUROPE • GREEK ISLANDS • LOIRE VALLEY
MILAN & THE LAKES • MUNICH & THE BAVARIAN ALPS
NAPLES WITH POMPEII & THE AMALFI COAST • NEW ENGLAND
PROVENCE & THE CÔTE D'AZUR • SARDINIA • SEVILLE & ANDALUCIA
SICILY • SOUTHWEST USA & LAS VEGAS • A TASTE OF TUSCANY
VENICE & THE VENETO

CITY GUIDES

AMSTERDAM • BERLIN • BOSTON • BRUSSELS • BUDAPEST
CHICAGO • CRACOW • DELHI, AGRA & JAIPUR • DUBLIN
ISTANBUL • LISBON • LONDON • MADRID • MOSCOW
NAPLES • NEW ORLEANS • NEW YORK • PARIS • PRAGUE
ROME • SAN FRANCISCO • STOCKHOLM • ST PETERSBURG
SYDNEY • VIENNA • WARSAW • WASHINGTON, D.C.

ALGARVE • AMSTERDAM

BARCELONA • BERLIN • BOSTON

CANCUN & THE YUCATAN • CRETE

DUBLIN • HONG KONG • LONDON

MADRID • MALLORCA • MIAMI & THE KEYS

MILAN & THE LAKES • NEW YORK

ORLANDO • PARIS • PRAGUE

PROVENCE & THE CÔTE D'AZUR

ROME • SAN FRANCISCO • SCOTLAND

SICILY • TUSCANY • VENICE

VIENNA • WASHINGTON D.C.